Sexual Feelings

CROSS CULTURES

Readings in Post / Colonial Literatures and Cultures in English

174

Sexual Feelings

Reading Anglophone Caribbean Women's Writing Through Affect

Elina Valovirta

Rodopi

Amsterdam - New York, NY 2014

COVER IMAGE
Gordon Collier (based on a motif by Verneri Kontto)

The paper on which this book is printed meets the requirements of "ISO 9706:1994, Information and documentation - Paper for documents - Requirements for permanence".

ISBN: 978-90-420-3860-8
E-Book ISBN: 978-94-012-1102-4

Printed in The Netherlands

Contents

Acknowledgements

MANY THANKS are due to Professor Lynne Pearce of Lancaster University for being my key inspiration in questions of feminist reader theory and for acting as my generous opponent in the dissertation stage of this book. Furthermore, I would like to thank Dr Angeletta Gourdine of Louisiana State University for her detailed comments, which greatly improved the coherence of my argument. I would also like to extend my warmest thanks to my technical editor at Rodopi, Gordon Collier, for his patience and promptness with the manuscript.

My late supervisor, Professor John Skinner, first introduced me to Caribbean literature in his postcolonial fiction seminar, and I owe him my gratitude for that and for always being open for questions. As I became 'orphaned' after John's passing, Professor Lydia Kokkola adopted me as her supervisee, and our cooperation has continued ever since. My warmest thanks and the deepest debt of gratitude go to Lydia for her guidance, support, and friendship.

My travels to the Caribbean have brought me in contact with scholars who have greatly influenced my work, and I thank attendees of the ACWWS conferences for being crucial to my thinking. In particular, Dr Orville Taylor of the University of the West Indies has been an invaluable source of information and friendship for years.

Back home, I would like to thank all my colleagues at the Department of English, University of Turku. In particular, Professor Risto Hiltunen has kindly supported my scholarly endeavours. My wonderful colleagues, Professor Joel Kuortti, Janne Korkka, Elina Siltanen, Mari–Liisa Varila, Ira Hansen, Anna Kalpio, Pekka Lintunen, and Janne Skaffari, among others, are a delight to work with. Similarly, the Department for Gender Studies has been my other home for years, and has given me the collegiality and support of Professor Marianne Liljeström. Most of my deepest friendships were forged at her research seminar over the years: Kaisa Ilmonen, Mari Pajala, Sari

Miettinen, Anu Laukkanen, Katariina Kyrölä, and Mona Mannevuo, to name but a few, have long been staples of this circle.

I also wish to thank my pub quiz team, Steam (Joel, Kaisa, Janne, and Teemu), for the recreation and my cousin Tilda for supplying me with ice cream and her lovely company.

I would like to close by thanking my family: my parents and my brothers, Jaakko and Heikki, and Maija and Katri, my sisters-in-law, and Pauli, my brother-in-law. My nieces and nephew, Myy, Vertti, and Hertta, are a constant source of joy and wonder to all of us. Thank you, Ville, for your love, support, and never-ending endeavours to create the best possible life for us.

Finally, the person who best exemplifies the preposition 'beside' on which I place emphasis in this book is my identical twin, Irene. You always make me aware of how "we live with and beside each other, and yet we are not as one."[1] Thank you for always being beside me.

⌘

Earlier versions of some of the material in the present book are listed below, with thanks to the publishers and editors involved:

"Blowing the love-breath: Healing men in Caribbean women's writing," *Feminist Review* 104 (Special Issue: "Affect and Creolisation," 2013): 100–18.

"Reading the intimacies of shame in Edwidge Danticat's *Breath, Eyes, Memory*," in *Scenes of Intimacy: Reading, Writing and Theorising Contemporary Literature*, ed. Jennifer Cooke (London: Bloomsbury Academic, 2013): 37–53.

"Ethics of empathy and reading in Shani Mootoo's *Cereus Blooms at Night*," in *Working with Affect in Feminist Readings: Disturbing Differences*, ed. Marianne Liljeström & Susanna Paasonen (London & New York: Routledge, 2010): 140–50.

"'Caribbean passion' as a reparative practice: The hypersexual and the asexual woman in the fictions of Opal Palmer Adisa and Erna Brodber," in *Seeking the Self – Encountering the Other: Diasporic Narrative and the Ethics of Representation*, ed. Tuomas Huttunen, Kaisa Ilmonen, Janne Korkka & Elina Valovirta (Newcastle upon Tyne: Cambridge Scholars, 2008): 182–97.

⌘

[1] Sara Ahmed, *The Cultural Politics of Emotion* (Edinburgh: Edinburgh UP, 2004): 39.

1
Sexual Feelings Beside(s) Each Other

Reading and Situating Caribbean (Literary) Sexualities

CONFUSION MUST HAVE BEEN THE BEST WORD to express my feelings when encountering Caribbean women's writing for the first time. It was in my undergraduate years at a postcolonial writing seminar, and customarily we were all to select a novel or two for our term papers. So intriguing was this story of a Jamaican young woman crumbling under but overcoming colonial and sexist pressures that I happily spent the better part of the academic year engaged with it. Confusion gave way to other feelings such as joy (of reading and discovery), anxiety (over writing a paper), shame (over my whiteness), and a myriad of other emotions I do not even have names for. Over the course of the seminar I began to develop an understanding of the fact that we make sense of who we are, where we are coming from, and where we are going to by way of how we *feel*. This means that affectivity, emotions, and feelings play a role in both subject-formation and meaning-production. The way we feel is an indicator of ourselves, and when I was first presented with the prospect of reading Erna Brodber's *Jane and Louisa Will Soon Come Home*, I was baffled by how difficult a novel it was. Granted, I may not have been thrown into the shallow end of the pool, as Brodber's writing is notoriously difficult for native and non-native reader alike, but it gave me something invaluable: a consideration of how emotions and knowledge, affect and cognition are intextricably linked. But before that I grasped the fact that there is no reading like a political reading.

The question of politicized readings becomes pertinent in postcolonial literary studies, the very existence of which rely on the global export of cultural products to wide and varied interpretative readerships. In the case of the (post) colonial Caribbean, Mimi Sheller details how, throughout its history, the region has been *consumed* in the form of, for example, raw materials such as coffee and sugar, tourism, and (various) cultural products such as music and literature to form Atlantic modernity and its hegemonic status in the world.[1] The ways in which "Caribbean culture has travelled" manifests itself in the fields of literature and literary studies as growing corpora of fiction and poetry are debated by members of the Western academy; in the context of both teaching and research.[2] Shalini Puri also notes that Caribbean literature on the global market is an example of how the "'local' is consumed 'globally'."[3] Puri calls for a careful reorientation of our reading practices, as oftentimes foreign readers do not have sufficient knowledge to understand the Caribbean postcolonial (with magical realism as its preferred genre).[4] This demand to reorientate reading is echoed by Patricia Saunders' comment on the lack of critical tools available for interpreting Caribbean women's writing.[5]

This study is one contribution to filling the gaps indicated by Puri, Saunders, and others. In this context, Sarah Brouillette, through Graham Huggan's views on the postcolonial exotic, explains that the proliferation of postcolonial literature on the global literary consumer market not only produces certain types of authors and texts, but it also produces audiences.[6] This means that we must consider the role of the reader in the meaning-making process. How do we *read* postcolonial literature, and in the case of the present study, how do we *read* Caribbean fiction in English by women? My motivation therefore arises from a need to understand some of the ways in which we read and negotiate meaning-production within a cross-cultural reading event involving a multiplicity of differences (including geographical, cultural, linguistic, racial, and religious). And my plea is for a more active reading of sexuality, emotions, and ethics in the postcolonial literary arena.

---

[1] Mimi Sheller, *Consuming the Caribbean: From Arawaks to Zombies* (New York & London: Routledge, 2003).

[2] Sheller, *Consuming the Caribbean*, 175.

[3] Shalini Puri, *The Caribbean Postcolonial: Social Equality, Post-Nationalism, and Cultural Hybridity* (New York: Palgrave Macmillan, 2003): 139.

[4] Puri, *The Caribbean Postcolonial*, 140.

[5] Patricia Saunders, "The Project of Becoming for Marlene Nourbese Philip and Erna Brodber," in *Caribbean Cultural Identities*, ed. Glyne Griffith (Lewisburg PA: Bucknell UP, 2001): 133.

[6] Sarah Brouillette, *Postcolonial Writers in the Global Literary Marketplace* (Basingstoke & New York: Palgrave Macmillan, 2007): 15.

The title of this book, *Sexual Feelings*, operates on two related levels that should not be understood as disparate taxonomies or separate blocs. Rather, to borrow Eve Kosofsky Sedgwick's idea of resistance to "origin and telos" found in linear logic, I urge that these levels be perceived in terms of "planar relations" that may be best described with the help of the preposition "beside."[7] Thinking of *sexual feelings* from two related perspectives existing alongside one another may help us to see how, in fact, we cannot separate them even if we decided to (for clarity's sake) discuss them singly. First, sexual feelings are a frequent theme in the present selection of Caribbean women's writing and are obviously my objects of enquiry. As such, sexual feelings can be seen as discourses or ideologies.[8] Second, sexual feelings are affective forces which serve to move, attach, and position their readers and are a tool of reading. From this twofold understanding of sexual feelings it follows that the object and subject of knowledge, in this instance, cannot be held at arm's length from one other; rather, they are engaged in an intimate relationship, operating together by the power of affect as their driving force and binding glue.

Sexual feelings as a literary motif in this selection of writing may be seen as belonging to the larger frame of their very sociality. Indeed, Sara Ahmed reminds us that, in this view of the emotions, they are seen as relational and social; not as simply private or insular.[9] Here, sexual feelings refer to the ways in which sexuality is represented as belonging to the affective domain. At the same time, the idea of sexual feelings refers to the ways in which the fictional characters in this particular selection conceive of sex and sexuality as always intimately connected with multiple, overlapping, contradictory, and powerful emotions. Sexual feelings thus indicate the thoughts, emotions, and embodied experiences of the novels' (female) characters with regard to sex and sexual encounters.

Considered in the context of meaning-production, sexual feelings serve to intensify the experiencing of narrative as a relationship between reader and text. By drawing on affect both as a literary theme and as an episteme of reading, I hope to show how thematic analysis and a theory of reading coexist. Reading affect is interactive, in that it generates the differences at play in the

[7] Eve Kosofsky Sedgwick, *Touching Feeling: Affect, Pedagogy, Performativity* (Durham NC & London: Duke UP, 2003): 8.

[8] See Lynne Pearce, *Romance Writing* (Cambridge: Polity, 2007): 1.

[9] Sara Ahmed, *The Cultural Politics of Emotion* (Edinburgh: Edinburgh UP, 2004): 8–9.

sense-making event, but also recognizes how such differences produce instances of affect in the first place. Thus, a scrutiny of emotions in reading invests emotions in text and reader alike, and lends them greater salience. My focus is on the ways in which affect can be employed in reading literature and other cultural products, not only on what it *does* and how it comes to signify.

The study aims to construct a version of postcolonial feminist theory that is affective, dialogic, and reparative for the purposes of reading sexual feelings in a selection of contemporary anglophone Caribbean women's writing. Sedgwick's proposal regarding the privilege of 'beside' then becomes a way of understanding this particular way of conducting feminist research; as openness to the simultaneous existence of several different forms of experience, such as "desiring, identifying, representing, repelling, paralleling, differentiating."[10] The element of 'beside' can refer to the multiplicity and deferral of meaning: there is no authenticity or 'correctness' of meaning or interpretation in this cross-cultural reading – rather, meaning slides across or slips away by necessity: not quite there but, with any kind of luck, beside meaning.

Affective feminist reading

The role of the reader in the act of reading has been under discussion in literary studies for decades. Since the heavy investment in semiotics in the 1960s at the latest, literary studies have viewed literature as a form of communication and, in the wake of reader theory (including US-based reader-response criticism and German-based reception aesthetics), the act of reading has been viewed as an act of textual interaction – rather than the earlier, implied, passive reception of a literary message. Much of the early debate turned on the level of readers' activity vs. passivity as theorists attempted to explain the mechanics of meaning-making and reading processes. The focus has increasingly shifted away from the centrality of the text's role in the reading process towards considering *how* readers interact with the text. Readers, in fact, have agency; they do not merely 'receive' or 'respond' to texts.

The way in which the New Criticism approached textual interaction stressed close reading for a good reason: texts require intimate engagement. However, in "paying attention to the literary text in and of itself," the New Criticism failed to account adequately for the affective dimension of the interactive

[10] Sedgwick, *Touching Feeling*, 8.

nature of reading.[11] Traditional theories of reading have a tendency to privilege the cognitive (the mechanics of interpretation) at the expense of the affective ("the role of 'feeling' within the reading process itself"[12]). In fact, W.K. Wimsatt's dreaded "affective fallacy" – the tendency on the part of readers to naively interpret texts according to their own feelings – was to continue influencing theories of critical reading over half a century later.[13] This aversion from accepting the reader as someone who feels led to the eradication of emotions from reading and literary theory altogether. The New Criticism entertained the idea of a reader approaching "the literary text in and of itself."[14] At least from the later perspective of feminist literary criticism, this notion is anomalous.[15] Affects are far from peripheral to the process of sense-making. On the contrary, affectivity is central to the meanings readers gain from textual encounters: the ways in which how we *feel* as readers impacts on the ethical and political choices we make, the way we *do* things. In fact, affects can be used to increase understanding, which reflects on how we can make the affective bear upon the cognitive.

In the past decade or two, feminist theory has witnessed an emphasis on the role of "affects, emotions and embodied experiences."[16] Feminist scholarship is also equally preoccupied with questions of ethics, particularly in cross-cultural contexts.[17] The affective and ethical turns in feminism have been

---

[11] Andrew DuBois, "Close Reading: An Introduction," in *Close Reading: The Reader*, ed. Frank Lentricchia & Andrew DuBois (Durham NC: Duke UP, 2003): 4.

[12] Pearce, *Feminism and the Politics of Reading*, 4.

[13] W.K. Wimsatt, *The Verbal Icon: Studies in the Meaning of Poetry* (Lexington: U of Kentucky P, 1954.)

[14] Dubois, "Close Reading: An Introduction," 4.

[15] Lea Rojola, "Sukupuolieron lukeminen: Feministinen kirjallisuudentutkimus" [Reading gender difference: Feminist literary criticism], in *Feministinen tietäminen: Keskustelua metodologiasta* [Feminist knowing: Conversations on methodology], ed. Marianne Liljeström (Tampere: Vastapaino, 2004): 36.

[16] Anu Koivunen, "Preface: The Affective Turn?," in *Conference Proceedings for Affective Encounters: Rethinking Embodiment in Feminist Media Studies*, ed. Anu Koivunen & Susanna Paasonen (Turku: University of Turku, School of Art, Literature and Music, Media Studies, Series A, 2001): 7.

[17] See Linda Hogan & Sasha Roseneil, "Gendering Ethics/The Ethics of Gender," *Feminist Theory* 2.2 (August 2001): 147. See also Sara Ahmed, *Strange Encounters: Embodied Others in Post-Coloniality* (London & New York: Routledge, 2000); Jane Haggis & Suzanne Schech, "Meaning Well and Global Good Manners: Reflections on

conflated, not only due to their temporal proximity of emergence, but also due to the inextricable link between ethics and politics as imbued with affect. Feminist scholars of affectivity such as Sue Campbell, Rei Terada, Sara Ahmed, Elspeth Probyn, Clare Hemmings, and Eve Kosofsky Sedgwick have deliberated upon the role of emotions and affects in connection with political and ethical questions.[18] Common to these writers is the understanding of affectivity as linked to larger contexts, rather than as merely being seen as the private property of an individual's psychology.

As Sara Ahmed has noted, the central issue of this type of inquiry is the way in which "emotions are crucial to politics."[19] Elsewhere, Ahmed further elaborates on the emotional ways in which we become invested in feminism as invoking an emotional response because it involves a critical rethinking of an individual's relation to social norms.[20] As we become politically invested, we *feel*. Indeed, Ahmed subverts and revalorizes the sexist assumption that "emotions are associated with women, who are represented as 'closer' to nature, ruled by appetite, and less able to transcend the body through thought, will and judgment."[21] Similarly, feminists are often seen as clouding issues by expressing hostility and anger, for instance (as though these were not a pre-eminently male precinct).[22] These politically motivated fallacies are put to a different use in feminist affective work, where Ahmed depicts the relevance of politics as affective. She writes that although emotions and feelings serve

---

White Western Feminist Cross-Cultural Praxis," *Australian Feminist Studies* 15/33 (2000): 387–99; and Chandra Talpade Mohanty, "'Under Western Eyes' Revisited: Feminist Solidarity Through Anticapitalist Struggles," *Signs* 28.2 (Winter 2003): 499–535.

[18] See Sue Campbell, *Interpreting the Personal: Expression and the Formation of Feelings* (Ithaca NY & London: Cornell UP, 1997); Ahmed, *The Cultural Politics of Emotion*; Elspeth Probyn, *Blush: Faces of Shame* (Sydney: U of New South Wales P, 2005); Clare Hemmings, "Invoking Affect: Cultural Theory and the Ontological Turn," *Cultural Studies* 19.5 (September 2005): 548–67; and Sedgwick, *Touching Feeling*.

[19] Sara Ahmed, "Communities That Feel: Intensity, Difference and Attachment," in *Conference Proceedings for Affective Encounters: Rethinking Embodiment in Feminist Media Studies*, ed. Anu Koivunen & Susanna Paasonen (Turku: University of Turku, School of Art, Literature and Music, Media Studies, Series A, 2001): 10.

[20] Ahmed, *The Cultural Politics of Emotion*, 170–71.

[21] *The Cultural Politics of Emotion*, 3.

[22] *The Cultural Politics of Emotion*, 170.

to move us, they also keep us in place by binding us to a place and a community.[23] Within this simultaneity lies the force of affectivity, since its mechanisms cannot merely be contained by viewing feelings as originary or ontological, residing in objects as such.

Inspired by the affective turn, my reading here follows "intensities of feeling, emotional attachments and gut reactions" which have been increasingly in the focus of feminist theory.[24] Theories of affectivity help counteract the decades-long influx of bodily textual metaphors circulating in literary and cultural theory, which do not take into account the very materiality of bodies and objects.[25] For example, Paravisini–Gebert is particularly critical of white Western readings of the representation of Caribbean women's bodies, in that the interpretations tend only to see the body as a symbolic construct and fail to account for their very materiality; their 'flesh-and-blood quality'.[26] This failure to account for the materiality of the body can be paralleled with how traditional reader theory privileged the cognitive at the expense of the affective, resulting in antipathy towards the reader as someone who feels.[27]

By embracing the affective fallacy in reading by emphasizing emotional interaction in the reading process, feminist critics also invite closer consideration of the various emotional and embodied experiences emerging during the reading event. Lynne Pearce moves discussion of the act of reading beyond the earlier, rather hermeneutic, debates of text–reader relations[28] in order to deal with reading within an affective framework. She reveals the power and implications of reading as a dialogic and affective process, where textual

---

23 Ahmed, "Communities That Feel," 11.

24 Marianne Liljeström & Susanna Paasonen, "Introduction: Feeling Differences – Affect and Feminist Reading," in *Working with Affect in Feminist Readings: Disturbing Differences*, ed. Marianne Liljeström & Susanna Paasonen (London & New York: Routledge, 2010): 1.

25 Liljeström & Paasonen, "Introduction: Feeling Differences – Affect and Feminist Reading," 1.

26 Lizabeth Paravisini–Gebert, "Women Against the Grain: The Pitfalls of Theorizing Caribbean Women's Writing," in *Winds of Change: The Transforming Voices of Caribbean Women Writers and Scholars*, ed. Adele S. Newson & Linda Strong–Leek (New York: Peter Lang, 1998): 164.

27 Pearce, *Feminism and the Politics of Reading*, 4.

28 Here I am referring to, for example, debates relating to the reader's 'activity vs. passivity' and the text–reader power hierarchy, which are not of primary relevance in this project.

positioning moves and evokes feelings in the reader. This means that the question in this model is not about what we can do to texts, but also what they can do to us.[29] Texts have the capacity to position their readers in many ways, just as readers can position the text in a variety of ways. As a result, the reading event is always a personal, emotional, and embodied encounter between the reader and the text. Reading with an understanding of the role of affect in the process of sense-making can enable the politically motivated reader to open herself up to the potential of change as she engages with, for instance, texts that demand a reading across difference such as postcolonial and transnational literature.

As I engage in this discussion, I sometimes employ the terms 'affect', 'emotion', and 'feeling' interchangeably, and at other times as specified (and varied) embodied and sensory experiences to describe the ways in which we come to *feel*. The word 'feeling' refers to an emotional, embodied experience which in a more general sense belongs to the larger family of affect. Thus, feeling is one possible way to express and conceptualize an affect. According to Rei Terada, affect refers to the physiological dimension of a psychological emotion, but at the same time the two remain indivisible.[30] The words 'emotion' and 'feeling' are used to denote the different modes of an affect's sensory perception: the latter involves a more embodied sense of affective experience. Terada uses the word 'feeling' when she wishes to stress the inseparability of the physiological and the psychological, and I share this view.[31] At the same time, however, I see no reason why emotions – as named affects in literary expressions – cannot contain a corporeal dimension.

The relationship between affect and sense-making is not unidirectional, as affects and their readers are co-dependent. The recognition and reading of affects depicted in the text calls for the reader to move, or to be moved. Thus, affects need readers and readers need affects in order to grasp literature and to be grasped by it. In fact, emotions are communicative in nature and are thus always dependent on their interpreters.[32] Emotions are not just located in the body or in the mind of those who are feeling: the way something feels to us is

---

[29] Pearce, *Feminism and the Politics of Reading*, 2.

[30] Rei Terada, *Feeling in Theory: Emotion after the "Death of the Subject"* (Cambridge MA & London: Harvard UP, 2001): 4.

[31] Terada, *Feeling in Theory*, 4.

[32] Sylvia Burrow, "The Political Structure of Emotion: From Dismissal to Dialogue," *Hypatia* 20.4 (Autumn 2005): 29.

already subject to a process of reading and attributing significance to it.[33] As such, emotions are relational in terms of both their subjects and their audiences. In this view, sense-production is wholly dependent on the mutually active role of the reader, as well as the text.

In other words, theorizing the act of reading as a relationship prompts discussion of the interactive nature of meaning-formation with its multiple affective processes. With the concept of 'the textual other' fashioned on the model of reading as a romance, Pearce notes that the satisfaction gained from the text depends on the dialogue between the reader and his or her textual other.[34]

The textual other in Pearce refers to that element (or those elements) in the text that the reader adopts as her 'love object' in reading. The textual other can be a character in the text, but also a larger texture such as stylistics, the author figure, or the interpretative community.[35] Drawing on Pearce, I suggest that a reader's commitment to a specific form of politics (or ethics) can become a textual other and her dialogic interlocutor in the reading process.

Understanding the differences generated between text and reader reminds the latter of the need to at times step back from projecting her potential feminist attachment or emotional investment onto the novels by Caribbean women writers such as those I examine in this book.[36] At times, she must exercise restraint by reflecting on her situatedness in the reading event. Affectivity is thus always connected with ethics: how we *feel* as readers has a bearing on the ethical and political choices we make, the way we *do* things.

Situating the Caribbean

The history of the Caribbean region at the centre of the slave trade (the Middle Passage) led to a sexual genealogy unlike anywhere else. Sexuality in the Caribbean has a complex and problematic history, yet despite its centrality in colonial oppression in the past and in today's global sex tourism, this has not invited extensive scholarly attention until recently.[37] We can detect growing

[33] Ahmed, *The Cultural Politics of Emotion*, 171.

[34] *The Cultural Politics of Emotion*, 181.

[35] Pearce, *Feminism and the Politics of Reading*, 15.

[36] Ahmed, *The Cultural Politics of Emotion*, ch. 8.

[37] Kamala Kempadoo, "Theorizing Sexual Relations in the Caribbean: Prostitution and the Problem of the 'Exotic'," in *Confronting Power, Theorizing Gender. Interdis-*

critical interest in the ambivalent nature of sexuality as a site of repression as well as possibility in the Caribbean.[38] Linden Lewis remarks that Caribbean literature is an important site for discussions of sexuality, in the face of scholarship on the subject that tends to be "cautious and conservative."[39]

My readings in this study seek to challenge this cautious conservatism. Contemporary anglophone Caribbean women's writing is inextricably linked with diaspora, which manifests itself along a continuum of thought ranging from a primary identification with the African diaspora as a result of the legacy of slavery to a New World migrant experience that has to negotiate itself in relation to "the Caribbean-Atlantic passage between America and the various islands.[40] The inherent "fromness" of the idea of diaspora, as criticized by Ien Ang, is then challenged by the implications of diaspora in contemporary Caribbean fiction by women, alongside its critical reception.[41]

---

ciplinary Perspectives in the Caribbean, ed. Eudine Barriteau (Kingston, Jamaica: U of the West Indies P , 2003): 182.

[38] See Evelyn O'Callaghan, "'Compulsory Heterosexuality' and Textual/Sexual Alternatives in Selected Texts by West Indian Women Writers," in *Caribbean Portraits: Essays on Gender Ideologies and Identities* ed. Christine Barrow (Kingston, Jamaica: Ian Randle, 1998): 294–319; Denise DeCaires Narain, "Standing in the Place of Love: Sex, Love and Loss in Jamaica Kincaid's Writing," in *Gendered Realities: Essays in Caribbean Feminist Thought*, ed. Patricia Mohammed (Kingston, Jamaica: U of the West Indies P and Centre for Gender and Development Studies, 2002): 334–57; Angeletta K.M. Gourdine, *The Difference Place Makes: Gender, Sexuality and Diaspora Identity* (Columbus: Ohio State UP, 2002); *The Culture of Gender and Sexuality in the Caribbean*, ed. Linden Lewis (Gainesville: UP of Florida, 2003); Donette A. Francis, *Fictions of Feminine Citizenship: Sexuality and the Nation in Contemporary Caribbean Literature* (Basingstoke & New York: Palgrave Macmillan, 2010); *Sex and the Citizen: Interrogating the Caribbean*, ed. Faith Smith (Charlottesville & London: UP of Virginia, 2011); and Donna Aza Weir–Soley, *Eroticism, Spirituality, and Resistance in Black Women's Writings* (Gainesville: UP of Florida, 2009).

[39] Linden Lewis, "Exploring the Intersections of Gender, Sexuality, and Culture in the Caribbean: An Introduction," in *The Culture of Gender and Sexuality in the Caribbean*, ed. Linden Lewis (Gainesville: UP of Florida, 2003): 9, 5.

[40] Cynthia James, *The Maroon Narrative: Caribbean Literature in English Across Boundaries, Ethnicities, and Centuries* (Portsmouth NH: Heinemann, 2002).

[41] Ien Ang, *On Not Speaking Chinese: Living Between Asia and the West* (London: Routledge, 2001).

Migrant authors who write 'about' the Caribbean define and negotiate themselves multilaterally in relation to the Caribbean as a physical, political, and cultural space, as well as their New World homeland.[42] The correlation between language and nation in the formation of the literary tradition is further unsettled by authors who hail from the non-English-speaking islands, but who write in English. Caribbean women's migrant writing may best be viewed as a tradition of writing that emerges in and of the Caribbean as an imaginary *diasporic construct,* in addition to being a concise physical point of origin. There, both the new and old homelands become imaginary constructs – rather than a fixed state. This diasporic condition as an underlying setting in the authors' work is profoundly gendered and sexualized (not to mention intersectional), and is therefore always connected to relations of power.

Such relations of power can be seen in the literary tradition of Caribbean women's writing, which – despite its heterogeneity – features a number of common themes, such as mother–daughter relationships, a young girl's formation or developmental *Bildung*, colonial education, and racism. Sexuality is another key theme which receives frequent attention in this body of writing. Sexuality in Caribbean literature (as treated by women in particular) is an ambivalent and contested terrain. Evelyn O'Callaghan comments:

> female sexuality in the work of West Indian women prose writers is either shrouded in secrecy and shame, or a matter of casual and unfeeling acquiescence to male pressure. In most cases, it has negative consequences for the woman's economic, social and psychological well being.[43]

Sexuality in this description is given a range of attributes that have affective associations: "secrecy," "shame," "casual and unfeeling" terms that clearly signal the intimate connections between affectivity and sexuality. Furthermore, the interconnections of sexuality and affectivity in Caribbean women's writing emerge laden with polarizations on a continuum of ambivalence, fluctuation, and inconclusivity. According to Denise deCaires Narain, attitudes toward sex and sexuality in the Caribbean context "shuttle between a frank and raucous explicitness about sex and almost Victorian prudery and deco-

[42] See Helen Scott, *Caribbean Women Writers and Globalization: Fictions of Independence* (Aldershot & Burlington VT: Ashgate, 2006): 2.

[43] O'Callaghan, "'Compulsory Heterosexuality' and Textual/Sexual Alternatives in Selected Texts by West Indian Women Writers," 297.

rousness."[44] As the above quotations attest, sexuality in Caribbean women's writing has an affective base ("shame," "casual," "unfeeling," "frank," "raucous," "prudery," "decorousness"). Hence, there is an aura of obscurity around sexual feelings in this body of writing. This obscurity needs to be mapped and taken seriously in an effort to differentiate between the reader's and the texts' respective and sometimes shared sexual feelings.

Caribbean feminists have offered critical perspectives on gender relations in the region. While doing so, they have problematized the legacy of white mainstream feminism in the Caribbean context. The relationship between white, largely middle-class and heterosexual, feminist thought was challenged by black feminist scholars already thirty years ago; such as in bell hooks' criticism of Betty Friedan's 1963 feminist classic *The Feminine Mystique*.[45] However, the African-American social and political context differs from that of the Caribbean to a considerable extent. Indeed, Rhoda Reddock remarks that the black feminist critique of white feminism did not resonate in the Caribbean, mostly due to the fact that women in the Caribbean have felt little relevance in the overarching concept of feminism.[46] Anita Haya Patterson writes that in Jamaica there has been a much greater degree of socio-economic equality between the sexes historically compared to other countries of the Commonwealth Caribbean and the US South; mostly traceable to women and men's unsegregated roles in slave labour.[47]

In addition, women were responsible for keeping provision grounds, giving them agency as entrepreneurs and market sellers or higglers, from which stems the near-archetypal features of a Caribbean woman's life: social authority, a larger degree of independence, verbal prowess, and matrifocal households. Perhaps in accordance with these historical factors, women in Jamaica (and indeed the rest of the Caribbean) have traditionally been sceptical towards European and American feminism (as seen in Patterson's reading of the

---

[44] Narain, "Standing in the Place of Love," 336.

[45] See bell hooks, *Feminist Theory: From Margin to Center* (Cambridge MA: South End, 1984).

[46] Rhoda Reddock, "Conceptualizing 'Difference' in Caribbean Feminist Theory," in *New Caribbean Thought: A Reader*, ed. Brian Meeks & Folke Lindahl (Kingston, Jamaica: U of the West Indies P, 2001): 201.

[47] Anita Haya Patterson, "Contingencies of Pleasure and Shame: Jamaican Women's Poetry," in *Feminist Consequences: Theory for the New Century*, ed. Elisabeth Bronfen & Misha Kavka (New York: Columbia UP, 2001): 254–82.

poetry of Louise Bennett). Patterson's brief historical account of differences between enslaved women across the Caribbean-Atlantic serves to exemplify "the difficulties of engaging Caribbean women's literature through contemporary feminist theory."[48] For this reason, Patterson proposes that we should examine the applicability of each theory in the specific historical context of the Caribbean. This ensures critical awareness of the limits of theories that originate in a different cultural, social, and political context than the environment to which they are applied.

Janet Momsen also notes the specific historical context in and due to which Caribbean women came to be categorized. She characterizes Caribbean gender relations as

> a double paradox: of patriarchy within a system of matrifocal and matrilocal families; and of domestic and state patriarchy coexisting with the economic independence of women.[49]

Momsen cites as a further paradox the fact that the Caribbean patriarchy is often "patriarchy in absentia," resulting from large numbers of migrant males and absentee fathers (or "gender-specific patterns of social behaviour"[50]). For example, between 1881 and 1921 a large number of Jamaican men were forced to migrate to Central America in search of work, leaving women in charge of the household and family.[51]

By and large, this male migrancy has meant that the Caribbean family can most often be described as "woman-headed."[52] In accordance with the women's central role in families, both Patterson and Momsen write about the long history of women's access to land ownership. Momsen adds, to Patterson's historical account of women's agricultural work, that, at the same time, education has traditionally been an important aspect of Caribbean women's lives. Perhaps because they did not have opportunities to those of the *Windrush* men who departed the islands for the UK in a 'colonization in reverse',

---

48 Patterson, "Contingencies of Pleasure and Shame," 258.

49 Janet Momsen, "The Double Paradox," in *Gendered Realities: Essays in Caribbean Feminist Thought*, ed. Patricia Mohammed (Kingston, Jamaica: U of the West Indies P and Centre for Gender and Development Studies, 2002): 45.

50 Momsen, "The Double Paradox," 51.

51 Patterson, "Contingencies of Pleasure and Shame," 257–58.

52 Marietta Morrissey, "Explaining the Caribbean Family: Gender Ideologies and Gender Relations," in *Caribbean Portraits. Essays on Gender Ideologies and Identities*, ed. Christine Barrow (Kingston, Jamaica: Ian Randle, 1998): 78–90.

women generally place great value on the opportunity to provide education for their children. The historically strong role of Caribbean women in both public and private life led to a view of Caribbean women as "overburdened superwomen."[53] The image of the strong matriarch represents "a homogenous typeface of Caribbean womanhood."[54] These problematizations of the "strong Caribbean woman" further indicate that the centrality of women in areas of society does not mark an equal – let alone a matriarchal – regime.

In a rather more critical tone, Lizabeth Paravisini–Gebert expresses scepticism about the fashion in postcolonial scholarship of seeing Caribbean women as marginal – a fashion that makes them "the other's other, a valuable commodity."[55] For Paravisini–Gebert, postcolonial feminist theories are inapplicable to the Caribbean context, where insular (rather than Euro-American) cultural forms play the most significant role in the shaping of a response to patriarchal colonialist oppression (163). Paravisini–Gebert is particularly critical of white Western readings of the representation of Caribbean women's bodies, in that these tend to be seen as a symbolic construct without materiality; their "flesh-and-blood quality" (164) (such as military rapes in Haiti and violence against women throughout the Caribbean) commonly neglected in Western theories of the textual body. In fact, the status of the "other's other" foisted on Caribbean women by postcolonial theory grants them nothing but voicelessness; there is little of benefit for them or us from such theorizations (168). Caribbean women's writing ought instead to seek inspiration from its own "creative spaces," such as the long history of active women asserting their bodies and sexuality in a manner with markedly different meanings from those in the West (among the insular strategies named by Paravisini–Gebert are 'slackness' and the central role played by Haitian peasant women in goods marketing). However, as we will see in the following introduction to the texts under scrutiny in this book, the inspiration behind Caribbean women writers has far greater latitude than we might at first assume.

---

53 Momsen, "The Double Paradox," 51.

54 Michelle Rowley, "Reconceptualizing Voice: The Role of Matrifocality in Shaping Theories and Caribbean Voices," in *Gendered Realities: Essays in Caribbean Feminist Thought*, ed. Patricia Mohammed (Kingston, Jamaica: U of the West Indies P and Centre for Gender and Development Studies, 2002): 22.

55 Paravisini–Gebert, "Women Against the Grain." 161. Further page references are in the main text.

Women writing the Caribbean: The selection of texts

With a noted "historical absence of the woman writer's text in Caribbean literary canons,"

> the term *Caribbean women's writing* arises from the need to depict and promote Caribbean women's literary and critical endeavours that have largely been silenced despite their long history.[56]

The political alliance termed 'Caribbean women's writing' serves as a signifier for a complex body of writing which is a "tradition already well-established in important ways."[57] However, this transnational and postcolonial writing cannot simply be classified by national or regional boundaries;[58] rather, it can be characterized as "from and about" the Caribbean.[59] This flexible designation involves both unity and complexity: despite the differences in Caribbean nations and cultures, the umbrella term 'Caribbean women's writing' has served to institutionalize and establish this literature as important and worthwhile in its own right.[60] These fictions, according to Carine Mardorossian, "radically reformulate[s] the meanings of the national, geographical, sexual, and racial concepts" that have been used as "foundational terms" in postcolonial literature studies.[61] My discussion of a selection of anglophone Caribbean women's writing from 1980 to the present accordingly treats works by authors whose themes and personal background reach beyond the carto-

---

[56] Carole Boyce Davies & Elaine Savory Fido, "Introduction: Women and Literature in the Caribbean: An Overview," in *Out of the Kumbla: Caribbean Women and Literature*, ed. Davies & Fido (Trenton NJ: Africa World Press, 1990).

[57] Saunders, "The Project of Becoming for Marlene Nourbese Philip and Erna Brodber," 133.

[58] Carine Mardorossian, *Reclaiming Difference: Caribbean Women Rewrite Postcolonialism* (Charlottesville: UP of Virginia, 2005): 1.

[59] Scott, *Caribbean Women Writers and Globalization*, 2.

[60] The Association for Caribbean Women Writers and Scholars, ACWWS, is the main academic and literary organ dedicated to the critical discussion of Caribbean women's writing. Denoting the international, geographically fluid nature of the association and its actors, ACWWS's biennial conference is held alternately in the Caribbean and elsewhere; usually in the USA.

[61] Mardorossian, *Reclaiming Difference*, 1.

graphic limits of the English-speaking Caribbean islands to their French and Spanish neighbours, the USA and Canada, and the UK.

I have not undertaken to provide an exhaustive survey of the body of writing in question, since this would assume an unreasonable degree of similarity between women of the Caribbean. Instead, selection has been made on the basis of how these novels intimate their respective reading practices, with content and theme providing the glue. The complex themes of sexuality and emotions, both in the reading process and in the texts themselves, have involved a rather subjective approach to selection criteria. For this approach, texts that have no impact on the reader would fail to illustrate the problematics of reading from an affective perspective. Texts that challenge the reader to test the limits of her understanding while engaging her in an affective strange encounter are needed. In this way, the selection process is determined by how the texts are read, not by what they represent. Another important factor in this selection (based on the reading strategies that the novels suggest) is the way in which certain novels complement one another in their treatment of sexuality. Here, what again becomes central is *how* these novels represent sexuality; rather than *what* that sexuality contains as a theme.

The novels discussed in this book take up the dilemma of sexuality in various ways, but in each case sexuality is assigned meanings ranging from ambivalence through negativity to the positive, healing aspects of sexual identities and actions.

Chronologically, the first novelist in this selection is the Jamaican Erna Brodber with her novels *Jane and Louisa Will Soon Come Home* (1980) and *Louisiana* (1994), along with the short story "Sleeping's Beauty and the Prince Charming" (1989). The next is the Haitian Edwidge Danticat with her first novel, *Breath, Eyes, Memory* (1994). Shani Mootoo, of Trinidadian-Canadian background, is the author of *Cereus Blooms at Night* (1996). Likewise writing in North America is the Jamaican Opal Palmer Adisa, with her first novel, *It Begins with Tears* (1997). The final author to be treated is the Guyanese Oonya Kempadoo, with her first novel, *Buxton Spice* (1998). As mentioned above, the Caribbean diaspora in fiction by women can be conceptualized as a continuum ranging from an afrocentric Caribbean feminist consciousness to more recent, transnationalist visions of the New-World experience.

The first example of this continuum is Erna Brodber, whose fiction and scholarship can be broadly defined as "Afro-Caribbean diasporic feminism," which brings to the fore the simultaneity of gender and race in a profoundly intersectional manner.[62] Brodber's approach to writing also ties her to issues of affectivity, as she herself notes: "I believe that our emotional relationship to the space about which we want to write, colours our approach to the work."[63] The creative imagination, in other words, evokes the senses and emotions as gateways to new and forgotten histories, serving to highlight the ways in which the Afro-Jamaican experience as related by Brodber is profoundly affective.

There were numerous important precursors to Brodber in the 1970s, including such authors as Olive Senior, Merle Hodge, and Beryl Gilroy. From the 1970s and early 1980s onwards, the Caribbean women writers' literary tradition experienced a considerable boom, with "increased attention to women writers of earlier periods" and "the emergence in greater numbers of new women writers of the Caribbean and its diaspora."[64] In Brodber's fiction, following this boom, we most interestingly witness notions of sexuality and emotions emerging and offering political insights.

Erna Brodber's fiction bridges the second wave of Caribbean women's writing (roughly from Sylvia Wynter's *The Hills of Hebron*, 1962, to the above-mentioned authors from the 1970s and 1980s) and the current wave of transnationalist authors from the mid-1980s to the 1990s and onwards (such as Shani Mootoo, Dionne Brand, and Jamaica Kincaid). In addition to this generational in-betweenness, Brodber can be situated as a mediating figure between afrocentric and creole or hybrid views of Caribbean culture and experience.[65] Incidentally, Brodber's *Jane and Louisa* was the first novel by a Caribbean woman writer I encountered in a postcolonial writing seminar, and a novel I have not managed to put down since first reading it. Indeed, its merits as a novel that 'sticks' cannot be undermined.[66]

Jane and Louisa Will Soon Come Home exhibits one of the most elusive and intriguing metaphors yet employed in Caribbean literature, the kumbla – the influence of which was so great that the first theoretical anthology on

---

[62] Myriam J.A. Chancy, *Searching for Safe Spaces: Afro-Caribbean Women Writers in Exile* (Philadelphia PA: Temple UP, 1997): 23.

[63] Erna Brodber, *The Continent of Black Consciousness: On the History of the African Diaspora From Slavery to the Present Day* (London: New Beacon, 2003): 160.

[64] Scott, *Caribbean Women Writers and Globalization*, 4.

[65] June E. Roberts, *Reading Erna Brodber: Uniting the Black Diaspora Through Folk Culture and Religion* (Westport CT: Greenwood, 2006).

[66] On stickiness, see Ahmed, *The Cultural Politics of Emotion*, 11, 13.

Caribbean women's writing was named after it.[67] Because of its polysemy and versatility, the kumbla as a metaphor is bound to pose the most problems for a reader who reads across differences, and its ambiguity and polyvalence are a great starting point. I do not find the metaphor outdated despite its having floated around for thirty years now, because it has not been considered from the point of view of feminist reader theory, affectivity, and sexuality.

Jane and Louisa Will Soon Come Home has its origin in a fictional case study for a sociology seminar on black identity crumbling under colonialist pressure. It was the very first of Brodber's attempts to express her uncertainty regarding the apparent paradox between objective sociological methods and her own need to focus on a specifically Jamaican, insider view on society. Stylistically, *Jane and Louisa* is a multivocal and multifocal, fragmented or quilted narrative (Afro-Caribbean women writers use the revisionary term 'quilted' to refer to a narrative lacking in the "linear, phallocentric form of the male text"[68]). It is the non-chronological story of the protagonist, Nellie Richmond's, journey from sheltered childhood and mystified puberty through to adult breakdown, charting a healing process and a struggle for maturation.

As postcolonial feminist texts, Brodber's writings do not simply break the master-narratives, rather, they create new sites of struggle and liberation in and from which an African-identified feminist (and feminine) minority discourse may be articulated.[69] As widely recognized by various critics, code-switching, vernacular vocabulary, and folklore imagery in Brodber's works – the standard, albeit demanding, textual strategies of postcolonial writing – do not qualify the texts as 'easy reads' for a non-native speaker of English situated thousands of miles from the setting of the novel.[70]

---

[67] *Out of the Kumbla: Caribbean Women and Literature*, ed. Carole Boyce Davies & Elaine Savory Fido (Trenton NJ: Africa World Press, 1990).

[68] Davies & Fido, "Introduction: Women and Literature in the Caribbean," 6.

[69] Along with the previously mentioned novels, *Jane and Louisa Will Soon Come Home*, *Louisiana*, and the short story "Sleeping's Beauty and the Prince Charming," Brodber has published the following fictional texts: the novels *Myal* (London: New Beacon, 1988) and *The Rainmaker's Mistake* (London: New Beacon, 2007); the story "One Bubby Susan," in *The Penguin Book of Caribbean Short Stories*, ed. E.A. Markham (Harmondsworth: Penguin, 1998): 48–53 (originally published in the *Jamaica Journal* 22.4 [1989–90]: 52–53; and the short-story collection *The World is a High Hill: Stories about Jamaican Women* (Kingston, Jamaica: Ian Randle, 2012).

[70] Bill Ashcroft, Gareth Griffiths & Helen Tiffin, *The Empire Writes Back: Theory and Practice in Post-Colonial Literatures* (London & New York: Routledge, 1989): 38.

Brodber's third novel, *Louisiana*, is discussed for its unique occurrence of an *asexual* woman.[71] I read asexuality as an oft-neglected expression of sexuality; as something other than simply a target-oriented desire for some-bodies that are similarly oriented. *Louisiana*, in other words, may have much more to tell us about sexuality and its related feelings than, for example, the overt treatment of sexuality in the fiction of Jamaica Kincaid, whose novels fall beyond the purview of this study precisely for their obviousness in this respect.[72] Perhaps more than any of Brodber's other novels, *Louisiana* focuses on alternative ways of knowing, beyond the five senses.[73]. Set in the American state of Louisiana in the 1930s, the novel is the story of the young anthropologist Ella Townsend's being taken on 'a spiritual journey' while in the midst of collecting oral data about old black Louisiana inhabitants with the help of a tape recorder. However, her interviewee, Mammy, dies before the completion of the project, although in this case death does not mark the end of life but, rather, a new beginning. When listening to the tapes, Ella discovers voices, topics, and things never said in the interviews. In other words, Mammy Sue Ann King and her friend Louise (who had died decades earlier) communicate to Ella via the tape recorder.

Brodber's short story "Sleeping's Beauty and the Prince Charming" includes a particular sexual-political comment by the story's narrator. The portrayal of a tragic love affair between two black idealists – a writer and a globetrotting prince – highlights the erasure of black female corporeality in the masculine context of the Rastafari religion and philosophy. The story is veiled in the frame of the eponymous Western fairytale, where the inability of the black man to deal with the female body (specifically the menstruation taboo, a recurring theme in Brodber) leads to the failure of the whole black project of diasporic emancipation and 'return to Africa', be it spiritual or physical. Sleeping's Beauty's wish for support from Charming as she struggles

---

[71] Denise DeCaires Narain, "The Body of the Woman in the Body of the Text: The Novels of Erna Brodber," in *Caribbean Women Writers: Fiction in English*, ed. Mary Condé & Thorunn Lonsdale (London: Macmillan, 1999): 113.

[72] See Narain, "Standing in the Place of Love."

[73] Nellie McKay, with reference to Toni Morrison, "Introduction" to Critical Essays on Toni Morrison, ed. McKay (Boston MA: G.K. Hall/Twayne, 1988): 3, Marc C. Conner, "Introduction: Aesthetics and the African American Novel," in *The Aesthetics of Toni Morrison: Speaking the Unspeakable*, ed. Conner (Jackson: UP of Mississippi, 2000): xi, and La Vinia Delois Jennings, *Toni Morrison and the Idea of Africa* (Cambridge & New York: Cambridge UP, 2008): 180–81.

with menstrual pain is too much for Charming to handle, and he takes off into the horizon, leaving "her to be a woman alone."[74] The narrator remarks that this is the reason for the failure of emancipation, since Sleeping's Beauty is unable to reintegrate mind and body without the help of Charming, thus remains asleep. Since she cannot operate alone, Charming is also unable (on his own) to settle black people in the promised land (i.e. Africa).

The Guyanese author Oonya Kempadoo's first novel, *Buxton Spice*, is set in approximately the same period of political turmoil in the 1960s and 1970s as Brodber's *Jane and Louisa*. Like Brodber's novel, *Buxton Spice* deals with the ambivalence of sexual formation, explicitly mirrored in the political race riots in 1970s Guyana.[75] As Helen Scott remarks, the novel offers a view of "the emotional and sensual experience of 1970s Guyana" with its powerful natural imagery tied to expressions of structural political violence.[76] Kempadoo's fiction remains the least studied of the authors in this selection.[77] Interestingly, *Buxton Spice* offers a textual structure that can often be detected in novels by Caribbean woman writers. In a kind of micro- and macro-structured novel, something occurring on an individual (female) level reflects larger societal upheavals. This mirroring technique prompts us to consider the stories of girls and women erased from the national master-narratives.

The first novel by the Jamaican-American Opal Palmer Adisa, *It Begins with Tears*, takes its place in my selection due to its abundance of affectivity in issues relating to sexuality. Adisa's writing is deeply committed to exploring sexuality, passion, and desire in an Afro-Caribbean context. Adisa is also a poet and essayist, and her collections *Caribbean Passion* and *Eros Muse* highlight a politics of sensuality and sexuality not far removed from her project of creating and discussing the black erotic and erotica.[78] Perhaps the most sexually explicit of the texts I read in this selection, *It Begins with Tears*

---

[74] Brodber, "Sleeping's Beauty and the Prince Charming," *Kunapipi* 9.3 (1989): 4.

[75] Although Guyana is, geographically speaking, situated at the northern end of the South American continent, culturally it has more in common with the Caribbean. Thus, Guyana is generally treated here as belonging to the Caribbean.

[76] Scott, *Caribbean Women Writers and Globalization*, 20.

[77] See *Caribbean Women Writers and Globalization*, 94.

[78] Opal Palmer Adisa, *Caribbean Passion* (Leeds: Peepal Tree, 2004), and *Eros Muse: Poems & Essays* (Trenton NJ: Africa World Press, 2006); as well as *Caribbean Erotic: Poetry, Prose & Essays*, ed. Opal Palmer Adisa & Donna Weir–Soley (Leeds: Peepal Tree, 2010).

contains sexual violence, polyamory, and various sexual encounters between the novel's characters. As Weir–Soley observes, "unlike some Caribbean women writers, Adisa does not shy away from dealing with adult female sexuality."[79] Despite the novel's portrayal of the power of sexuality as a positive force, sexuality also becomes expressed in negative terms through jealousy and rage. The magical-realist novel tells of the life in the fictional village of Kristoff in rural Jamaica, where the community is shaken by the return of the sensuous former prostitute, Monica, from her years as a sex worker in Kingston. After embarking on a relationship with the married Desmond, Monica is attacked by a group of three women in her village, who violently shove hot peppers into the adulterous woman's bodily orifices. This West-African-derived tradition of peppering is an example of how sexuality operates under a strict regime of discipline and punishment – despite its positive associations with liberation and power.

As mentioned earlier, sexuality is frequently represented as a negative force in Caribbean women's writing. Perhaps the most famous expression of this can be seen in Haitian-American Edwidge Danticat's first novel, *Breath, Eyes, Memory*.[80] For my reading of *Breath, Eyes, Memory*, what becomes central is not its commercial status but its status as *the* cross-over novel from the Caribbean – making it a relevant example of how to read across differences. Danticat's novel is a story of migrancy highlighting survival despite individual and collective traumas in the past. Four generations of Haitian women are forced to address their relationships with each other, as well as their violent legacies. The historical tradition of mothers 'testing' their daughters' virginity by inserting a finger into the child's vagina is a source of trauma for the novel's protagonist, Sophie Caco. A child born of rape, Sophie has to endure her mother's obsession with her chastity, and, later, to find ways of coping with her mother's mental illness. As a violent practice, testing is worth considering from the perspective of feminist sexuality, as it has been read as

---

[79] Weir–Soley, *Eroticism, Spirituality, and Resistance in Black Women's Writings*, 153.

[80] Danticat's novel has been the best selling of all Caribbean women's novels, thanks to its being featured in 1998 on Oprah Winfrey's Book Club television show and website. This highlights the power of mass-reading events and communities and how they shape our reading practices. See Danielle Fuller, "Reading as Social Practice: Beyond the Book Research Project," *Journal of Popular Narrative Media* 1.2 (October 2008): 211–17.

"unequivocally oppressive" by Western readers, while Haitian-American women have criticized testing as an obsolete cultural practice.[81] These contesting knowledges need to be considered in an effort to read the novel as an expression of sexuality imbued with negative affect.

These two acts of violence, *testing* (always in italics, as the hymen-testing tradition is referred to in *Breath, Eyes, Memory*) and peppering (in *It Begins with Tears*), find their horrific counterparts in rape, isolation, and incest in *Cereus Blooms at Night* by Shani Mootoo, a Trinidadian-Canadian author. The novel's flashbacks tell of the events leading to the social reclusion of its protagonist, Mala Ramchandin, after growing up under her father's incestuous sexual tyranny. Despite – or perhaps due to – the taboo of same-sex relationships and non-heterosexual identities in the Caribbean, gay, lesbian, and queer topics have been intensively focused on in Caribbean literary studies in the past decade or so.[82] This interest is in part thanks to a proliferation in fiction which, through its creative imaginings, has served to generate more conceptual space for non-normative sexualities. In particular, expatriate authors such as Mootoo, Patricia Powell, and Thomas Glave have drawn creative as well as critical attention to the issues at stake in a social and cultural setting that generally allows for little (or no) queer expression or experiences in everyday life.[83]

---

[81] Mardorossian, *Reclaiming Difference*, 127.

[82] For example, the website for J-Flag, the Jamaica Forum for Lesbians, All-Sexuals and Gays, cites several articles of Jamaican law that are enforced to persecute homosexuals (see http://www.jflag.org/bodyspirit/rights.htm). A similar aversion can be detected in academic thought, such as in Fanon, who, according to Jonathan Goldberg, contends that "there is no homosexuality indigenous to the Antilles," thereby deeming queer lives in the Caribbean to be unnatural and imported. See Goldberg, *Tempest in the Caribbean* (Minneapolis: U of Minnesota P, 2003): 20.

[83] I use the term 'queer' following Kekki and Ahmed: as an umbrella term for the lives, identities, and experiences of (as well as research on) gay, lesbian, bisexual, and transgendered people. Queer theory seeks to question and challenge heteronormativity and offer different political and sexual positions conceived as vital for non-heterosexual people. However, few scholars would venture to rob the term of its multiple meanings with a strict definition. Thus, entirely different understandings of 'queer' from those offered here circulate and are used in the field of Queer Studies. See Lasse Kekki, *From Gay to Queer: Gay Male Identity in Selected Fiction by David Leavitt and in Tony Kushner's Play Angels in America I–II* (Bern: Peter Lang, 2003): 28, and Ahmed, *The Cultural Politics of Emotion*, 166.

Mootoo's novel, set on the fictional Caribbean island of Lantanacamara,[84] is narrated by Nurse Tyler, who cares for Mala "PohPoh" Ramchandin; an elderly woman taken into custody at the nursing home after the discovery of the decomposed body of her sexually abusive father. Gradually, Nurse Tyler discovers Mala's life story, and relates it to the reader. In coming to terms with Mala's story, Tyler begins to make sense of his gender and sexual identity. At the beginning of the novel, Tyler refers to himself as a man, but by the end of the novel, s/he no longer uses such a term.[85] Instead, Tyler decides to "unabashedly declare myself" by wearing lipstick, powder, and a flower-patterned scarf.[86] The caregiver–patient relationship in the novel becomes reciprocal, as it is through caring for the elderly and mentally deranged Mala at the nursing home that Tyler begins to find his/her true self as a transgendered individual. Through this storytelling event, the novel brings heteronormativity under scrutiny and invites its readers to engage with non-normative sexualities which have hereto largely escaped representation in the Caribbean literary imagary.

Bearing in mind Paravisini–Gebert's overtly critical tone about the study of Caribbean women's writing by Western scholars, it is important to scrutinize the conditions of each attempt at knowledge production as well as the subjects of that knowledge. In other words, who reads these texts I have just described? Paravisini–Gebert's rejection of Western feminist theories of corporeality thus evokes the problems of both epistemology and ontology for a Western reader unable to claim 'insular' Caribbean methods of meaning-making; whatever they might be. Who, then, is the reading subject and where is she situated? This question is the topic of discussion in the following section.

⌘

---

[84] According to Grace Kyungwon Hong, Lantanacamara is fashioned on pre-independence colonial Trinidad, where Mootoo spent her childhood. In addition, Mala Ramchandin's family background as the descendants of South Asian indentured labourers hints at an Indo-Trinidadian context. See Grace Kyungwon Hong, "'A Shared Queerness': Colonialism, Transnationalism, and Sexuality in Shani Mootoo's *Cereus Blooms at Night*," *Meridians: Feminism, Race, Transnationalism* 7.1 (2006): 74.

[85] Mootoo, *Cereus Blooms at Night* (London: Granta, 1996), 12.

[86] *Cereus Blooms at Night*, 247.

Situating the reader

In order to account for the role of the reader as someone who feels while engaging with the textual scenarios of healing described above, the figure of the reader needs to be situated in relation to the region as well as the reading event. It would be too hasty to reduce the equation of reading the local globally to a matter of simple physical geography. Certainly, it would be easy – albeit entirely unsatisfactory – to reduce the question of difference to a matter of physical distance: for instance, here is a reader located in Turku, Finland, reading novels set in Kingston, Jamaica. As this reading is premised on difference as a challenge to the reading process, the question is thus not one of difference as de-facto distance which the reader would strive to overcome or deem impossible to bridge. Certainly, this would reduce matters to (merely) geographical location as the signifier of difference. Instead, defining the reading subject in this endeavour entails a keen interrogation of the production of differences in the reading process as intersectional.[87]

The concept of difference has been instrumental to feminist thought throughout its history. Initially, difference was understood almost exclusively in terms of gender. The political agenda of second-wave feminism had to expand the discussion of difference considerably.[88] As Rita Felski notes, "female difference has fragmented into multiple differences."[89] This condition is generally referred to as the feminist politics of difference, where gender, race, class, sexuality, and other categories are seen as co-articulated. Helen Scott argues that literary criticism on Caribbean women's writing is preoccupied with gender and fails to account for class as a relevant category of social differentiation.[90] Scott highlights class and materialist theory in her account of post-independence struggles in the Caribbean nations of Haiti, Guyana, Grenada, and Antigua. Class conflicts between women provide a theme often seen in Caribbean women's writing, and thus, following her materialist premise, calls for a foregrounding of class in critical analysis.[91] In turn, I suggest that, in

[87] See Avtar Brah & Ann Phoenix, "Ain't I a Woman? Revisiting Intersectionality," *Journal of International Women's Studies* 5.3 (2004): 75–86.

[88] Chris Weedon, *Feminism, Theory and the Politics of Difference* (London & Malden MA: Blackwell, 1999): 1.

[89] Rita Felski, "The Doxa of Difference," *Signs* 23.1 (Autumn 1997): 1.

[90] Scott, *Caribbean Women Writers and Globalization*, 9.

[91] *Caribbean Women Writers and Globalization*, 17.

reading Caribbean women's writing, an intersectional feminist approach will enable us to view categories of social differentiation as convergent and produced in constant interaction with each other.[92] This idea of differences then means that class or gender alone does not provide us with access to plausible meaning-production, but that they work together in an intersectional manner.

One of the first critics to use the term 'intersectionality' in feminist theorizations of difference was the black feminist lawyer Kimberlé Crenshaw. Crenshaw states that identity-politics failed to account for differences within a specific social group, and that it is of the utmost importance to pay attention to the intersections of race and gender in the analysis of violence against women of colour. According to Crenshaw,

> through an awareness of intersectionality, we can better acknowledge and ground the differences among us and negotiate the means by which these differences will find expression in constructing group politics.[93]

Central to intersectionality as a means of conceptualizing difference is the manner in which its multiplicity lies in the *articulations* of social categories of difference. Avtar Brah and Ann Phoenix theorize this condition of 'intersectionality' as

> the complex, irreducible, varied and variable effects which ensue when multiple axis (sic) of differentiation – economic, political, cultural, psychic, subjective and experiential – intersect in historically specific contexts.[94]

Conceptualizing difference as intersectional is vital for my approach to fiction, which is, by necessity, laden with differences; all discursive, articulated, and intersectional.

A keen awareness of the intersectional condition as constitutive of the novels' dynamics will enable us to scrutinize these texts with more understanding and sensitivity. An intersectional reading may even take us further than serving to point out random intersections of social categories in various material contexts. Instead, an intersectional approach – which is, by necessity,

---

[92] See Avtar Brah, *Cartographies of Diaspora: Contesting Identities* (London: Routledge, 1996), and Brah & Phoenix, "Ain't I a Woman? Revisiting Intersectionality."

[93] Kimberlé Crenshaw, "Mapping the Margins: Intersectionality, Identity Politics, and Violence Against Women of Color," *Stanford Law Review* 43.6 (July 1991): 1299.

[94] Brah & Phoenix, "Ain't I a Woman? Revisiting Intersectionality," 76.

also a materialist approach – is bound up with the processes of reading. In other words, intersectionality is always subject to interpretation and is thus contextual and situational.

The text–reader relationship has to be seen as intimate, because meaning production requires close contact in which the production of differences, affects, and meanings becomes possible. This paradoxical position forms in accordance with a transgressive logic, as difference is not simply produced on the premise of distance; rather, meanings (and differences at the same time) are constantly produced in the reading process; in the contact between text and reader, the two strangers.

In her book *Strange Encounters*, Sara Ahmed poses the question "how do you know a stranger?" – appealing to how, in the establishment of strangerhood, you in fact *recognize* strangers as *some-bodies* whom you actively do-not-know, rather than being something or somebodies as essentially, ontologically unknown in themselves.[95] The question of knowing a stranger also refers to the problem of how to produce knowledge and meaning from someone or something unknown to and from your cultural context and perspective, and what kinds of knowledge and meanings are produced in each attempt at getting to know (and, thus, producing) the stranger; be it an everyday, face-to-face, or literary–scholarly encounter. These strange encounters, according to Ahmed, are "mediated and partial" (15) meetings involving surprise and conflict, where the element of surprise arises from a potential inability to read the 'Other' and the element of conflict arises from the power-relations at play in each encounter, enabling the 'Other' to exist (8).

What is strange in a reading process thus becomes a constant subject of negotiation – a factor that underlies the dynamic of the current study. The question is therefore not that of deeming a text to be 'strange' and subsequently seeking to 'know' it, but is, rather, that of possessing the will and the means to scrutinize the ways in which strangerhood – in this case, affectivity and sexuality – is produced and constructed textually and situationally in a reader's dialogue with the material. While Ahmed does not always have a literary encounter in mind when theorizing strange encounters, she illustrates what she means in terms of encounters as the coming-together of elements by offering an example of reading "as a meeting between reader and text" (7). In this meeting, meaning becomes constituted as a form of sociality (15), because we

---

[95] Ahmed, *Strange Encounters*, 55. Further page references are in the main text.

do not recognize strangers by their distance but through their very proximity – which denotes to us that they do not 'belong' (22).

Ahmed writes about the process of recognition involved in contact with strangers as that which occurs, not from afar, but from being (too) close. The encounter has already taken place in the establishment of strangerhood, and it is there that differentiation of subjects takes place (23). This, according to Ahmed, is the precise moment when a subject comes to "inhabit or dwell in the world" (24); that is to say, to claim its locationality. In the same way, the reader becomes aware of his/her place in the world, and of "the immense 'distance' between author and reader in the cross-cultural or subcultural text."[96] Yet, as suggested by the stranger's proximity in the act of recognition, the distance mentioned in the above quotation from Bill Ashcroft fails to explain everything. Granted, the potentially large geographical distance or the cultural gap that is often at play in postcolonial reading[97] is important, but reading texts is not just geography. To me, methodologically more interesting is the *negotiation* between proximity and distance or sameness and difference in the reading process.

In terms of social differentiation within the reading process, Elizabeth Abel remarks that white feminist readers often overlook race in literary studies. In her article on the problematics of race in feminist literary interpretation, Abel recounts her troubling reading experience of Toni Morrison's "Recitatif," when she was unable to determine whether the protagonist was black or white, as the text provided only contradictory evidence on the matter. This leads her to ask a series of critical questions regarding white women reading black texts, bodies, and textual bodies. Abel argues, through a careful consideration of three critical texts by white feminists on black women's writing, that there is a tendency among white feminists to read black women's writing while neglecting the ways in which the texts are inscribed in black political and cultural traditions; instead, aligning the texts with white feminist agendas.[98] Abel concludes by calling for cautious readings that position themselves self-

[96] Bill Ashcroft, *Post-Colonial Transformation* (London & New York: Routledge, 2001): 66.

[97] Ashcroft, *Post-Colonial Transformation*, 75.

[98] Elizabeth Abel, "Black Writing, White Reading: Race and the Politics of Feminist Interpretation," in *Female Subjects in Black and White: Race, Psychoanalysis, Feminism*, ed. Elizabeth Abel, Barbara Christian & Helene Moglen (Berkeley: U of California P, 1997): 118.

critically with respect to black feminist criticism, in order to arrive at a balanced outcome that reduces the risks of creating a phantasm of the "others."[99]

This rather conciliatory view is further challenged by Jane Haggis and Susanne Schech's analysis of how the white Western trope of benevolence operates in feminist praxis, in which they establish that the 'white woman's burden' has been instrumental in shaping feminist thought. In addition, Haggis and Schech articulate a need to deconstruct the discourse of 'meaning well' which still dominates many white approaches to intercultural and interracial encounters. Despite the fact that "mantras of difference are incantated," global feminism continues to be determined according to white parameters and is fuelled by motivations which can be traced back to the figure of the "good Christian white woman," the "Lady Bountiful" as the benefactor of the 'other' woman.[100]

Instead, Haggis and Schech urge white feminists researching non-white women to consciously "risk being BAD, not (only) as 'girrrrls' contesting conventions of patriarchy, but as makers of powerful knowledges about others."[101] Another Australian feminist scholar, Aileen Moreton–Robinson, joins Haggis and Schech's bold declaration; arguing that white race privilege has not been sufficiently questioned within feminism, and, since the aim of feminists should be "to be effective trouble makers," such troublemaking should be extended to white feminist theory in a project which re-interrogates and reconfigures its premises openly – much like Haggis and Schech's project – without avoiding risk-taking.[102]

If white feminists attempting a dialogue with the 'Other' woman have at times been unnecessarily cautious about their subject-positions as knowledge producers, so, too, has traditional reader theory been somewhat conservative in dealing with the role of the reader. In addition to the aforementioned privilege of the cognitive at the expense of the affective, theories of reading have produced a gap between the reader as a theoretical figure, on the one hand, and the reader as an empirical subject to be studied on the other.[103] For ex-

[99] Elizabeth Abel, "Black Writing, White Reading," 120.

[100] Haggis & Schech, "Meaning Well and Global Good Manners," 387.

[101] "Meaning Well and Global Good Manners," 397.

[102] Aileen Moreton–Robinson, "Troubling Business: Difference and Whiteness Within Feminism," *Australian Feminist Studies* 15/33 (2000): 348, 343.

[103] Lea Rojola, "Puhetta *siitä*: Lukijuuden rakentuminen Maria Jotunin novellissa Rakkautta" [Speaking about *it*: The construction of readership in Maria Jotuni's short

ample, Wolfgang Iser, in his book *The Act of Reading*, formulates a reader-response theory according to which the literary text is replete with gaps which the reader attempts to fill during the process of an aesthetic response. For Iser, the implied reader is clearly separated from its empirical counterpart, the actual reader. He writes that the implied reader "has his roots firmly planted in the structure of the text; he is a construct and in no way to be identified with any real reader."[104] In other words, the implied reader is the reader presupposed by the text, "a textual structure anticipating the presence of a recipient without necessarily defining him" (34). According to Iser, the implied reader is an ahistorical concept without a social context. Rather, he believes that texts themselves already carry meaning potential, which will be actualized by the reader's response to the text. Thus, the reader's role consists of three factors: the text's guidance; the reader's point of view; and the coming-together of the two (36). It is at this point of convergence that the actual reader becomes important. The 'real' reader is the person who picks up the book and begins to read and interpret it, and this is the point at which textual structure becomes a structured *act*.

The reader as an empirical figure has been studied in turn by scholars concentrating on audience reception through discussing the mass-reception of certain literary and cultural phenomena. These "actual readers," to borrow Iser's term, were not so much about the textual coding of reading positions in the text's structure as about the everyday situations in which different readings take place. Recently, however, these views have been bridged in empirical work. One important instance of such an approach is provided by the research project 'Beyond the Book: Mass Reading Events and Contemporary Cultures of Reading in the UK, the USA, and Canada'. In the transatlantic collaboration of different reading communities, shared reading practices were examined according to feminist epistemologies.[105] Caribbean women's writing has also received scholarly attention within the Beyond the Book project,

---

story Rakkautta], in *Kohtauspaikkana kieli. Näkökulmia persoonaan, muutokseen ja valintoihin* [Language as a meeting place: Aspects of persona, change and choices], ed. Taru Nordlund, Tiina Onikki-Rantajääskö & Toni Suutari (Helsinki: SKS, 2006): 475.

104 Wolfgang Iser, *The Act of Reading: A Theory of Aesthetic Response* (Baltimore MD & London: Johns Hopkins UP, 1978): 34. Further page references are in the main text.

105 Fuller, "Reading as Social Practice," 2008.

as Anouk Lang, Daniel Fuller, and James Procter have explored the mass-readerly responses to Andrea Levy's novel *Small Island*.[106]

One of the pioneering approaches in the field of cultural studies was provided by Liebes and Katz, who conducted a reception survey of *Dallas*, the globally popular prime-time television soap opera, broadcast in the 1970s and 1980s. The research spanned ninety countries in order to make sense of *Dallas*'s universal appeal, but the authors found that received perceptions were too complex to generalize according to individual nations. Similarly, Ien Ang in her now classic study on the pleasures of watching *Dallas* collected data from Dutch *Dallas* aficionados; seeking views on what constituted their viewing-pleasure.[107] Based on the data, Ang concluded that the pleasures provided by each *Dallas*-watching event were connected to the viewer's moment of freedom "from the prohibitions and demands of society."[108] This cathartic function of the TV show reflects Ang's view of the text–reader relationship as interactive, and is thus one of the first reader-oriented models of interpretation to points to a merging of the theoretical and the empirical.[109]

Feminist reader theorists like Lynne Pearce have successfully discussed these seemingly disparate figures together within the affective model of reading.[110] In fact, there is an active relationship between the two figures with which Pearce holds a balanced dialogue. The theoretical reader is also always an empirical, 'actual' reader, and vice versa. This is highlighted by Pearce's decision to use her own reading notes and experiences, along with those of other readers, as material for her formulations of reading as a romance. This "autobiographical method" includes Pearce's use of the first-person personal pronoun in discussing the "readerly guinea pig."[111] In my readings, I employ a

---

[106] Anouk Lang, "Reading Race in *Small Island*: Discourse Deviation, Schemata and the Textual Encounter," *Language and Literature* 18.3 (August 2009): 316–30; Anouk Lang, "'Enthralling but at the Same Time Disturbing': Challenging the Readers of *Small Island*," *Journal of Commonwealth Literature* 44.2 (June 2009): 123–40; and Danielle Fuller & James Procter, "Reading as 'Social Glue'? Book Groups, Multiculture and the *Small Island Read 2007*," *Moving Worlds* 9.2 (2009): 26–40.

[107] Ien Ang, *Watching Dallas: Soap Opera and the Melodramatic Imagination*, tr. Della Couling (1985; London: Routledge, 1991).

[108] Ang, *Watching Dallas*, 22.

[109] Pearce, *Feminism and the Politics of Reading*, 16. Further page references are in the main text.

[110] See Rojola, "Speaking about *it*," 480.

[111] Pearce, *Feminism and the Politics of Reading*, 3.

similar discursive strategy in attempting an introspective, reflexive reading and writing process. At the same time as such a personalist 'I' is employed, we must, however, bear in mind that, in discursive practices, pronoun-use performs multiple functions.[112] Pearce details the uses of the "autobiographical 'I'" in terms of feminist rhetorics by analysing the multiple pronoun uses in feminist texts.[113] In her account, the use of first-person singular 'I' can be divided into the "first person personal" and the "first person strategic," where the latter is a somewhat more decentered writing self than the former.[114] As in feminist writing at large, these two figure in my text alternatingly, but individuating between their different uses need not be deemed entirely crucial for the sake of reading this study.

The fundamental reason why this approach incorporates the readerly 'I' as a crucial component of the analysis is that, in this model, the reader is always *articulated* within the text.[115] This unique position results from Pearce's model of affective reading, where each moment of theorizing reading is also a moment of *actual* reading which, as affective, impresses itself upon the reader's embodied knowledge-potential.[116] The active theoretical/empirical reader-relationship is resolved by Pearce's idea of reading as dialogic[117] in the Bakhtinian sense, in which there is a "dialogic interdependence of speaker and addressee."[118] When the text and the reader are in a perpetual dialogic relationship, the earlier rigidity between the text and the reader (or the reader

---

[112] Lynne Pearce, *The Rhetorics of Feminism: Readings in Contemporary Cultural Theory and the Popular Press* (London: Routledge, 2004).

[113] Pearce, *Feminism and the Politics of Reading*, 25, and Pearce, *The Rhetorics of Feminism.*

[114] *The Rhetorics of Feminism*, 47, 86, 88.

[115] *Feminism and the Politics of Reading*, 24.

[116] See Vivian Sobchack, *Carnal Thoughts: Embodiment and Moving Image Culture* (Berkeley: U of California P, 2004).

[117] Note that here I am not so much interested in dialogism as a stylistic feature, although that dimension also (re)appears later in my reading. Some of these authors' narrative techniques can be placed in the polyphonic, dialogic or double-voiced African (American) tradition, as exemplified by Zora Neale Hurston. For a discussion of polyphony, see Henry Louis Gates, Jr., *The Signifying Monkey: A Theory of African-American Literary Criticism* (New York & Oxford: Oxford UP, 1998). Rather, my interest in dialogic reading in this instance is primarily methodological.

[118] Lynne Pearce, *Reading Dialogics* (London: Edward Arnold, 1994): 4. Further page references are in the main text.

in the text) becomes challenged by their interplay. In the dialogic model, we can no longer clearly distinguish between individual readers or individual texts, as each utterance is constituted on the principle of simultaneity of the speaker's and the addressee's voices in a *dynamic* relationship.

Pearce emphasizes that dialogic interdependence is a dynamic always "inscribed by *power*" (4–5). Accordingly, the dialogic principle in its "radical, politicized" form cannot be understood without an awareness of power, as there is inevitably a power-marked relationship between speaker and addressee. Dialogue is not simply based on the principle of democratic reciprocity, yet we inevitably become "alerted to the inequalities between the terms/subjects under consideration" in textual and non-textual voices (12). Indeed, Pearce asserts that feminist critics "have simply no investment in a depoliticized reading" of Bakhtin and dialogic theory (13); particularly as gender is a question neglected by "Bakhtin's own formulation of dialogic relations, be these linguistic, textual or interpersonal" (19). Similarly, in his account of post-colonial reading, Ashcroft turns to a model of dialogic reading, asserting that meaning is "a product of the dialogic situation of reading," which then becomes "a social accomplishment."[119] In her conclusion (written in the form of a dialogue between the author and the reader), Pearce maintains that the dialogic contract is dependent on difference as a condition and a consequence.[120] Dialogism's dependence on difference reasserts its usefulness for a cross-cultural feminist politics of reading, which in itself cannot exist without an awareness of and willingness to work with inter- and intrasubjective differences between women.

Difference as a condition and consequence of reading becomes highlighted by the idea of the reader as a ghostly presence in reading a text.[121] By ghostly readers, Pearce refers to the ways in which the reader can wander about the textual landscapes while textual characters are always "fixed in the historical moment of their first inscription" (24). This also means that, despite her ability to "*move about texts*" (25), the reader has no power to change the story's events; no matter how she haunts the story that she reads and romances. We can be active readers, who "voyeuristically explore our textual others from all angles, desperately looking for ways in which we may make them

---

[119] Ashcroft, *Post-Colonial Transformation*, 60.

[120] Pearce, *Reading Dialogics*, 202.

[121] Pearce, *Feminism and the Politics of Reading*, 24. Further page references are in the main text.

respond to us and include us in their script" (25). Yet, by constructing such intimate relationships in reading, more often than not the reader becomes cognizant of herself as involved in a "ghostly romance" of disconnection and loss – despite "moments of connection and fulfillment" (25) which typically provide the reader(s) most pleasure in reading.

In addition to a romantic relationship (central in Pearce's framework) there are other possible relationships (such as sexual ones) involved in the reading process. In this study, I view feminist attachment as one such potential textual other.[122] The reader's feminist attachment, in my view, refers to an attachment and emotional commitment to feminist politics, including various emotional responses such as "withness," wonder, love, and empathy.[123] Here, as elsewhere in cross-cultural feminist thought, the notion of empathy needs to be clarified in order to differentiate between the seemingly similar (but, in my treatment, disparate) affective experiences of sympathy and empathy.

In her analysis of affective responses in the reading of literature, Susan Feagin discusses the affective imaginings of empathy and sympathy: she asserts that empathy is a simulation of what another person is going through, whereas sympathy is a somewhat milder affective response, in that it only "requires having feelings or emotions that are in concert with the interests or desires" of the fictional character with which the reader sympathizes.[124] In Feagin's reading of empathy, the reader adopts the perspective of the other person (i.e. character), in the sense that she compares her own, similar experiences and attributes the emotions experienced at that time to the fictional character and his/her experiences. Feagin explains: "To empathize with someone is to know what it's like for them, to experience things as they do."[125] The problem for a feminist reader, however, is to consider how she may experience "things as they do" in an ethical way, as it entails the inhabiting – even colonizing – of another person's subject-position. As Ahmed asserts, at worst, empathy can in fact sustain "the very difference it may seek to overcome."[126]

A different reading of empathy may help us to move further away from Feagin's rather crude conceptualization of a reader's affective responses as

[122] Ahmed, *The Cultural Politics of Emotion*, 171.

[123] *The Cultural Politics of Emotion*, 160.

[124] Susan Feagin, *Reading with Feeling: The Aesthetics of Appreciation* (Ithaca NY: Cornell UP,1996): 83.

[125] Feagin, *Reading with Feeling*, 101.

[126] Ahmed, *The Cultural Politics of Emotion*, 30.

reserved solely for the fictional characters with whom she identifies. As such, Feagin's view cannot account for textual others as larger formations, such as a feminist attachment in the form of empathy. Her view is also precarious in its refusal to engage with the idea of text and reader in a dialogic, communicative relationship.[127] This unilateral view of reading emotions does not allow us to clarify the very circulation of affects as a force constitutive of, and constituted in, the text–reader interaction. Instead, we need to recognize empathy as an interactive affect. Milton J. Bennett, a scholar in cross-cultural communication, offers an in-depth consideration of the differences between the notions of sympathy and empathy that I find useful for my discussion.

To Bennett, sympathy refers to a projection where "we are referencing how we ourselves might think or feel in similar circumstances," but the problem with sympathy (as with Feagin's use of empathy) is that it always involves an assumption of similarity, and this potentially acts as a form of epistemic violence.[128] In addition to being "insensitive to difference," Bennett lists the dangers of sympathy, in asserting that it is "patronizing" and "breeds defensiveness" – akin to what Richard Dyer famously terms "me too-ism"– which hinders communication.[129] In contrast, the term 'empathy' in Bennett refers to a perspectival change that resists ethnocentric, homogenizing uses of sympathy and results in an awareness of the plethora of different perspectives through *participation* in the other person's experience.

Bennett stresses the importance of participation, as opposed to the placing of oneself into another person's experience in sympathy. However, sympathy and empathy might not operate at such opposite ends of the spectrum of sameness (identification in sympathy) and difference (participation in empathy). They may therefore be conceived not as exclusive but, rather, as mutually influential. As Elspeth Probyn remarks, "instead of posing sameness and difference as opposing and static blocks, we might find it refreshing to think about the varying degrees and hues of similarity and difference that constantly inform human life."[130] I choose to use the term 'empathy' to highlight Bennett's

---

[127] Pearce, *Feminism and the Politics of Reading*, 19.

[128] Milton J. Bennett, "Overcoming the Golden Rule: Sympathy and Empathy," in *Basic Concepts of Intercultural Communication*, ed. Milton Bennett (Yarmouth and London: Intercultural, 1998): 197.

[129] Bennett, "Overcoming the Golden Rule," 202, and Richard Dyer, *White* (London: Routledge, 1997).

[130] Probyn, *Blush: Faces of Shame*, 22.

emphasis on participation, but, like Probyn, I recognize the hues of identification that it may contain. Participation echoes the politics of partiality – as called for by Ien Ang – to be adopted by feminism operating with difference.[131] Examining "'multicultural desire' in feminism," Ang suggests that the incommensurability of a feminist politics of difference means that we cannot expect to have an impact on the lives of the Other in any other way than by limited participation, "which does not absorb difference within a pregiven and predefined space but leaves room for ambivalence and ambiguity" (178). Awareness of this fundamental ambivalence is, according to Ang (187), a lifeline for ethical knowledge-production.

This method of reading as committed to the political and the ethical in an affective way is further motivated by Eve Kosofsky Sedgwick's methodology of paranoid and reparative reading practices. Sedgwick's notions of paranoid and reparative reading are "changing and heterogeneous relational stances,"[132] where paranoid reading refers to the tendency of queer studies (and, one might add, feminist scholarship at large) to simply expose oppressive strands in texts and other social phenomena. Paranoid reading, in other words, emphasizes the depressive position (borrowed from the psychoanalyst Melanie Klein) and is thus a negative affect theory (136). However, despite detailing paranoid readings in full, Sedgwick does not give an account of what a reparative reading might look like. This study takes on the challenge of elaborating on reparative reading practices. According to Sedgwick, reparative reading refers to an open attitude – a stance exposed to the potential of surprise in a text. Sedgwick explains that a reparative reading should be seen as a position, rather than as an outcome:

> [Reparative reading] undertakes a range of affects, ambitions, and risks. What we can best learn from such practices are, perhaps, the many ways selves and communities succeed in extracting sustenance from the objects of a culture – even of a culture whose avowed desire has often been not to sustain them. (150–51)

Reparative reading thus strives to add and to accumulate; to find strength in positive resources and to allow multiple, simultaneous processes open to feelings of surprise and wonder. The benefits of such openness for my reading would be a new kind of intellectual desire; a will to know, and an access of knowledge itself. An openness to alternative readings created by a reparative

[131] Ang, *On Not Speaking Chinese*, 178. Further page references are in the main text.

[132] Sedgwick, *Touching Feeling*, 128. Further page references are in the main text.

motivation may also be helpful in negotiating literary borders. A paranoid reading works by anticipating a self-explanatory, oppressive outcome to any given phenomenon, whereas a reparative reading is not so eager to jump to conclusions. A reparative practice places its hope in a variety of surprises (good or bad). Some of these surprises, then, within the incommensurability of a feminist politics of difference, may enable the spaces of living "together-in-difference" to become more livable.[133]

In practising reparative reading, this book seeks solutions to a problem that can be simply summarized as follows: how can a white feminist reader read and understand Caribbean fiction written by women from a white cross-cultural feminist perspective? I look for ways in which meaning production and understanding can be negotiated within and through the reading process taking place across multiple intersecting differences. In an effort to combine the preoccupations of feminist reader theory and Caribbean sexualities in literature, I ask the following questions: How does a Caribbean cultural context in literature respond to – and become constructed by – this reading practice, which charts the "contradictory ways in which sex is viewed in the Caribbean"?[134] What are the ways in which sexuality becomes a scene or site of affect in anglophone Caribbean women's writing? How should we read sexuality as and through affect? How can affects be used as reading tools or strategies? What are the ethical implications of an affective text-reader relationship?

The cyclical narrative arch of this study moves from sexual ambivalence to the negative and the destructive side of sexuality (in terms both of literary theme and of reading), then proceeds via the positive and the liberatory view of sexuality to a reparative view of ambivalence. Having set out the background for reader theory and its situation in this particular context in this introductory chapter, the limits of a reader's knowledge are then tested in a discussion of sexual liminality and ambivalence in Chapter 2, "Reading the Ambivalence of Sexuality in Transition." This discussion charts the ways in which sexuality is the scene, or site, of affect expressed in terms of ambivalence and liminality, as connected to a young girl's sexual formation in Brodber's *Jane and Louisa Will Soon Come Home* and Kempadoo's *Buxton Spice*. Brodber's influential image of the kumbla and Kempadoo's expression of "the four-o'clock feeling" serve as similar examples of adolescent sexuality

---

[133] See Ang, *On Not Speaking Chinese*, 184, 193.

[134] Narain, "Standing in the Place of Love," 336.

set in a liminal space and time. This induces the reader's engagement in a sexual logic which is teased out through the use of silences, secrecy, and taboos. These affects create an interpretative open-endedness where monologic readings become impossible and knowledge is revealed only by an engagement with that which is yet unclear, in formation, or concealed. As such, this air of uncertainty serves as our first key to meaning-production as affective.

From ambivalence as a force of reading, the discussion proceeds to the texts in my corpus where sexuality and its affects are clearly negative and violent. Chapter 3, "The Possibilities of Reading Sexual Shame, Violence and Pain," asks how we should read sexuality as imbued with negative affect. In particular, shame features in this reading of sexual violence and abuse. Sexuality as a destructive force is depicted in the form of testing in Danticat's novel and of peppering in Adisa's novel, where the two novels are paired by their comparable yet completely different understandings of shame. Furthermore, the destructive sexuality of the whisper circle in Brodber's *Jane and Louisa* and the short story "Sleeping's Beauty" highlights how the reader needs to engage with shame and negative affect in order to understand it as a productive, affective force that creates not only differences between subjects but also potential for change.

Chapter 4, "Communities that Heal: Reading Sexual Healing," offers a reading of sexual healing and self-discovery as the antidote to the perils discussed in the preceding chapter. The rituals of naming in Adisa's *It Begins with Tears* and Danticat's *Breath, Eyes, Memory*, and the successful quest for the past in Brodber's *Jane and Louisa*, serve to interpellate their readers to a discourse of reparative liberation that emphasizes the communal and the ancestral as the foundation of liberation.

In Chapter 5, "Shadow(ing) Men – Visions of Caring Masculinities," the emancipatory quests read here become understood in a different light, as I read the "shared queerness" in Mootoo's *Cereus Blooms at Night* as an example of queer sharing and baring as a new and different way of imagining community in Caribbean women's writing. Such a community would not then be based on a presupposition of sameness of ancestral lineage, for example, but on the premise of queer difference as a credible basis for communal relations. My reading of Mootoo's novel thus unsettles the correlation between liberation and the collective and the communal as always based on sympathy (that is, sameness of feeling), and teaches us instead that empathy (shared participation without imagined sameness) is the ethical response in a shared process of healing. Likewise, in Brodber's *Jane and Louisa Will Soon Come Home* and in Adisa's *It Begins with Tears* women's healing processes are aided with the helping men, Baba and Desmond, who take on the role of caregiver or healer in the women's pain and anguish. The men's engagements as helpers in the women's quests for emancipation and survival denote a new paradigm of men's participation in the lives of Caribbean women.

The final chapter, "'Caribbean Passion': The Hypersexual and the Asexual Woman as Reparative Tropes," engages with a case study of reparative reading.[135] The two sexual prototypes, Brodber's asexual Ella in her *Louisiana* and Adisa's hypersexual Monica in her *It Begins with Tears*, are read through passion as the affective force which highlights the two opposite women's similarities. I argue here that, in a reparative reading, both of these prototypical representations are freed from the constraints of their respective categories, and we come to see them as examples of non-normative sexualities that carve out new sexual spaces and evoke new reparative affects. They clarify our understanding of desire (in the form of Caribbean passion) as something *beyond* mere desire and towards a particular type of human body. This final attempt at reading sexual feelings amalgamates sexuality and affectivity with spirituality and desire as a force far more powerful than a simple anchoring of sexual affect to particular bodies and objects.

My aim is not to provide an instructive, instrumental methodology of reading, which might seem frustrating for those readers awaiting my didactic answer to the 'how to' questions posed above. Instead, my project has ambitions that point to the theoretical and the philosophical, as I hold that an instructive reading of these novels would do them an injustice by reducing their reading to simple step-by-step instructions. Instead, this reading may serve to clarify the complexity, polysemy, and fluidity of feelings in the text–reader relationship. As such, the results of this reading help to clarify the very cultural nature of emotions in general and Caribbean, non-Western, complex feelings in particular.[136] Affects in the reading process do not lend themselves to a monologic reading or uniform meaning. An ability to coexist with ambivalence – with textual ambiguity and a consciousness of the limits of our knowledge in each literary encounter – may in fact enable a more equal dialogue to take place. The matter is not simply one of celebratiing complexity

---

[135] See Sedgwick, *Touching Feeling*.

[136] On complex feelings, see Campbell, *Interpreting the Personal*.

over simplicity or ambiguity over clarity; it involves, rather, acknowledging these elements as vital conditions for producing knowledge across difference.

Reading in an affective and dialogic strange encounter takes us to the proposal of affect(s) as vital for readings taking place within the feminist politics of difference, as in this study. This is my starting point for the discussions that follow in the next four chapters, and it therefore warrants some further clarification. I hold that the potential for change resides in the process of being moved by a text. However, as Ahmed states in her reading of Deleuze and Guattari, there is, and should be, a greater reason to read than simply for the purpose of being "moved, or worked upon, by the text."[137] This is a potential pitfall of any affective reading. In fact, if a reader's only motivation for reading is to surrender her agency and allow the text to take her for a ride, then the only motivation for reading would be for the goals and interests of this particular literary methodology (i.e. what a text 'does'). In that process, we would therefore fail to ask the text to answer certain questions (i.e. what it 'means'). The success of said methodology would then rely on the presumption of the capacity of the text to move the reader, whereas it is entirely possible for a text to leave its reader entirely unmoved – or for a reader to be unwilling to *be* moved. Yet, in the event of not moving or having been moved, one could still ask the text a number of questions and ponder its potential readings.

In such an event, a figure of what Ahmed terms the "failed reader" would then be constructed as the unfortunate side-product of the triumph of the successful reader, who, obediently taken for a ride by the text, is thus moved by the act of reading.[138] This is hardly my objective in this study. The crucial question becomes, rather, how these reading strategies, used in part to mobilize their reader, avoid the risk of keeping the 'object' in place while simultaneously allowing the Western reading subject to move and be moved. This not only fetishizes movement, as criticized by Ahmed, but also turns it into a mechanism of privilege, where the movement of some-bodies is made possible by keeping others in place.[139]

Instead, like Ahmed, I do not want to concentrate on the binarism of "you ask either what the text means, or what it does," because in fact these are not

---

[137] Sara Ahmed, "Phantasies of Becoming (the Other)," *European Journal of Cultural Studies* 2.1 (January 1999): 48.

[138] Ahmed, "Phantasies of Becoming (the Other)," 48.

[139] Ahmed, *The Cultural Politics of Emotion*, 152, and *Strange Encounters*, 85.

mutually exclusive tasks.[140] Each meaning-producing attempt involves a rethinking of how a text works and why – and for what kind of a reader. While opening to the Other and being moved by the Other in a way that "one ceases to inhabit the same place," my affective reading provides a way of responding to the Other, and having a dialogue over meanings with the Other, with which or whom the reader is in power-laden contact; "a strange encounter."[141] Following this affective model of meaning and subject-formation, then, we arrive at the provisional conclusion that, in the act of reading, something always takes place – something that moves, although we do not always know in advance who it is, or, indeed, where it moves. Nor do we know in advance what the merits gained, lessons learned, and losses faced in each act of moving or being moved will be. Therefore, the act of reading as a movement is always subject to risk, and such a risk is one well worth taking – for questioning the contours of movement in reading itself may reveal new paths for negotiation and interpretation, and even, perhaps, paths that are yet to be trodden.

⌘

[140] Ahmed, "Phantasies of Becoming (the Other)," 48.

[141] Ahmed, *Strange Encounters*, 156.

2 Reading the Ambivalence of Sexuality in Transition

Erna Brodber and Oonya Kempadoo

FEW TEXTUAL METAPHORS have invited such critical attention in the field of Caribbean literary studies as the polysemically elusive figure of the kumbla in Erna Brodber's first novel, *Jane and Louisa Will Soon Come Home*. It is therefore only appropriate, if not crucial, that this cultural figure which has surely expanded many emotional and intellectual horizons begins my foray into anglophone Caribbean women's writing, sexuality, and affectivity. In the early 1990s, scholars such as Carolyn Cooper, Daryl Cumber Dance, and Evelyn O'Callaghan were occupied with explaining the contours of this infamously difficult textual and thematic motif.[1] The kumbla, importantly, came to depict the whole tradition of Caribbean women's writing,

[1] Carolyn Cooper, "Afro-Jamaican Folk Elements in Brodber's *Jane And Louisa Will Soon Come Home,"* in *Out of the Kumbla: Caribbean Women and Literature*, ed. Carole Boyce Davies & Elaine Savory Fido (Trenton NJ: Africa World Press, 1990): 277–88; Carolyn Cooper, "'Something Ancestral Recaptured': Spirit Possession as Trope in Selected Feminist Fictions of the African diaspora," in *Motherlands: Black Women's Writing from Africa, the Caribbean and South Africa*, ed. Susheila Nasta (London: Women's Press, 1991): 64–87; Daryl Cumber Dance, "Go Eena Kumbla: A Comparison of Erna Brodber's *Jane and Louisa Will Soon Come Home* and Toni Cade Bambara's *The Salt Eaters*," in *Caribbean Women Writers. Essays from the First International Conference*, ed. Selvyn R. Cudjoe (Wellesley MA: Calaloux, 1990): 169–84; and Evelyn O'Callaghan, "Interior Schisms Dramatised: The Treatment of the 'Mad' Woman in the Work of Some Female Caribbean Novelists," in *Out of the Kumbla: Caribbean Women and Literature*, ed. Carole Boyce Davies & Elaine Savory Fido (Trenton NJ: Africa World Press, 1990): 89–109.

as is revealed by the title of the influential 1990 anthology *Out of the Kumbla: Caribbean Women and Literature*.

The 2000s saw another kumbla renaissance in the scholarly reception of Caribbean women's writing, this time with an attempt to link the kumbla to further literary interests. Elina Valovirta, Antonia McDonald, and June Roberts re-read the kumbla as a device in *écriture féminine*, creative fellowship, and black folk culture, respectively.[2] The kumbla, unexplainable and yet in need of explanation, is a textual figure as well as an emotional, lived experience involving social psychology and elements of folklore; utterly ungraspable for those unfamiliar with Afro-Caribbean psychopathology and cultural tradition – and often even for those familiar with it. Evelyn O'Callaghan explains the kumbla in a way which may here function as our provisional introduction: it is "a kind of protective enclosure, calabash or cocoon, made up of layers of assumed roles and evasions, behind which the fragile self hides its vulnerability."[3] While a powerful textual strategy, the ways in which the kumbla conditions the reader and can be used as a literary reading method has, however, only now become a subject of scrutiny.

Brodber explains the creative process behind *Jane and Louisa* in an article while reflecting on the multi-dimensional nature of her "study," as well as enabling readers to understand why the work takes its particular form:

> This study had also to be short enough, sharp enough, and topical enough to make its point quickly because as a poor, half-illiterate people we have neither the time, the skills, nor the paper to deal with long works. It had to have space in which people could do their own dreaming, their own thinking and their own planning. These considerations account for the format, content, and the style of the piece.[4]

---

[2] Elina Valovirta, "The Kumbla Revisited: Reading Erna Brodber's *Jane and Louisa Will Soon Come Home* as Post-Colonial Ecriture Feminine," *Atlantic Literary Review* 3.2 (April–June 2002): 130–42; Antonia McDonald, "Coming Home to Mama's Garden: Creative Fellowship in *Jane and Louisa Will Soon Come Home*," *MaComère* 6 (2004): 13–18; and Roberts, *Reading Erna Brodber*, 13–18.

[3] O'Callaghan, "Interior Schisms Dramatised," 107. The 'kumbla', it is assumed, refers to the calabash; a plant with eponymous pumpkin-like fruit which may be carved and dried into a bowl or vessel. As such, the calabash is a very functional fruit, as it can be used for cooking, as a container, and as a musical instrument.

[4] Erna Brodber, "Fiction in the Scientific Procedure," in *Caribbean Women Writers. Essays from the First International Conference*, ed. Selvyn R. Cudjoe (Wellesley MA: Calaloux, 1990): 166.

Ironically, the author posits her novel's conciseness as the prerequisite for its accessibility to the audience she had intended the novel to reach: Jamaicans at home but also in the diaspora. However, the novel is notoriously difficult for both native and foreign reader alike.[5] The format of the piece in the above quotation refers to the essentially hybrid nature of the novel. In fact, referring to *Jane and Louisa* as a novel is inherently unsatisfactory, as the work is a hybrid of many genres: fictional autobiography, novel, prose poem, folktale, and ring game. As a Caribbean *Bildungsroman*, *Jane and Louisa* can be characterized as a novel of ethnic and feminist formation which, in the end, reaches an understanding on the importance of family history, ethnic roots, and the importance of coming to terms with one's sexuality.[6] In the novel, this last matter is seen as analogous to finding one's language. Reading Brodber's kumbla motif together with the idea of an ambivalent hybridity helps clarify the role of the kumbla, not only as a defensive strategy but also as a linguistic and thematic tool or strategy through which a postcolonial feminist minority discourse can be articulated and read.

Brodber's *Jane and Louisa Will Soon Come Home* (henceforth *Jane and Louisa*) along with Oonya Kempadoo's *Buxton Spice* can be read through the idea of a dialogic relationship between the reader and the text, where affects function as literary devices. Affects leave their imprint on the text–reader relationship and also on the text, in which sexuality is in constant transition. In other words, the novels' affects mobilize and move the reader in an interactive way, as the dialogic principle dictates. Seen as tools or devices, affects also *do* things to the reader in the text, while at the same time undergoing a process of interpretation by the reader. In such an interactive scenario, reader and text are mutually influential. Navigating and negotiating strategies for reading through this affective ambivalence of sexuality becomes my task in this chapter, where the reader needs to assert what Puri calls an "interpretive flexibility" in order to make sense of the affects at play in Brodber and Kempadoo's novels.[7]

---

[5] The novel's difficulty was mentioned several times in discussions at the Erna Brodber symposium entitled "From Kumblas to Blackspace," held at the Mona campus of the University of the West Indies in Jamaica, 2002.

[6] On the Caribbean *Bildungsroman*, see Curdella Forbes, "Fracturing Subjectivities: International Space and the Discourse of Individualism in Colin Channer's *Waiting in Vain* and Jamaica Kincaid's *Mr Potter*," *Small Axe* 12.1 (2008): 16–37.

[7] Puri, *The Caribbean Postcolonial*, 160.

Scott notes that *Buxton Spice* "centers around [the protagonist]'s emergent sexuality," while, in an interview, Kempadoo herself names "the end of sexual innocence" as her theme.[8] Like Brodber's kumbla, Kempadoo's novel has a myriad chain of affects associated with sexuality. In fact, one review states that the feelings through which the novel's sexual awakening is expressed will "certainly seem alien to most North American readers."[9] Since the novel has been translated into five languages and is widely read outside the USA and Canada, we can also assume that an international readership will profit from a consideration of the ways in which the novel's complex affects are, in fact, sexually formative. In this respect, the affects in *Buxton Spice* connect with Brodber's kumbla, as both novels foreground a sense of ambivalence relating to nascent sexuality. More critically than by their somewhat shared themes, however, my reading of the novels illustrates and exemplifies the types of reading strategies required by their readers. The key question, then, becomes how we should negotiate that very ambivalence as an integral element of the reading-event itself.

In Kempadoo's novel, the girl protagonist's sexual awakening is depicted in conjunction with the volatile political context of the post-independence race riots in 1970s rural Guyana. As Kempadoo states in an interview about her novel, "The girls' relationship [to the outside world] is comparable to that of the people and the government."[10] Such a parallel structure is also a feature of the black[11] British novel of transformation, which according to Mark Stein is not only "about the *formation* of its protagonists" but is also about "the

---

[8] Scott, *Caribbean Women Writers and Globalization*, and Harald Leusmann, "An Interview With Oonya Kempadoo," *World Literature Written in English* 39.1 (2001): 110.

[9] Patrick Markee, "The tree that knew too much," *New York Times* (11 July 1999): 12, http://query.nytimes.com/gst/fullpage.html?res=9A0CE7DD143DF932A25754C0A96F958260 (accessed 26 August 2013).

[10] Leusmann, "An Interview With Oonya Kempadoo," 110.

[11] It needs to be noted here that Mark Stein defines 'Black' (his capitalization) according to the British context of his literature to also encompass novels written by Asian British authors such as Hanif Kureishi. The term 'Black' in Stein's treatment thus encompasses a largely heterogeneous sample of ethnicities. See Mark Stein, *Black British Literature: Novels of Transformation* (Ohio: Ohio State UP, 2004): xv, 8. In my discourse, however, 'black' refers to Afro-Caribbean (and, at times, African-American) ethnicities.

transformation of British society and cultural institutions."[12] The novel projects a similar dynamic of (trans)formation, where Lula's sexual formation is parallelled with the surrounding Guyanese society's ongoing turmoil in its process of (trans)formation from a British-ruled colony to the independent state (within the Commonwealth), divided by ethnically aligned political parties. Stein refers to this double structure as "the performative function" of black British novels of transformation, which are not merely "inscribed by cultures they inhabit [but] in turn mold those very cultures."[13] This dimension of the performative politics of literature serves to highlight how Kempadoo's novel comments on (and carves a space for) a young girl's existence within a society in crisis.

Tamarind Grove, the fictional home village of the novel's protagonist, Lula, is located on the coast of post-independence Guyana. There, the People's National Congress, led by the authoritarian black prime minister Forbes Burnham, clashes with the country's Indo-Guyanese population, plunging the multiethnic yet racially segregated Tamarind Grove into turmoil. The novel foregrounds divisions within Guyanese society arising from intertwining and conjoined categories of social differentiation. At the same time, Lula and her friends Rachel, Sammy, and the tomboy Judy explore their pre-teen sexuality. In this respect, the novel is about knowing and not knowing, secret knowledge, rumour, and hidden facts that the young girls do their best to uncover in order to satisfy their curiosity on all things sexual. An air of ambiguity is inherent to the novel's general atmosphere as the girls try to make sense of sex the only way that they can: by outsider observation. Lula, the offspring of a middle-class family with a mulatto Creole mother and Indian Coolie father, has multiple encounters with sexual awakening ranging from the stagnant "four o'clock feeling" through to the abrupt end of childhood in the discovery of Judy's sexual meddlings with a black boy, André, during a night of political violence and rioting. In the course of the novel, Lula and her friends' sexual awakening progresses from sex-talk to voyeurism, masturbation, playing husband and wife, sexual harassment, and, finally, intercourse. This progression of sexual awakening engages the reader in the novel's sexual ambivalence, which can be described in kumblan terms: sexuality is itself something that is hidden, as well as something from which one feels the need to hide.

---

[12] Stein, *Black British Literature: Novels of Transformation*, xiii.

[13] *Black British Literature: Novels of Transformation*, 36.

My aim in this chapter is not to offer a definitive, hermeneutic vision of the kumbla as an entity (because I am not sure it can be defined as such), nor do I wish to pin down the sexual affective experiences and events in Kempadoo's novel leading to a predictable outcome. Rather, I offer an understanding of their fluidity and polysemy as productive and performative in determining the myriad associations that are created between sexuality and affectivity. Through this performative function, sexual affects do not simply name something that exists, but they also generate and mould what they name. A similar argument is made by Sue Campbell, who claims that affects become formed in and by their expressions: i.e. come into existence only when they are uttered.[14] In fact, affective discourse as performative produces effects through repetition, citing norms and conventions, thereby creating something new, just as Stein suggests occurs with novels of transformation.[15]

Rather than simply undertaking the reductive task of addressing what these affects actually *are*, it makes more sense to ask,what do they *do* to the reader, and to the text? How do they position their reader? How are these positions related to affectivity and sexuality? Further, how is the reader to escape the grasp of the kumbla, which, like any hiding place, if dwelled in for too long, fails to work?

The kumbla is a "complex emotion"[16] similar to the sexual affects in *Buxton Spice* that range from the "four o'clock feeling" to the "bombing-up feeling" to the emotions related to Judy's being caught having (interracial) sex. They can be seen as transitory affective formations, which, at once temporal and temporary, transport the narrative and the reader into a new time, place, and state of mind. In other words, these complex affects are vehicles with which the reading may proceed. But how to interpret them intersectionally? Whither does this affective chain in fact transport the reader? These affects, although they evade strict meaning-formation and categorization, are expressions of a sensually affective moment which, while fleeting, leave their imprint on the reader. The kumbla and *Buxton Spice*'s chain of sexual affects from four-o'clock feeling onwards shun monologic readings by way of their openness and ambivalence. Instead, they teach the reader to adopt a more refined sensibility open to elements of surprise, conflict, and change.[17]

---

[14] Campbell, *Interpreting the Personal*, 6.

[15] See Stein, *Black British Literature: Novels of Transformation*, 36.

[16] Campbell, *Interpreting the Personal*, 3.

[17] See Ahmed, *Strange Encounters*, 6.

The kumbla as refuge and trap in Erna Brodber's *Jane and Louisa Will Soon Come Home*

As O'Callaghan's introduction to the kumbla denotes, it is a self-created defence mechanism which hides an individual's insecurity or prevents him/her from facing certain issues (such as sexuality) which are experienced as damaging to the self.[18] The frequent occurrence of the kumbla imagery in Brodber's novel indicates the need to be hidden from threatening situations in an enclosed physical space or mental state. The polysemic figure of the kumbla operates on the level of both the narrative and the characters, and avoids strict definitions and categorizations, as is made obvious by the following passage describing it in the novel:

> [A] kumbla is like a beach ball. It bounces with the sea but never goes down. It is indomitable. [...] It bounces everywhere. Unlike the buoy, it is not tethered. [...] But the kumbla is not just a beach ball. The kumbla is an egg shell, not a chicken's egg or a bird's egg shell. It is the egg of the August worm, It does not crack if it is hit. [...] Your kumbla will not open unless you rip its seams open. It is a round seamless calabash that protects you without caring. [...] Your kumbla is a helicopter, a transparent umbrella, a glassy marble, a comic strip space ship. You can see both in and out. You hear them. They can hear you. They can touch you. You can touch them. But they cannot handle you.[19]

A closer look at the passage allows us to draw certain conclusions about the nature of kumbla. First, it is described as a material, spatial entity; an enclosed space as an object such as a beach ball, an egg or a calabash. Like the egg of the August worm, the kumbla is a protective space, a calabash within which one can dwell in peace. The idea of the kumbla as a state of mind indicates the multiple associations of spatiality which at times may even be in conflict. The kumbla image can in fact be seen as a prime example of theorizations of space as geographical, social and psychological.[20] According to Gwin, space does not simply refer to "an entity that contains something else but the swirl of social relations and productions in particular locations, whether these loca-

[18] O'Callaghan, "Interior Schisms Dramatised," 107.

[19] *Jane and Louisa Will Soon Come Home* (London: New Beacon, 1980): 123.

[20] Minrose Gwin, *The Woman in the Red Dress: Gender, Space and Reading* (Urbana & Chicago: U of Illinois P, 2002): 5.

tions be material, cultural, or even psychological."[21] With this dimension of space in mind, we can see interconnections between the cultural, the psychological, and the feminine in the case of the novel's protagonist, Nellie. For her, the kumbla also becomes a state of mind, when she inhabits a series of kumblas and hovers in the uncertainty of threatening and distorted images of sexuality and womanhood. Nellie adopts different roles as coping mechanisms for the pressures she faces, such as becoming a promiscuous young woman who engages in an act of oral sex in a movie theatre, and later as a dry intellectual denying her sexuality.

But reducing the kumbla to a psycho-spatial entity does not project its endless implications, as the kumbla does not merely perform spatially. In addition, the description in the above passage points to both mobility and motility: the kumbla is depicted as a helicopter which is able to move around on account of its rotating blades. Like a beachball, which moves in the air or bounces around, the kumbla as a helicopter involves cyclical motion. This highlights the round, cyclical shape of the figure as it envelops the narrative. At the same time, like the helicopter, it is a vehicle with which the narrative advances and, like the space ship, it is a vessel that enables travel across space and time (as we know them). The idea of movement is fundamental to the kumbla, because the reading of it initiates a process of perpetual resignification. Thus, the word 'vehicle' in its double sense usefully describes the elusive metaphor of the kumbla: it is used in the sense both of a means of transportation and of a means of expression – as that particle of a metaphor in which the referent is imaged; the vehicle of metaphor itself. Using poetic terms, we can see that the kumbla is a metaphor (for affect and effect) without a straightforward, clearly identifiable tenor.

As vehicle, the kumbla moves and floats around as a signifier, and constantly runs the risk of entrapping its inhabitant. Despite its productive safety, the kumbla is, at best, a temporary survival strategy, as it can turn destructive if one dwells in it for too long. One kumbla, which is easily replaced by another, may become an imprisoning trap; ultimately, then, one has to emerge from the kumbla or run the risk of psychosis, or loss of contact with social reality. The narrator warns that, once one has inhabited a kumbla, it cannot be exited easily:

> The trouble with the kumbla is the getting out of the kumbla. It is a protective device. If you dwell too long in it, it makes you delicate.

---

[21] Gwin, *The Woman in the Red Dress*, 6.

> Makes you an albino: skin white but not by genes. Vision extra-sensitive to the sun and blurred without spectacles.[22]

As O'Callaghan notes, a self dwelling in the kumbla for too long may turn against itself: "Eventually, the self must emerge into the threatening world or risk psychic fragmentation."[23] This denotes how, by necessity, the kumbla is a fleeting state or space.

In addition to the visual, spatial, and mental dimensions of the temporary kumbla, the section of the novel entitled "The Kumbla" characterizes the tactile dimension of the protective device: "They can touch you. You can touch them. But they cannot handle you."[24] In other words, although you are safe in the kumbla, where no one can handle you, you are also unable to handle 'them'. The impenetrable shelter of the kumbla may result in the loss of agency through losing touch with oneself as a functioning individual. The kumbla can only make you untouchable for so long.

The two famous trickster tales, or Anancy stories, in Brodber's novel further illustrate how the kumbla can be used or abused as a vehicle, tool or strategy. Like the kumbla, no Brodber scholar has left these embedded folktales undiscussed. June Roberts remarks that Brodber's writing makes use of a number of elements, including:

> the folktale, the proverb, the trope of storytelling, indirect discourse, voiceovers, folk dialect, indirect points of view, and other rhetorical tropes of the oral tradition, but she often assigns these discursive valences to the subtext until they uncontrollably and uncannily erupt to the surface as haunting yet vestigial historical and cultural signifiers, only to disappear again equally suddenly and without warning.[25]

In the first story, Anancy's cunning survival strategy turns against itself, when echo traps Anancy in the woods in an endless downward spiral of his lies.[26] The second story, however, shows how language and kumbla can be used as a strategic device for ensuring a safe passage home. The downsides of the kumbla are displayed in the teaching of the novel's tragic trickster tale, where Brer Anancy, the spider, becomes trapped in the kumbla of language. In order to create an alibi after killing his sawing partner, Anancy shouts into the

---

[22] *Jane and Louisa Will Soon Come Home*, 130.

[23] O'Callaghan, "Interior Schisms Dramatised," 107.

[24] *Jane and Louisa Will Soon Come Home*, 123.

[25] Roberts, *Reading Erna Brodber*, 11.

[26] *Jane and Louisa Will Soon Come Home*, 36–38.

woods, demanding to be told whether anyone knows who killed his partner. He thus uses language to protect himself, but does so for selfish ends, which ultimately leads to his destruction: through echo, the question keeps returning to Anancy and he becomes, as Cooper notes, "trapped in the subterfuge of the kumbla."[27] The narrator depicts Anancy's fate: "Twirling madly in a still life"[28]. This highlights one of the kumbla's most frustrating capacities; the failure to move while in motion.

Go eena kumbla: Into the safe kumbla-space and state of mind

According to Cooper, the title *Jane and Louisa Will Soon Come Home* originally refers to a Jamaican children's ring game, which is derived from a British quadrille dance.[29] In the context of the novel, it depicts "the adaptive capacity of Neo-African folk culture in Jamaica, its conscription of English folk traditions for its own enrichment."[30] In an altered order, the lines from the song serve as chapter headings for the novel: My dear will you allow me / To waltz with you / Into this beautiful garden / Jane and Louisa will soon come home. This highlights the fact that the narrative itself follows the cyclical nature of the ring game. "Cyclostyled" is how Brodber characterizes her narrative.[31] In addition to being a reference to the children's song, the title has several other meanings.

The names Jane and Louisa refer to Nellie's two cousins who come to stay with Nellie's family during childhood summers, which is when the girls take their first steps towards sexuality through talking about "sex and babies."[32] Janey and Louise are supposed to be more enlightened when it comes to sexuality, because they live with their Granny Tucker, whom the girls have often overheard praying aloud and talking to herself about family woes. The three girls crave more information, which they do not get from their favorite aunt:

---

[27] Cooper, "Afro-Jamaican Folk Elements in Brodber's *Jane and Louisa Will Soon Come Home*," 285.

[28] *Jane and Louisa Will Soon Come Home*, 38.

[29] Cooper, "Afro-Jamaican Folk Elements," 280.

[30] "Afro-Jamaican Folk Elements," 280.

[31] Brodber, "Fiction in the Scientific Procedure," 166.

[32] *Jane and Louisa Will Soon Come Home*, 96.

> Aunt Alice knew what we wanted to know but she only smiled and when we pestered her too much, she sang:
>
> Jane and Louisa will soon come home
> Into this beautiful garden.
>
> And that was that.[33]

By singing a children's ring song to the girls, Aunt Alice reminds them that they are only children and should not stick their noses into adult matters. The lines can also be interpreted as offering reassurance. As the reference to a 'beautiful garden' is a common allusion to sexuality, Aunt Alice also insinuates that, in the ongoing process of learning and growing, the girls will soon find their share of adult knowledge. A division between child and adult sexuality becomes established here through Aunt Alice's use of the ring game's song as a euphemism for sexual knowledge to which children need not have access. This air of secrecy recalls Michel Foucault's elaborations of the history of sexual knowledge. According to Foucault, the discourse of not speaking directly about sexuality in front of children developed in the early Enlightenment. There, the question was not about silence but, rather, about silences as the different ways of not speaking directly, and so preventing children's exposure to sex.[34]

As such, the song actually initiates the girls into sexuality, wherein the precedent set by the future tense hints at a process of becoming that the prepubescent girls are to encounter in due course. The song does not serve its intended purpose of repressing the girls' 'will to knowledge'. The opposite in fact happens, as the girls continue to search for answers in the only ways available to them: by eavesdropping and gossip. In Foucauldian terms, the girls become implanted within a sexual discourse through the ambivalence of indirect speech and the silence imposed on them. At the same time, the song arising from the adaptive Afro-Jamaican cultural repertoire provides a resistant commentary on the girls' will to knowledge: as rural Jamaican children, their time of leisure should be dedicated to playing the ring game that they have learnt at home, not to something deemed to be foreign to children, such as sexuality.

---

[33] *Jane and Louisa Will Soon Come Home*, 97.

[34] Michel Foucault, *The History of Sexuality*, vol. 1: *An Introduction*, tr. Robert Hurley (*Histoire de la sexualité*, I: *La Volonté de savoir*, 1976; New York: Vintage, 1980).

The novel's central symbol, the kumbla, emerges in the first section of the novel soon after the description of Nellie's childhood setting, and the onset of puberty in the safe environment of a small village in rural Jamaica. Nellie depicts her surroundings as protective and protected, where childhood games take place in the romantic idyll of the Caribbean countryside:

> We lived in a mossy covert, dim and cool and very dark. And we could make it darker still when we played dolly house in our sink hole searching for treasures which the sea washed up or when we stared into the iridescent black ink that made our night [...]. Ever see a fowl sitting on eggs in a cold December rain. We knew the warmth and security of those eggs in the dark of her bottom. [...] Mountains ring us round and cover us, banana leaves shelter us and sustain us [...]. You should see the poor insipid sun trying to penetrate us! [...] Poor insipid sun. Fighting the banana leaves to come in.[35]

In this passage, the sun is considered to be the only threat to the safe haven of home, which is itself dark and unexposed. The nest-like surroundings and resulting atmosphere change abruptly when Nellie's neighbour, Mass Mehiah, cuts down his cedar trees to make room on his land for a religious meeting house, about which Nellie points out knowingly: "and the American bishop is going to open it" (15). The cutting-down of trees results in the loss of protection from the threatening sunshine, and Nellie notes: "the sun is walking bravely now and has cracked my neighbour's calabash," followed by the command: "Go eena kumbla" (15). Mass Mehiah has broken the kumbla that protects him and Nellie from the sunlight; an analogy for anything damageable, not only here but throughout the novel. It is again important to note the recurring nature of the kumbla: it is easily replaced by another one. In the case of Mass Mehiah, his protective trees are replaced by his religion in the form of the congregation house. Religion serves to break the safe environment, the kumbla of Nellie's childhood, twice: first, physically, in the form of a religious meeting house; and later, ideologically, by Aunt Becca's teachings about sexuality.

Throughout the novel, in order to escape what she experiences as the threatening nature of sexuality, Nellie retreats into her kumbla. As mentioned before, this ultimately transforms the self into an unprofitable and unfruitful being prone to self-destruction. In other words, as Nellie escapes from sexual

---

[35] *Jane and Louisa Will Soon Come Home*, 9–10. Further page references are in the main text.

repression into the kumbla, the protective device, when abused, ultimately becomes self-repressive. For example, in an attempt to find solace and purpose, the adult Nellie retreats yet again into an evasive role, this time as secretary to a black-activist movement. However, Nellie's boyfriend, Robin, dies in a metaphorical fire (the novel remains ambiguous about whether this is the case of an actual fire or burn-out through exhaustion). Nellie does not let this stop her: "But I went on as before. I took the minutes with a stiff upper lip" (52). By dwelling in her kumbla for too long, Nellie becomes its victim and her health begins to crumble. Ultimately, action becomes impossible when one stays locked in the alternative order. Nellie expresses her frustration by crying uncontrollably, but continues in her activities within the movement. Not long after this, she goes into shock and walks to and fro, while scratching her itchy skin: "So I scratched and walked. Walking fast and scratching, I know I looked like a fowl in an ants' nest but I didn't mind" (66). What Evelyn O'Callaghan finds in three other novels by Caribbean female novelists is also true of this novel: for Nellie, too, "confusion and guilt associated with varying models of female sexuality lead towards mental breakdown."[36] The warning rings loud and clear.

Getting out of the reading as a kumbla

June Roberts sets strict parameters to a non-indigenous reader's position on reading Brodber. These parameters entail an acknowledgement of "Brodber's understated cultural privilege and knowledge of her subject matter as well as the moral authority her position as a diasporan intellectual represents."[37] The foreign reader needs to be "morally positioned" in order to begin reading Brodber.[38] While I wholly agree with Roberts on Brodber's merits, and while it might be understandably profitable for a foreign reader to cling to the venerable author's figure for the kind of 'proper' reader's position called for by Roberts, it also runs the risk of reducing fictional meaning to its author's body, thereby hindering the interplay of affectivity and sexuality in the reading event.

In my interactive approach, it is not simply the reader who assumes a position from which to begin to read, but it is also the text that positions the reader

[36] O'Callaghan, "Interior Schisms Dramatised," 99.

[37] Roberts, *Reading Erna Brodber*, 11.

[38] *Reading Erna Brodber*, 11.

throughout the reading process. The point is that these positions cannot in fact be locked up in advance, a priori. The dialogic reader who wishes to read across differences would do better to pay heed to the ongoing production of affective encounters in a dialogic text–reader relationship and the ensuing communication.

Reading the kumbla as an element that positions the reader while the latter simultaneously attempts to position the kumbla in a reading may offer an insight into the kumbla's contingencies. In addition to being a textual metaphor serving as a defence mechanism for the protagonist, Nellie, and various other characters in the novel, the kumbla also has relevance at the level of the text–reader relationship. The novel itself has been characterized as a kumbla on the cover of the 1998 edition: it "is like a kumbla – the central symbol of this novel." The constraints of an enclosed space have to be broken when considering the novel as a potential kumbla. As an open text, the novel necessitates a reading cognizant of the dangers of kumbla, an entrapping device which eventually leads to its own destruction. In fact, a monologic reading would simply end up revolving in a similar downward spiral to that which causes Anancy's demise.

One should thus pay heed to the problem of how to avoid the threat, in this reading, of the novel's turning into a trap. The idea of an 'open text' introduced by reader theory and used to characterize a narrative lacking a linear, coherent structure and ending can be compared to Hélène Cixous's idea of the book as 'round'.[39] According to Cixous, the book has "only to await resurrection."[40] It is the reader's task to breathe life into it and not let it be destroyed by a suffocating, enclosing reading. In fact, one can read in Brodber as well as in Cixous a resistance to monologic analysis or mechanic interpretation. Both write 'escaping texts', which is also the subtitle of Cixous's essay collection *Stigmata*.[41] By their very nature, these escaping texts resist reductive, paranoid readings. It is as if the texts escape the mind of the reader.

Reading the kumbla requires the reader to abandon all expectations of a straightforward realist narrative and instead prompts her to be willing to be

---

[39] I have discussed the connections between Brodber and Cixous in my reading of the kumbla as an example of postcolonial *écriture feminine*. See Valovirta, "The Kumbla Revisited."

[40] Hélène Cixous, *Stigmata: Escaping Texts*, foreword by Jacques Derrida, preface "On Stigmatexts" by Hélène Cixous (London & New York: Routledge, 1998): 146.

[41] Cixous, *Stigmata: Escaping Texts.*

placed in whatever positions she finds herself fashioned in by the kumbla. For example, a passage in which Nellie's great grandmother Tia's denial of her native heritage is presented can be read as explaining what white-spun kumblas can do. Tia breaks all connections to her own culture by adopting white customs and ways of life through her white spouse, William. The expression "nine night" in the following passage shows how the text itself may provide a hint about its meaning by positioning the uncultured reader in an alienated, white position. The narrator observes that: "Very soon she did not know what a nine night was. My poor great grand Tia! She was a national laughing stock! She overdid things a bit!."[42] The meaning of the passage becomes understandable without previous exposure to the meaning of the cultural practice of the nine night, a wake held after an individual's passing. Tia has lost contact with her culture because she no longer even knows the meaning of the word. If the reader is not familiar with the concept, the text's message becomes further emphasized: Tia has become white, or whitened. In a pitying, sarcastic tone, Nellie recounts: "Tia Maria, in the prime of her life, had built a fine and effective kumbla out of William's skin."[43] In order to understand Tia's tragedy in her white marriage, the reader has to abandon her eurocentric meaning-production and turn instead to a more flexible process of signification.

Such a reading process does not distinguish (to any great extent) between the object and its method. Eve Kosofsky Sedgwick mentions the idea of ends and means as inseparable in Buddhist pedagogy on illness and dying, where means and ends are brought "into unaccustomed relations with each other."[44] In other words, what becomes central in the reading of the kumbla is precisely its circularity, which becomes here – unlike in Western thought – a useful and worthwhile thought-process.[45] This process follows its own cyclical logic, but does not fall prey to the kumbla's suffocating tendencies, because it simultaneously produces open readings that are not shielded from outside influence. The kumbla, as that which escapes the reading, dodges the reader's attempts to grasp what ultimately refuses to be graspable, and flows through the fingers. In turn, it is this very ungraspability and openness of the kumbla that itself grasps the reader, and opens up an affective relationship enabling the reader, to quote Sara Ahmed, "to respond to the other [...] and to have an encounter

---

42 *Jane and Louisa Will Soon Come Home*, 138–39.

43 *Jane and Louisa Will Soon Come Home*, 142.

44 Sedgwick, *Touching Feeling*, 167, 176.

45 *Touching Feeling*, 167.

in which something takes place."[46] As Ahmed notes elsewhere, on "sticky signs," an idea onto which we can easily project the kumbla, what sticks is always relational; items become sticky when they encounter other sticky items.[47]

Being stuck by and in the text thus requires the reader to be sticky in her approach and attitude in turn, which demands an openness to polysemy and an absence of mastery in the face of ambivalence aroused by a reparative impulse. Thus, it is important to note that being sticky (as a sign or by one's attitude) is not ontological. The idea of stickiness is not used here, as Ahmed reminds us, as a qualitative expression of an object's surface, but, rather, *"as an effect of the histories of contact between bodies, signs and objects."*[48] Thus, the kumbla's stickiness as a sign is precisely an effect of its contact with the reader, highlighting the interaction and reciprocity of dialogic, affective reading. Being helicoptered around by the kumbla's many meaning potentials is in fact how the text positions its reader and thus serves as a path to a reading. A negotiation between the kumbla's and the reader's strangeness to each other is the key.

It would be futile for the reader to attempt to grasp the kumbla; it will not "stick" for good but will slip through the reader's sticky fingers. Paradoxically, it is the kumbla's very slipperiness that causes its stickiness as an object to impresses itself on the reader and move her. For this reason, it is not useful to differentiate between passive or active – despite the impression that one or the other, the reader or the text, seems at times to be more sticky or more clingy.[49] Rather, we only have the kumbla's and its reader's endless, cyclical interplay of affect, meaning, and encounter. The only way out of the kumbla's restraining capacities to entrap and destroy lies in the potential(s) of each reading itself.

The idea of the kumbla as a tool for the articulation of identity-formation may prove helpful in considering its role in the reading process. Scott writes that cultural forms, when used as tools, have a useful role in cultural analysis. According to her, they are

> helpful for discussions of Caribbean literature, which even more obviously than other regional literatures is multifaceted and plural, draw-

[46] Ahmed, *Strange Encounters*, 147.

[47] Ahmed, *The Cultural Politics of Emotion*, 91.

[48] *The Cultural Politics of Emotion*, 90 (italics in original).

[49] *The Cultural Politics of Emotion*, 91.

> ing on and synthesizing multiple influences – from Amerindian, African, European, Asian traditions – to produce something unique. Concepts such as transnationalism, hybridity, nomadism, syncretism, creolization continue to be central to critical exploration of Caribbean culture.[50]

While Scott maintains that Marxist theory is a useful framework for her materialist approach to the theme of globalization in post-liberation Caribbean women's writing, here I discuss hybridity in connection with Brodber's writing in general, and with the kumbla in particular. As paradoxical as it may seem, the kumbla – despite its notoriety for being elusively difficult – has a function as a tool or a heuristic device for the reader. This can be seen in the kumbla's liberatory function in the novel.

The second Anancy story in the novel shows how language and the kumbla can be used as strategic devices for ensuring a safe passage home. This second story highlights the creative, protective, and healing powers of language and story. Anancy takes his son Tucuma to fish in Dryhead's waters, because otherwise they would starve. This is dangerous for them, as the waters are forbidden, but it is said right at the start that one should not worry, since "Anancy is a born liar, a spinner of fine white cocoons, a protector for his children."[51] After being caught, Anancy and his son play tricks on Dryhead so that they may be able to head home. They fool Dryhead into believing there are five more children, whom Anancy will give to Dryhead only if he lets Anancy go with the oldest (and in fact the only) son, Tucuma. While Anancy is giving away his imagined children one by one, he shouts out the command "Go eena kumbla" to Tucuma, so that he knows when to assume new, temporary camouflage. Dryhead mistakes the chant as a curse word, but for Tucuma it is a sign to assume different disguises.[52] In other words, he inhabits a series of kumblas temporarily, to ensure that they are allowed to leave for home safely. The kumbla, in this case woven from language, is a positive thing, something that enables one to survive when used in the right way. It expresses, according to Cooper, "a positive acknowledgement of subterfuge to ensure safe passage."[53]

---

[50] Scott, *Caribbean Women Writers and Globalization*, 11.

[51] *Jane and Louisa Will Soon Come Home*, 124.

[52] Dance, "Go Eena Kumbla," 171.

[53] Cooper, "Afro-Jamaican Folk Elements," 284.

The first Anancy story depicted the destructive aspect of language and how one can be trapped in the kumbla. The later Anancy story reveals the protective and healing capacities of language, where "linguistic masking" serves as a strategy for redemption.[54] Together, the two stories point out not only "the paradoxical meaning of the kumbla" but also how it is possible to create a kumbla out of language, whether protective or destructive.[55] As mentioned above, Scott discusses Caribbean cultural forms, including hybridity, as tools for the exploration and articulation of a unique cultural and political experience. Most famously discussed by Homi K. Bhabha, hybridity invites connections in the very liminality of Brodber's writing.[56] Introducing Bhabha's ideas about what lies in-between may also serve to illuminate the nature of Brodber's black feminine discourse in the form of the culturally syncretic and hybrid *Jane and Louisa*.

In his influential and much quoted article "DissemiNation," Bhabha constructs a theory of the writing of a nation by people of the diaspora.[57] It is in fact one of the political aims of Brodber's fiction to write 'community tales' for diasporic black people, and can thus be seen as an attempt to write the nation.[58] Bhabha states that when people scatter in the form of diaspora, they simultaneously gather in time and space. From their "myths and fantasies and experiences, a historical fact of singular importance" there emerges a "cultural construction of nationness as a form of social and textual affiliation."[59] A similar gathering can be read as taking place in Brodber's fiction and in her characters of diverse cultural origins (the protagonist Nellie's family, the Richmonds, like most African-Jamaican families, have a past of mixed black and white ancestry). Bhabha's formulations on the idea of 'cultural difference' which exists "at the frontiers of cultural hybridity" clarify the context in (and from) which Brodber's writing arises.[60] While using elements from

---

[54] McDonald, "Coming Home to Mama's Garden," 14.

[55] Cooper, "Afro-Jamaican Folk Elements," 284.

[56] Homi K. Bhabha, *The Location of Culture* (London & New York: Routledge, 1994.

[57] Homi K. Bhabha, "DissemiNation: Time, Narrative, and the Margins of the Modern Nation," in *Nation and Narration*, ed. Homi K. Bhabha (London: Routledge, 1990).

[58] Brodber, "Fiction in the Scientific Procedure," 164.

[59] Bhabha, "DissemiNation," 291–92.

[60] Bhabha, *The Location of Culture*, 162.

Jamaican folklore and indigenous life-forms in the employment of the kumbla and in the form of Anancy stories, *Jane and Louisa* presents the kind of everyday "scraps, patches and rags" which make up the writing of a nation a "reproductive process."[61] Simultaneously, Brodber absorbs influences from the Western tradition, with frequent intertextual references to its literature, culture, and other phenomena. Intertextuality is one manifestation of *Jane and Louisa's* hybridity, as seen, for example, in the connection between Plato's cave and the kumbla, or in the leader of the black-activist movement compared to Moses leading his people.[62]

As Bhabha writes, "Cultural difference must not be understood as the free play of polarities and pluralities in the homogeneous empty time of the national community"; rather, one should take heed of the multitude of voices and world-views.[63] In her fiction, Brodber intermarries different textual elements, genres, and themes to highlight the liberating potential of a hybrid narrative arising from precisely the kind of transgressive discourse that Bhabha writes about, where negotiation of authorities takes place and new forms of meaning are established.[64] Just as Bhabha makes clear that this kind of borderline activity calls for the transgression of disciplinary and cultural boundaries, Brodber's texts spring from a border pregnant with pluralities and potential for alternative ways of being a woman, being a scholar, being a black, and being a migrant.

Now, in and of itself, the idea of creating the marginal existence of a liminality is neither destructive nor protective, nor emancipatory. As far as I can see, there is nothing liberating in hybridity per se. I adopt this critique from

---

[61] *The Location of Culture*, 209, 208.

[62] In a conversation after Nellie's homecoming from her studies in the USA, the following intertextual links arise as motivation for action in the black-activist movement:

–[…]We were brought up to take to learning.
To take to Plato and Moses. –
–The cave and all that. Oh yes, you've seen the light–
–Yes I have seen the light and I shall lead my people–

(*Jane and Louisa Will Soon Come Home*, 43). Here, interestingly, the cave allegory in Plato and Moses leading enslaved Israelites to the promised land are evoked to highlight the plight of the black-activist movement to lead enslaved people out of the oppression of colonialism.

[63] Bhabha, *The Location of Culture*, 208.

[64] *The Location of Culture*, 162.

Sara Ahmed, who reminds us that not all border-crossings are transgressive and liberating, but that we should, rather, pay attention to their various conditions and modalities.[65] Instead, it is (at least) a dual project, in that one not only *chooses* to be in the margin but is also marginalized, as is the case with the kumbla. These states are born out of necessity. A kumbla is formed as a reaction to a looming threat or distress. In the same way, people "gathering at the frontiers," as Bhabha writes, are not simply living a liberating, multi-influential existence in a carnivalistic game where the minority discourse breaks free of the oppression of the majority discourse.[66] Rather, such a gathering is often a consequence of oppression and violence.

However, a liminal existence – whether the kumbla or Bhabha's hybridity – can become the kind of transgressive discourse that Bhabha writes about, where authorities are questioned and new forms of meaning are established.[67] The process must be kept ongoing. The flexibility of hybrid formations, like the kumbla, enables mediation between different meanings by different readers. Mediation and flexibility also become crucial for sexual affects in different contexts. Reminiscent of the ambivalence of the kumbla, a unique set of affects are involved in the following reading of a young girl's sexual formation in another Caribbean setting; Guyana. While different, these affects also fall under the purview of transitory sexuality and the idea of reading as a liminal activity negotiating across borders of meaning.

The chain of sexual affects from "four o'clock feeling" to "taking man" in Oonya Kempadoo's *Buxton Spice*

Two parallel plot-lines run through *Buxton Spice*, which denotes a micro–macro-structure on the level of the plot, while the individual experience merges with the larger political setting of the novel. Lula and Judy, along with their friends, search for sexual knowledge in the uncertain social setting of Guyana in the 1970s, where Forbes Burnham's rise to power divided the country along ethnic lines instead of the earlier class-based power struggles.[68] Such

[65] Ahmed, *Strange Encounters*, 80–81.

[66] Bhabha, "DissemiNation," 291.

[67] Bhabha, *The Location of Culture*, 162.

[68] Scott, *Caribbean Women Writers and Globalization*, 90.

parallel structuring of the novel can be seen as a feature of the anglophone Caribbean *Bildungsroman* in the 1960s and 1970s, but the description also applies to certain novels written later, such as *Jane and Louisa* or *Buxton Spice*.[69]

The novel's parallel structure requires a turn to intersectionality, which may teach a new literacy when addressed on the level of the text–reader relationship. A multi-locational intersectional reading of difference allows for a micro- as well as macro-level analysis (as famously called for by Chandra Mohanty in her 2003 revision of "Under Western Eyes"). This means that, apart from the novel's parallel structure, there are in fact two levels of intersectionality at play in this type of reading. First, we have the individual subject-level of the text's fictional characters, whose identities are intersectionally produced throughout the novel in various scenarios that all contain a multitude of differences, yet each can be read by foregrounding certain differences over others when we bear in mind the theme of sexuality. At the same time, the novel positions its reader in an atmosphere of learning by uncovering difference through various intersectionalized encounters and experiences. This larger, macro-level exploration of the cross-cultural reading process may provide insight into how each fictional sexual/textual encounter is always a site of differentiation, and that sites of differentiation teach invaluable lessons on the ways in which the people in Tamarind Grove live "together-in-difference."[70] This micro- and macro-level approach enlists us in looking into larger contexts besides our specific material, while at the same time keeping a close eye on the everyday politics of the lives we are exploring.

The seemingly stagnant 'four-o'clock feeling' as an expression of liminality

Just as in Brodber's *Jane and Louisa Will Soon Come Home*, trees have an important function in Kempadoo's *Buxton Spice* to describe its protagonist's childhood surroundings, and to establish a personal relationship between her and the natural world. In *Jane and Louisa*, Nellie describes her childhood home surrounded by sheltering trees and the mountainous landscape. In *Buxton Spice*, Lula also relies on the trees in her yard, this time as keepers of secrets and sources of sensory experience. Scott notes:

[69] Forbes, "Fracturing Subjectivities," 17.

[70] Ang, *On Not Speaking Chinese*, 193.

> Lula has tangible relationships with the different trees and especially with the eponymous mango that knows but refuses to reveal the secrets of her confusing world.[71]

The novel begins with Lula's remark "I got to know all the secrets of the house – like I knew all the trees in the yard."[72] According to Scott, in Guyanese literature, there is a pervasive association between landscape and female sexuality, and nowhere is this more prominent than in *Buxton Spice*.[73] The novel's varied affective and sensual encounters often take place in connection with, or become expressed through, the nature and landscape: "Lula's emergent sexuality is projected onto trees, animals, the weather, every aspect of the physical world" (115).

All of Lula's trees have a name symbolizing their importance as partners-in-crime who become personified, and exist in a close relationship with the characters (104). As in the other novels Scott discusses, *Buxton Spice*'s Sweet Dungs Tree, Male Genip Tree, Small Mango Tree, and the sinister Buxton Spice all "bear witness, provide shade, shelter, and comfort, and sometimes also represent unnamed fears and ominous secrets" (104). Like *Jane and Louisa*'s protective cedar trees, the trees in *Buxton Spice* serve the purpose of providing a kumbla-like shelter to the young girl exposed to the threats of the outside world.

In an early passage in the novel, Lula wanders around her surroundings as the day's heat turns into a cooling afternoon. My focus here is on the ambiguous and ambivalent "four o'clock feeling," which depicts Lula's state of mind as she wanders around aimlessly, without much of a goal or objective:

> House quiet. Even the yard quiet. The heat of the day cooling to four o'clock feeling. Mums and Dads still resting. My sister Sammy helping Judy and Rachel DeAbro bag off sugar in their father's shop. I slipped out the small front gate, four o'clock feeling inside me. Sun still too hot to move fast. […] I straightened up. Looked around with my four o'clock feeling. Nobody on the street. Not a dog or a fowl-cock.[74]

---

[71] Scott, *Caribbean Women Writers and Globalization*, 104.

[72] Kempadoo, *Buxton Spice* (London: Orion, 1998): 3.

[73] Scott, *Caribbean Women Writers and Globalization*, 88. Further page references are in the main text.

[74] *Buxton Spice*, 20.

How should we interpret this feeling? Is it simply the matter of an individual's private emotions ("four o'clock feeling *inside* me," my italics), or is the four-o'clock feeling the text's ethos serving to highlight the other characters' states of mind, and the community's expectant political atmosphere? As Lula looks around with her four-o'clock feeling, affect serves as a lens through which she sees and experiences the surrounding world, and in this way, it serves as her perspective on life. The hard-to-grasp affect corresponds to emotions defined by Sue Campbell as too complex and multifaceted to be divided and placed in the so-called classical categories of emotion (for example, love, fear, anger, and envy).[75] Campbell writes that the naming and reading of these complex emotions is difficult, as they often receive their expression in ways that differ from the so-called classic emotions.[76] Their ability to be transmitted thus relies on their interpretative communities' ability to individuate and interpret them.

The four-o'clock feeling that overcomes Lula as she walks around in and outside her family's yard depicts an ambivalent state of mind. It cannot be interpreted as referring to any single, identifiable emotion; rather, it is a slightly obscure affect that casts its aura over the scene's stagnant atmosphere. The four-o'clock feeling can be individuated as an affect conveying a growing young girl's sense of place in, and awareness of, her world. She is on the cusp of sexual consciousness, yet she is aware of experiencing something new and depicts it as a "four o'clock feeling." The fact that the word 'feeling' is attached to affect makes it clear that it is in fact an affect which also involves physical sensations, and so it cannot simply be captured by the word 'emotion'. The ambivalence of the four-o'clock feeling in the novel is a metaphor reaching further than the individual's private mental state: it has a role as a figure of speech depicting the text's undertone at a moment of stagnation before the onset of large-scale events.

The physical space and surroundings of Lula's yard is closely tied to the four-o'clock feeling. In fact, it is an affective formation born of the place and time in question. For example, the "two o'clock air" that precedes the four-o'clock feeling is "thick with the milky, nutty smell of crushed beans and the room around us [is] half dark."[77] The scent and the darkness of the room

---

[75] Campbell, *Interpreting the Personal*, 2–3.

[76] *Interpreting the Personal*, 165.

[77] *Buxton Spice*, 19.

merge with the sensation of two-o'clock air; the time and place for making tofu and performing household chores.

The ensuing four-o'clock feeling is as much a temporally motivated figure as it is a spatial one. In fact, the four-o'clock feeling is markedly attached to temporality as well as temporariness. During the affective experience of the four-o'clock feeling, the morning and midday have passed; it is time for the afternoon siesta. This, too, will pass. As a product of modernity, time plays a central role in the ways in which we experience the present. Caribbean space–time was, paradoxically, instrumental in the construction of Western modernity, yet it was fundamentally excluded from modernity's benefits.[78] The four-o'clock feeling (as Lula's experience of the present) has to do with a similar sense of fleeting unattainability. It connects the hazy vibrations of political unrest and sexual growth that converge in an ongoing tension in the life of Lula and her friends in Tamarind Grove. The poignancy of the four-o'clock feeling is born of the temporary halt that it implies, and yet, paradoxically, it offers a temporal leap as the futurity of the present – of things yet to come – is momentarily experienced inside the body ("the four o'clock feeling inside me"). Lula's process of differentiation between childhood and adolescence becomes lived in that moment. In order to explain the momentary nature of Lula's four-o'clock feeling as a force of differentiation, we can draw a connection between her process of becoming a desiring subject and Elizabeth Grosz's theory of temporal becoming.[79]

According to Grosz, processes of differentiation are always bound up with time, whereby virtual futurity is the time of sexual difference[80] as it will have taken place (the future anterior intended), as it has not had time to do so in the present, after Irigaray, in the phallogocentric order.[81] In other words, the four-o'clock feeling may in Lula's case be an affective equivalent to Grosz's

---

[78] Sheller, *Consuming the Caribbean*, 188, 191.

[79] See Elizabeth Grosz, *The Nick of Time: Politics, Evolution and the Untimely* (Durham NC & London: Duke UP, 2004), and *Time Travels: Feminism, Nature, Power* (Durham NC & London: Duke UP, 2005).

[80] Grosz insists that in her work the question is not that of gender, but that of sexual difference. For her purposes, 'gender' refers to the representation and "socialized ideal" of sexual difference. 'Sexual difference', in turn, refers to a conception of difference as constitutive and pre-existing "the entities that it produces": i.e. that which often becomes understood as gender. See Grosz, *Time Travels*, 171, 174.

[81] *Time Travels*, 175.

understanding of sexual difference as not existing in any concrete form(s). Instead, the anticipation of Lula's becoming a desiring subject through the four-o'clock feeling expresses how "that which has yet to take place exists only in virtuality."[82] In this way, time therefore becomes a "dynamic force" of affect, where desire, subjectivity, and the virtuality of the future congregate in one affective moment that serves as a catalyst of change, and thus of differentiation within the self.[83] In fact, the four-o'clock feeling may even be described as precisely a Groszian "nick of time," referring both to the urgency of time and to the untimely – as that which creates a nick or rupture in the seeming continuity of past, present, and future.[84] Thus, as a response to one of Grosz's conclusions, that "the virtual exists only in time," we may also note that it may be supplemented by affect, which also receives its force from the dynamism of time.[85]

The four-o'clock feeling is the affective moment in which, like in Grosz's thought, "temporality and change are lived and experienced."[86] In the liminal time of siesta, then, many events take place; instead of inhabiting its seeming stagnation, Lula's delicate pre-teen self takes active steps towards maturity. Reading the four-o'clock feeling as a textual strategy creating an effect of confusion and bewilderment in the text brings the reader closer to Lula's experience. At the same time, the ambivalence and air of stagnation implied in the four-o'clock feeling also serve to distance the reader from Lula's obscure experience. The narrative, in other words, works by the logic of Ahmed's strange encounter as an interplay of proximity and distance, with the temporal affect of the four-o'clock feeling as its driving force. At the same time, it sheds light on the novel's main theme; the enigmatic state related to the unravelling of sexual knowledge in (pre-)puberty, which has no straightforward emotional definition – just the obscure four-o'clock feeling. Its ostensible stagnation awakens Lula as well as the reader to look with anticipation toward what will happen when the four-o'clock feeling has passed.

⌘

---

[82] Grosz, *Time Travels*, 175.

[83] *Time Travels*, 181.

[84] Grosz, *The Nick of Time*, 14.

[85] *The Nick of Time*, 241.

[86] Grosz, *Time Travels*, 180.

From "bombing-up feeling" to "taking man": An intersectional reading

The protagonist, Lula, and her friends seek knowledge and understanding of sexuality with open curiosity. Both sexuality and the political volatility of Burnham's dictatorship in the village are strange, unknown issues to the girls, which they observe keenly as outsiders. For example, Lula watches through her window as a group of men punish another in an act of extreme violence.[87] Later on, she acknowledges that there are lessons her educated parents cannot teach her: "Was much more to see and learn though, through our windows, across the street. In other people's yards" (122). The questions pertaining to sexuality become answered through secrets, voyeurism, and the uncovering of hidden knowledge. A voyeuristic gaze serves as the satisfier of the girls' curiosity in various scenes throughout the novel.

The girls sneak out to take a look at and sniff of the mentally deranged Uncle Joe's penis through a hole in the crotch of his pants, when he falls asleep under the house after lunch: "In the middle of his crotch, where the stitching had bust, was a lovely big hole, just skinning up at us" (7). Fascination tinged with a little trepidation grants the girls access to the unknown sights, sounds, and smells of an adult male body as they point and giggle at the sleeping man's penis. Lula narrates the incident:

> Straight there we headed, pushing and jostling, gulping down our squeals and squeaks to get a better look. [...] Inside, the curve barely visible, was a wrinkled, wrinkled, thick dull brown almost black skin. (7)

Teasing Uncle Joe provides the girls with the opportunity to observe sexuality from a safe distance, but their curiosity is endlessly dissatisfied. After further teasing poor Joe to show them his "donkey lolo," the girls spy through a keyhole on the older boys engaged in a sexual act with a girl they call Sexy Marilyn in one of the rooms of the family's large house. In the dark of the schoolroom, according to Lula, "Sexy Marilyn get screw," and adds that she knows that the boys involved knew that Lula and her friends were watching (35). The girls peek and giggle at the event, yet they are slightly perplexed and possibly even scared by the puzzling act of sex. Gossiping ensues, where the girls' sexual ignorance is depicted as they converse about Marilyn's "big-woman body," her large breasts and allegedly wanton sexual appetite (36).

---

[87] *Buxton Spice*, 53. Further page references are in the main text.

As the girls begin to observe changes in their own bodies, Lula becomes endlessly fascinated by what she calls a person's "man-self," the masculine traits she finds in each person (129). The manner in which she gathers more information about the various man-selves of her home village is by staring out of the window and studying people, in order to imitate them. She observes "the way they pulled on the bright cigarette stub and then swung down the hand, grab the crotch, shift to the other leg" and then follows suit by prancing around in her room like the men on the street (129). Her fascination leads her to imitate her older brother Yan's "man-self" by going shirtless and wearing her father's trousers. After Lula has a sexual encounter with her friend Judy's brother, Iggy DeAbro, who corners and fondles Lula one day, Lula begins to wonder about her new sensations. She tries to downplay the incident in her mind: "It wasn't sex. Was just a feeling, more like an embarrassment" (103). From then on, her explorations with sexuality continue in full force.

The girls read the sexual education book *Man and Woman* (in secret, naturally), and soon afterwards Lula brings herself to her first orgasm with the help of the shower head (107). The experience of sexual arousal receives the name "bombing-up feeling" in Lula's mind, and from then on she continuously re-creates it when alone (107). Lula remarks:

> After that, the bombing went on whenever I could get enough time in the shower. The fear of somebody finding me like that with my legs up against the wall made it scarier. Better. (108)

The fact that Lula chooses to create a euphemism for the sensation of sexual arousal is fitting: she is not yet able to fully verbalize the new sensation. Various other emotions, affects, and embodied experiences also fall under Lula's expression. The bombing-up feeling is more than tinged with pleasure and shame:

> That big thing [the idea of a penis] and the bombing feeling, made a shame grow in me. Shame, if anyone was to find out I bombed up with it. […] It made the explosion bigger. Was something I couldn't explain to Judy. (110)

Lula, a desiring subject-in-formation, experiences her sexual pleasure in close connection with shame; an emotion that Anita Haya Patterson associates closely with pleasure in Jamaican women's poetry.[88] While the contours of shame are markedly distinct in Patterson's case, her associating of pleasure

[88] Patterson, "Contingencies of Pleasure and Shame," 269.

with shame is an important discovery for affective feminist work on Caribbean topics. Another complex affect, the bombing-up feeling, intertwines the feelings of arousal, fear, and shame of the possibility of being caught, pleasure arising out of that fear, and of Lula's own private achievement in the sensation of orgasm. Like the ephemeral four-o'clock feeling, the bombing-up feeling captures the developing and changing experience of Lula herself as a desiring subject at a moment in time that promises more, but that does not yet reveal all.

Eventually, the girls fail to remain outside their country's societal turmoil, as the race-related riots touch their young lives more intimately. As the mixed-raced daughter of an Indian father and a black and white mother, Lula is well aware of the segregation between the blacks and the Indians in Guyana, and it makes her life more difficult in her multiracial circle of friends. Towards the end of the novel, on the night that the political climate heats up into a riot, Judy, a middle-class white girl, is caught in the act with the black André. There, the articulation of class, race, and sexuality is made abundantly clear to the young girls at the same time as the equally race- and class-driven riots break out in the racially segregated village. After Judy's nightly encounter with André is discovered, her mother's reaction is profoundly violent and echoes the bleak vistas Burnham's regime presented to women.[89] Mrs DeAbro yells at her daughter as she lashes her with her cane:

> "Oh *God*! My daughter dere taking black man in de bus shed! Oh Lord! God, you have no mercy on me! *Taking man!* When people frighten to go outside, you dere *taking man by de roadside!*"[90]

Mrs DeAbro's violent outburst against her daughter continues with a physical testing of her daughter's genitals to look for signs verifying that she has had sexual intercourse (see 'testing' in the next chapter). André, for his part, is completely absent from the scene of Judy's discovery; he has probably fled into the dark of the night.

An intersectional reading may serve to (but does not condone) Mrs De Abro's violent reaction. The constant plea to God in the passage points to Mrs DeAbro's devout Catholicism, which adds the fear of sin to her fury (73). Furthermore, her antagonism has to do with her privileged Portuguese heritage; a small but significant ethnic minority in Guyana, and hence close to 'white' on the racial-ethnic social stratification (65). In this way, her

---

[89] See Scott, *Caribbean Women Writers and Globalization*, 93.

[90] *Buxton Spice*, 180. Further page references are in the main text.

daughter's interracial sex with a racial 'inferior' fuels Mrs DeAbro's outrage. At the same time, the mother's reaction reflects her middle-class aspirations described throughout the novel, as she expects her daughter to remain chaste for a future husband (64). To add insult to injury, Judy's breaking of the curfew associates her with the political turmoil, the class- and race-driven riots which Mrs DeAbro's (presumed) chaste, Catholic, white-Portuguese middle-class daughter should avoid. In fact, it is Mrs DeAbro's violent behaviour that allows the intersectionality of differences to be read. These differences become produced in and by Mrs DeAbro's affective reaction. The differences are not originary or affect-inducing in themselves; rather, it is the conflict between the effect and affect of differences that explains the scenario.

The complex intermarriage of social differences has a lesson to teach the young girls in the novel. As Scott notes, they now know of "the perils of sexual pleasure and danger."[91] Hence, intersectionality has an embedded pedagogy, most visible at points in the novel in which differences can be seen to clash. As Judy's secret is unexpectedly revealed, the girls become aware of what happens when wrongly intersectionalized individuals become sexually involved. The white middle classes and poor blacks do not match; upon the realization of this, these categories truly become constructed in the girls' minds. The guessing-game of sexuality is over; as Lula remarks, "Now the whole village knew."[92] The incident has further consequences for the rest of the girls, as they reach the end of an era of sexual innocence: everyone is now aware of the complexity of difference and the repercussions of sexual behaviour in a social context where race and sexuality are interconnected with power. Secret sexuality is made public knowledge, which marks the end of the girls' childhood era. In this way, the transition to a new era happens dramatically both on the individual and on the community level.

Claire C. Robertson gives an interesting account of the reciprocal relationship between theory and her research material on the gender systems of Ghana and Kenya, as well as St Lucia in the West Indies. Robertson explains that the term 'materialist' has two senses in her research, where it refers to both a revisionist Marxism and a close connection to the actual material, the research "data."[93] Robertson adds: "My materials also include my convic-

---

[91] Scott, *Caribbean Women Writers and Globalization*, 114.

[92] *Buxton Spice*, 182.

[93] Claire C. Robertson, "Cultural Materialism: Reflections on a Theoretical Odyssey from Africa to the West Indies," *Journal of Women's History* 11.1 (1999): 168.

tions, knowledge, and experiences."[94] Similarly, the reader *is* her own material, as the "convictions, knowledge and experiences" of the reader have an impact on which categories of difference become dynamic and which are left stagnant at each given interpretive act. Rather than simply read how differences are produced on a fictional subject level in literature, there is, therefore, another level of intersectionality at play here; that of social differentiation in the relationship between the reader and the text. In other words, the reader/researcher figure also becomes produced in the reading process as intersectionally differentiated in the encounter with the research material.

A reading is always dependent on the reader's ability to interact with the categories of difference, which, in turn, interact with each other. Therefore, it is important to question the selective process by which categories become foregrounded in a reading: how does this particular text speak its axes of difference to me and how, in turn, does it cause me to read certain differences into existence? As Sara Ahmed writes, "even the event of claiming some differences, is to refuse to admit to others."[95] Intersectionality always depends on our capacity and readiness to observe or give value to certain differences while we might be culturally and socially conditioned to overlook others. That is not to say that a 'native reader' would be better equipped to give an account of the factors at play in Judy's scenario described here; rather, it demonstrates that the concepts we choose to utilize are largely dependent on our capacities to use them, as well as on the material context in which we employ them.

The question, then, becomes how to conduct a balanced dialogue that gives voice to certain differences at certain points, while asking them to stay quiet at other times, and embodies certain materialities at select points while making them invisible at other times. If our ability to read intersectionality has largely to do with choice, then we can also choose to challenge each intersectional reading with a counter-reading. It is important to remember that intersectionality is not a concept that serves to reconcile the conflicts resulting from the complexity of a politics of difference. Always ultimately dependent on its material, not on its theoretical formulations, intersectionality as a tool can only take the reading as far as the material conditions allow. Unlike *Jane and Louisa*, *Buxton Spice* does not present a moment of liberation or progression

---

[94] Robertson, "Cultural Materialism: Reflections on a Theoretical Odyssey from Africa to the West Indies," 168.

[95] Sara Ahmed, *Differences That Matter: Feminist Theory and Postmodernism* (Cambridge: Cambridge UP, 1998): 196.

towards harmony. In fact, the novel ends in bitter disappointment when Lula's family leaves Tamarind Grove for England, as the disturbed Burnham era reaps its harvest in making futile attempts at national unity.[96] In the end, Lula takes her disappointment out on the Buxton Spice tree, which has failed to educate her despite its many years of keeping watch. Lula lashes out at Buxton Spice:

> "All dese years we here, you know bout t'ings and wouldn't tell me nothing. You the one always spying. Well we goin now! You could stay and watch people suffer more."[97]

For Lula, the tree embodies and personifies the adult experience that she cannot control or understand. The tree, a generator and facilitator of Lula's multiple sensations, feelings, and emotions, is in the end depicted as growing one "fat rosy mango," perhaps symbolizing the hope that the Guyanese land and nature carry with them as they sustains those who stayed through the difficult years.[98]

This chapter has concentrated on readings of and ways of reading affects, feelings, and complex emotions that are connected to the ambivalent nature of the onset of sexuality as transitory, in flux, undergoing constant change. Complicating a straightforward focus on age as the primary category of differentiation, this model of reading is based on those emotions that express and emerge from the unexplainable affective, embodied experience of sexuality and sex in cases where clear-cut meanings elude the protagonists and their readers. Erna Brodber's *Jane and Louisa*, with its notoriously difficult and elusive kumbla figure, shows us how the reader becomes positioned by its polysemy into a world of ambivalences where negotiations of new meanings and understandings of sexuality and emotions are negotiated. Bringing together the different implications of the kumbla, then, indicates that the kumbla can be protective and destructive, immobile and mobile, a space and a practice or a process, a role and an evasion, and indeed, indigenous and hybrid. Most importantly, it is Brodber's instrument whereby to describe with full awareness the multitudes contained by her experimental, alternative, and marginal ways of creating fiction and scholarship.

Oonya Kempadoo's *Buxton Spice*, on the other hand, presents its reader with a chain of affects from the four-o'clock feeling to the bombing-up

[96] See, for example, Scott, *Caribbean Women Writers and Globalization*, 87.

[97] *Buxton Spice*, 183.

[98] *Buxton Spice*, 183.

feeling, to the tragic discovery of sexual activity happening in secrecy. This affective formation does not as such offer the reader a teleological guideline to follow in order to understand the novel's portrayal of implicit and explicit sexuality. Instead, it serves as the text's ethos, which colours its protagonist's life, titillating and confusing her. At the same time, the reader is placed in conversation with sexuality in these embodied affective encounters, which refuse to be defined in clear-cut terms. From reading complex emotions as ambivalent and never fully definable from outside the reading process itself, we move on to discuss those affective experiences relating to sexuality that are marked as to be read in terms of negative-affect theory. There, we encounter sexualities and sexual experiences that seem only to further immerse the reader in the murky waters of reading sexuality as a source of shame, isolation, and destruction.

⌘

3
Ways of Reading Sexual Shame, Violence, and Pain

Edwidge Danticat, Opal Palmer Adisa, and Erna Brodber

THE EMOTION OF SHAME is probably the most-theorized of all classically categorized and named emotions in recent feminist theorizations of affectivity. In fact, Jill Locke asserts that there has lately been a veritable "surge of interest" in shame.[1] Kathleen Woodward goes even further by stating that "there has been an explosion of interest in the emotion of shame across a wide variety of disciplines."[2] In order to understand the salience of shame in the domain of affective feminist work, we need but consider Eve Kosofsky Sedgwick's assertion that shame is "the place where the *question* of identity arises most originarily and most relationally."[3] In other words, shame as an affect raises crucial questions about the very foundations of our identities in a way that is relational; thereby signalling a decidedly dynamic relationship between shame and identity. The two shape each other in a constant flux of signification, and it is this dynamism that leads the reader to a path of meaning-production. The idea of relationality works in dialogic reading, too, as the reader and the text are in a dynamic, affective relationship with each other. In fact, reader and text in this model do not even exist without the other, since, according to the dialogic principle, language itself always presupposes the existence of the simultaneity of two voices within each utterance. In an attempt to understand the language of shame, the reader therefore

---

[1] Jill Locke, "Shame and the Future of Feminism," *Hypatia* 22.4 (2007): 147.

[2] Kathleen Woodward, "Traumatic Shame: Toni Morrison, Televisual Culture, and the Cultural Politics of the Emotions," *Cultural Critique* 46 (Autumn 2000): 211.

[3] Sedgwick, *Touching Feeling*, 37 (emphasis in original).

needs to listen to the silenced voice of shame, and enter into dialogue with that which cannot always be explicitly articulated.

Sexuality has generally been seen as a site of shame, but not for everyone, nor is it a similar experience for all who feel it.[4] In other words, sexuality as a site of shame is also a site of differentiation. This also helps us to see differentiation within shame; not all shame is similar. Due to the subsequent complexity of shame, there is thus an urgent need to understand shame in its many forms.[5] In her reading of the poetry of the Jamaican women poets Una Marson, Vera Bell, and Lorna Goodison, Anita Haya Patterson discovers shame to have a "distinct cultural resonance" in Caribbean women's writing.[6] In these poems, shame is tied to issues of pleasure and respectability, where women's sexual pleasure is, on the one hand, seen as a self-recognized feature of Afro-Jamaican women's identities, but, on the other, is seen as shameful and unrespectable, largely as a consequence of the abuse of the (sexual) body under plantation slavery.[7] Furthermore, Patterson contends that "the act of putting a name to the experience of shame itself was a critical step in the historical development of women's literary emergence in Jamaica."[8] While I agree with Patterson on the importance of bestowing a name on an affect for it to be individuated as a discernible emotion in a particular cultural context and literary tradition, my concern in this chapter is with the ramifications of the expression *after* it has been named and transmitted to a reading audience. Along with shame as an expressed emotion in the novel, the reading event as a site of shame becomes central, as it is the time and place where shame's meanings are negotiated in the affective encounter between reader and text.

According to Denise DeCaires Narain, Caribbean women's writing since the 1980s has "increasingly recognized the ways in which female sexuality has been socially coded to signify limitation and *shame*."[9] Evelyn O'Callaghan makes a similar observation about the aura of shameful sexuality in Caribbean women's writing.[10] This chapter takes up those instances of shameful female sexuality which lead to negative consequences and loss of a sense

[4] Probyn, *Blush: Faces of Shame*, x.

[5] Woodward, "Traumatic Shame," 235.

[6] Patterson, "Contingencies of Pleasure and Shame," 269.

[7] "Contingencies of Pleasure and Shame," 275.

[8] "Contingencies of Pleasure and Shame," 275.

[9] Narain, "Standing in the Place of Love," 334. (My emphasis.)

[10] O'Callaghan, "'Compulsory Heterosexuality'," 297.

of self and is seen as shameful, damaging, and destructive. Shame circulates most poignantly in the sexual lives and bodies of girl and women characters. Again, the goal is not to determine what sexual shame in the novels under discussion *is*, but, rather, to explain the effects of being shamed to read shame from the vantage point of sexual violence, damage, and pain.[11]

The four texts dealing with shame in this chapter all link sexuality and shame; Edwidge Danticat's *Breath, Eyes, Memory*, Opal Palmer Adisa's *It Begins With Tears*, Brodber's *Jane and Louisa Will Soon Come Home*, and her short story "Sleeping's Beauty and the Prince Charming" ("Sleeping's Beauty") highlight physical and/or mental damage through sexual shame. They also invite or encourage similar ways of reading despite the various types of damage inflicted on the women: from women's sexual violence against women (Danticat and Adisa) and self-inflicted sexual violence (Danticat) to more symbolic damage in the forms of taboo and silence as destructive of voice and agency, where the mystification of the menstruating female body appears to destroy female identity (Brodber).

Danticat's *Breath, Eyes, Memory* relates the story of three generations of Haitian women who, in one way or another, must come to terms with their traumatizing pasts. Donette A. Francis examines five different scenes, or sites, of violence in *Breath, Eyes, Memory*, of which the two most relevant ones for the purposes of this chapter are entitled by Francis "Testing – traumatic heirlooms" and "The pestle – confronting trauma."[12] These designations refer to the two incidents of sexual violation and self-inflicted sexual violence by women in the novel. Testing refers to the Haitian tradition of mothers testing their daughters' virginity by inserting the pinkie finger into the girl's vagina in order to ensure the hymen is intact. The pestle, in turn, refers to the decision of the first-person narrator–protagonist, Sophie Caco, to take her own virginity by using a pestle in order to stop this traumatizing and humiliating ordeal.

Sophie spends her childhood with her mother's sister, Tante Atie, in Haiti, and at the age of twelve is sent to the USA to live with her mother, Martine. For Sophie, her new life growing up in New York means a struggle for inte-

---

[11] In this chapter, sexual shame is a concept similar to Woodward's naming of the shame in her reading of Toni Morrison's *The Bluest Eye* as racial shame. See Woodward, "Traumatic Shame," 224.

[12] Donette A. Francis, "'Silences Too Horrific to Disturb': Writing Sexual Histories in Edwidge Danticat's *Breath, Eyes, Memory*," *Research in African Literatures* 35.2 (Summer 2004): 77, 82, 84.

gration in American society. She becomes fluent in English, succeeds at school, and works hard for her education, but her mother is not so successful. Constantly haunted by nightmares of being raped by a Macoute – a soldier in the violent militia – as a young girl in Haiti, Martine has a living memory of the incident in her daughter (who was born of the rape, and who physically resembles no one in the Caco family). Paranoid about guarding Sophie's chastity, she continues the rural Haitian women's custom of "*testing*" (the word is italicized throughout the novel). Unable to endure the humiliating procedure any longer, Sophie breaks her hymen with a mortar pestle, thus failing the next testing and causing her mother to throw her out of their home to start an independent life.

A comparable scene of subjection takes place in Adisa's *It Begins With Tears*. Set in the fictional village of Kristoff in rural Jamaica, the novel recounts the story of Monica, a retired prostitute in her forties who returns home to live comfortably in a house paid for by a lover. To her misfortune, Monica enters into a love relationship with a married man, Desmond, which culminates in three village women – Desmond's abandoned wife, Grace, and her friends Peggy and Marva – unleashing an act of extreme sexual violence on Monica as punishment.The three women use the practice of 'peppering' to teach a lesson to Monica, who feels no shame for her past as a prostitute; nor for her adulterous actions with Desmond. In peppering Monica, the three women forcibly insert hot peppers into her bodily orifices: her mouth, nose, and vagina. The shame circulating before, during, and after these scenes in Adisa and Danticat's texts is my concern in the first part of this chapter.

The final part of this chapter is dedicated to the subtle and overt manifestations of shame in Brodber's texts, which has to do with the inarticulable taboo of menstruation. Evasion and dismissal produce shame, which works against the female protagonists' body–mind integration. Nellie, the protagonist of *Jane and Louisa Will Soon Come Home*, grows up in an environment that does not nurture her coming to womanhood and the arrival of what she calls 'it' (referring to the onset of puberty and menstruation). The uncertainties of becoming a mature sexual female are ultimately what lead Nellie to retreat to her kumbla. In the allegorical short story, "Sleeping's Beauty and the Prince Charming," a similar menstruation taboo hinders the re-integration of the distressed Sleeping's Beauty's mind and body, as Prince Charming is unable to cope with her period – and so abandons his black princess. Prince Charming's actions lead to the failure of the couple's plans to liberate black people, thereby evoking the partial blame that black men must bear for negative attitudes towards the sexual black female body.

These three authors thus confront the reader with an array of shaming scenes, in ways that might not be possible in non-literary contexts. Shame is an affect of intimacy; experienced as exposure which shapes (sexual) identities,[13] shame has been seen as a 'sticky' affect, something that is contagious.[14] By way of their stickiness, literary emotions may be transmitted and shifted to the reader in the affective text–reader relationship. The recurring argument that literary emotions also have the capacity to be transmitted and shifted to the reader then leads to the question of what we, as readers, can do to affects – and, indeed, what do they do to us. I am not referring here to the simple adoption of literary affects by the reader but to a more complex reading practice of reworking (with) affectivity for meaning and understanding. What does shame do to those who feel it, and to those who do not?

As the 'performance of shame' entails an interlink with various other emotions, shame needs to be read through a variety of associated emotions such as guilt, honour, responsibility, terror, and pain.[15] How do the sexual histories of Caribbean women explain the shame felt in the face of sexual violence, abuse, and the idea of sexuality as destructive? Shame functions as a differentiating device in these violent "intercorporeal encounters between others."[16] Simultaneously, shame exposes us to a "double movement" of individuation and relationality.[17] Thus, shame creates identities and relationships, alienation and community, and possesses a certain sociality.[18] Shame produces gaps, distances, and pain between women. In this, I ask: how can we read (through) shame? How does shame function in my reading of these texts?

I argue that shame in these texts possesses a "cognitive edge" for the reader, in that, while shame might not work as an epistemological tool for the characters in the texts, it may do so for readers who witness or experience it vicariously.[19] In other words, while the characters might not transcend shame on the textual level, the reader may do so. The work shame does to the text

[13] Ahmed, *The Cultural Politics of Emotion*, 103.

[14] Sedgwick, *Touching Feeling*, 36.

[15] Ahmed, *The Cultural Politics of Emotion*, 110, 103.

[16] *The Cultural Politics of Emotion*, 103.

[17] Sedgwick, *Touching Feeling*, 37.

[18] See, for example, Woodward, "Traumatic Shame," 212.

[19] Woodward, "Traumatic Shame," 213.

and its reader can be characterized in many ways, but the focus here is on two ways in which its function may be understood. First, shame is a motivator that incites sexual violence. It spurs actions of various kinds, and the effects of these actions are thus shame-related: the fear of being shamed is a cause of shame. Second, shame can be seen as a tool for reading, where readers, motivated by a reading of shame, can be prompted not only to witness the damage it does but also to understand its underlying power-structures. As a result of engaging with shame-fuelled processes of differentiation, new notions of the self may be negotiated within the affective text–reader relationship.

From the idea of shame's cognitive edge arises the notion of shame as an active agent of social being and doing. In a similar vein, Elspeth Probyn takes a refreshing approach to shame when she notes that it can be positive, in that it does things and is productive in making us re-envisage the constructions of our humanity.[20] According to Probyn, it "goes to the heart of who we think we are" (x). Shame is also productive in requiring "self-evaluation and transformation" and containing the promise of "a return of interest, joy and connection" (xiii). As such, shame therefore suggests that we *care*. Without shame, we fail to consider differentiation from and connection with other people (xiv). Like Probyn, I endeavour to discuss shame in productive ways. Shame, in my view, has a cumulative affect that, despite the tragedies for individuals or collectives it causes, may also be seen as a force for change and regeneration. It is not that all shame is productive, but we as readers can view it in a productive manner. Regarding shame as situational may allow shame to be seen as a tool which "demands that big questions be asked in a modest way" (xviii). It is my hope in this chapter that shame may be put to good (albeit modest) use in reworking it for the purposes of reading-for-change.

The sexual shame of 'testing' in Danticat's *Breath, Eyes, Memory*

Haiti's history of violence established by its colonial legacy and decades of dictatorship has been referred to as "state terror."[21] This traumatic history of

[20] Probyn, *Blush: Faces of Shame*, xviii. Further page references are in the main text.

[21] Myriam Chancy, "'No Giraffes in Haiti': Haitian Women and State Terror," in *Écrire en pays assiégé: Haïti / Writing Under Siege*, ed. Marie–Agnès Sourieau & Kathleen M. Balutansky (Francopolyphonies 1; Amsterdam & New York: Rodopi,

sexuality in Haiti is "a living presence" in all of Danticat's writing, not least in *Breath, Eyes, Memory*.[22] The novel is concerned with the gendered and sexualized side of the country's structural violence, which projects its sombre shadow onto the lives and bodies of Haitian women and girls. Indeed, this violence is so pervasive that it reaches women and is inflicted by them on themselves; 'state terror', in its gendered nature, is "the violation endured by Haitian women because of their sex."[23] Sexual violence against women and girls under the Duvalier regime was openly perpetrated by his militia henchmen, the Tontons Macoutes.

In the scenes set in Haiti (in Sophie's childhood and when she returns to see her grandmother, Grandmè Ifé, and Tante Atie as an adult), according to Helen Scott, "we see the casual brutality of the Macoutes, whose presence is overtly sexualized and intimidating."[24] For example, young Martine is raped by a masked Macoute who "kept pounding her until she was too stunned to make a sound," while threatening to kill her.[25] Sophie feels threatened by them when she rides in the same van in Haiti (97). When Sophie goes to the market with her grandmother, a vendor wrongly accused of stepping on a Macoute's foot is beaten to death by the militia while "every one watched in shocked silence, but no one said anything" (118). Tante Atie's friend Louise reminds Atie that they might be next to be taken by the Macoutes, demonstrating the randomness of these acts and threats of violence (138). Sophie recounts what she has learnt of the Macoutes: "they did not hide" and "if a

---

2004): 304. Dictators François "Papa Doc" Duvalier and his son, Jean–Claude "Baby Doc" Duvalier, ruled Haiti in the latter half of the twentieth century (1954–71 and 1971–86, respectively). During that time, thousands of dissenters were brutally murdered, and Duvalier "encouraged foreign corporations to exploit Haitian workers in low-wage agriculture and industry" (Scott, *Caribbean Women Writers and Globalization*, 3). Historically, Haiti is the only country in the world with a successful black-led revolution in 1791. Despite (or perhaps even due to) this, Haiti remains one of the world's poorest countries.

[22] Helen Scott, "Ou libéré? History, transformation and the struggle for freedom in Edwidge Danticat's *Breath, Eyes, Memory*," in *Écrire en pays assiégé: Haïti / Writing Under Siege*, ed. Marie–Agnès Sourieau & Kathleen M. Balutansky (Francopolyphonies 1; Amsterdam & New York: Rodopi, 2004): 461.

[23] Chancy, "'No Giraffes in Haiti'," 316.

[24] Scott, *Caribbean Women Writers and Globalization*, 33.

[25] Danticat, *Breath, Eyes, Memory* (London: Abacus, 1994), 139. Further page references are in the main text.

woman refused, they would make her sleep with her son and brother or even her own father" (139).

The ubiquitous sexual violence in the novel is coupled with other bodily misfortunes, as Scott notes: Sophie's mother, aunt and grandmother all suffer from tumors (Martine's case is most severe in that she has breast cancer), and Sophie herself suffers from bulimia soon after her marriage.[26] These bodily manifestations of damage lead Scott to claim that, in the novel, "again and again bodies, especially women's bodies, are assaulted, mutilated, abused, become diseased, and die."[27] Showcasing the social history of rape and sexual violence in Haiti in *Breath, Eyes, Memory*, Danticat not only reveals the patriarchal, sexist power-structure of the aftermath of the Duvalier regime but also demonstrates how this power-structure is continued and supported by women in the families.[28] As grandmother Ifé explains to Sophie, her job was to keep her daughters' sexual purity intact until they find her a suitable husband.[29] The polarization of sex as either acceptable in matrimony or shamefully degrading outside marriage leads to sexual discipline fuelled by the ideals of respectability, responsibility, and honor.[30] Behind these three ideals, shame does its work to support and validate the practice of 'testing'.

Fuelled by shame

Against the background of structural sexual violence on the female body, *Breath, Eyes, Memory* brings the 'virginity cult' of testing to the fore as its key theme and recurring motif, where a girl's sexual chastity becomes a point of obsession for their mothers.[31] Sophie articulates her understanding of the preoccupation with virginity:

> I have heard it compared to a virginity cult, our mothers' obsession with keeping us pure and chaste. My mother always listened to the echo of my urine in the toilet, for if it was too loud it meant that I had been deflowered. I learned very early in life that virgins always took small steps when they walked. They never did acrobatic splits, never

[26] Scott, "Ou Libéré?," 466.

[27] Scott, *Caribbean Women Writers and Globalization*, 38.

[28] Francis, "'Silences Too Horrific to Disturb'," 79, 82.

[29] *Breath, Eyes, Memory*, 156.

[30] Francis, "'Silences Too Horrific to Disturb'," 82.

[31] *Breath, Eyes, Memory*, 154.

> rode horses or bicycles. They always covered themselves well and, even if their lives depended on it, never parted with their panties.[32]

The severity of this ideal of chastity is highlighted by the dependent clause "even if their lives depended on it," indicating that chastity in the novel does indeed become a matter of life and death.

As I read the affective ramifications of testing for Sophie, my attention is drawn to the self-perpetuating and recursive nature of state terror morphing into the ubiquitous affect of shame, with regard to the tradition of testing. Sophie realizes at the end of the novel how "nightmares are passed on through generations like heirlooms."[33] The many contingencies of shame are an integral part of these transgenerational nightmares.[34] The way shame circulates in the novel is tied up with other affective formations, serving to carry its weight. In *Breath, Eyes, Memory*, responsibility, honour, respect, and being 'good' are close relatives of shame. They help shame's work by further ambiguating and contradicting its mechanisms as they become evoked in the validation of testing; it is a mother's responsibility to take care of the family's honor by testing, and the daughters need to be respectful of their parents and be 'good' by abstaining from pre-marital sex.[35] Failure to adhere to these codes leads to shame.[36] Discussing shame in Toni Morrison's *The Bluest Eye*, Kathleen Woodward notes that it is passed down from one generation to the next.[37] This inter-generational circulation of shame means that it is not simply a temporary, passing emotion (as we tend to think of emotions), but that it is "not so much identifiable as a particular emotion as it is virtually inherent in the way that one responds to the social world."[38] In *Breath, Eyes, Memory*, the ramifications of shame are so pervasive that they do not need to be singled and named all the time. However, in the instances where it is named, it becomes clear how and why it is the central affect, worthy of discussion on its own terms, as well as in relation to other affects.

When Sophie is sent to the USA to live with her mother Martine in New York, the older woman inquires of her twelve-year-old daughter whether she

---

[32] *Breath, Eyes, Memory*, 154.

[33] *Breath, Eyes, Memory*, 234.

[34] Francis, "'Silences Too Horrific to Disturb'," 76.

[35] See Ahmed, *The Cultural Politics of Emotion*, 103, 105, 112.

[36] *Breath, Eyes, Memory*, 156.

[37] Woodward, "Traumatic Shame," 218.

[38] Woodward, "Traumatic Shame," 224.

has been "good."[39] She needs not explain further: the question "meant if I had ever been touched, if I had ever held hands, or kissed a boy" (60). Martine's control of her daughter's body works through concealed language, where there is no need to overtly state anything sexual. Martine then proceeds to inform Sophie about testing by telling of her own experience of the practice, as administered by her mother years earlier: "When I was a girl, my mother used to test us to see if we were virgins. She would put her finger in our very private parts and see if it would go inside" (60). Martine backgrounds the motivation for her daughter by telling her that testing was performed because it was the mother's responsibility to ensure her daughter's virginity until marriage. By evoking responsibility, Martine validates the future testing. After that, she explains to her pre-teen daughter how she was conceived of a rape in the cane field, when an anonymous, masked man attacked her on the roadside when she was "just barely older than" Sophie (62). Learning about rape as the origin of her conception, Sophie realizes that she is a constant reminder of the traumatic event for her mother.[40] Thus Martine's violation of rape and Sophie's testing become discursively linked, both being acts of sexual violence in the male exercise of control.

Throughout the novel, we are faced with characters being reminded of their pasts which, according to Scott, denotes the "historical continuities" at play.[41] Testing can be located in these haunting historical continuities of Haiti, as one instance of the importance of social respectability in a class society where a woman's worth was determined by her marriage value. As a woman's respectability was determined by her marriage, and her honour by her respectability[42] and as a woman's economic class was largely determined by her married status,[43] the dynamic relationship between these factors leads to a harsh sexual discipline; desperately monitored by mothers wishing a 'better' life for their daughters through marriage. According to Francis, the logic of this historical chain is that a "woman is property and her worth is determined by an exchange value that is measured by her virginity."[44] In testing, the virginal

---

[39] *Breath, Eyes, Memory*, 60. Further page references are in the main text.

[40] Scott, "Ou Libéré?," 462.

[41] Scott, "Ou Libéré?," 463.

[42] Francis, "'Silences Too Horrific to Disturb'," 82.

[43] Scott, "Ou Libéré?," 469.

[44] Francis, "'Silences Too Horrific to Disturb'," 82.

female body becomes the valuable good whose having remained intact ensures not only her own respectability but that of her entire family.

Foreshadowing the beginning of Sophie's testings, Martine alludes to this chain of honour by lamenting its loss among the new generation of Haitian girls in the New World.[45] She explains: "The problem with the new generation is that a lot of them have lost their sense of obligation to the family's honor"; instead of striving for respectability in the form of a middle-class occupation (particularly that of a doctor), they opt for unskilled menial jobs which bring in "quick cash."[46] Her daughter Sophie turns out to be a specimen of this new generation unconcerned with issues of honour and middle-class aspirations, when she fails to come home early from her visit next door to see her new friend; the African-American jazz musician, Joseph. At home, the eighteen-year-old Sophie is taken upstairs to her bedroom by her mother, where she has to lie down on her bed while being tested (84).

In the following weeks, Sophie undergoes a weekly testing in order to ascertain, in her mother's words, whether she is "still *whole*" (86). In this expression, wholeness and virginity become equated as a sign of the young woman's worth remaining intact until the anticipated marriage. Without her virginity, Sophie would be broken in a crucial way annulling the requirement of the goods exchange in marriage. The allusion to wholeness is particularly ironic: as the testing continues, Sophie's mind begins to disintegrate and she describes herself as follows: "My mother rarely spoke to me since she began the tests. [...] I was feeling alone and lost, like there was no longer any reason for me to live" (86–87). What for her mother is an attempt to guarantee Sophie's future security through virginity leading to respectable marriage, in fact for Sophie means the loss of a will to live and further alienation from her mother, with whom she never developed a maternal bond growing up in Haiti.

One night, when her mother goes out with her boyfriend, Marc, Sophie enters the kitchen and finds a mortar and a pestle in the cabinet (87). In an effort to save herself from further subjection to the traumatizing experience of testing, and in an act of sexual resistance, Sophie pushes the pestle inside herself in order to break her hymen – a domestic object employed for self-inflicted violence. Sophie, in immense physical pain, narrates in excruciating detail how her "flesh ripped apart" as she pushed the pestle into her vagina

---

[45] Martine never considers her own obligation to family honour, as she clearly considers herself a lost cause on account of her being raped as a young girl in Haiti.

[46] *Breath, Eyes, Memory*, 80. Further page references are in the main text.

and saw "blood slowly dripping on the bed sheet" (88). This act of self-inflicted violence can be seen as a drawing of a boundary in the form of breaking another – the hymen – in an effort to protect the surface of one's body from transgression. Knowing that it will result in disgrace and loss of honour in her mother's eyes, Sophie hurts herself to preserve her bodily integrity by herself determining its uses. This act of self-inflicted violence may thus be seen as an act of resistance, yet it is a hollow victory for Sophie, as it causes pain and trauma, landing her in the hospital, where stitches are needed to repair her wounded labia.[47]

In order to understand Sophie's choice, a closer look at the passages that explicitly evoke shame reveals the ramifications of sexual violence. Shame is first named in the novel when Sophie returns to Haiti about a year after the final incident of testing by her mother (which, of course, she fails).[48] After Martine casts Sophie out of their home, the latter marries Joseph. Experiencing sexual problems in her marriage due to pain, phobia, and lack of sexual desire, Sophie decides to return to Haiti in an effort to reconnect with her past. She brings her twenty-week-old baby Brigitte with her to meet her Tante Atie and grandmother Ifé, and it is in Haiti that Sophie begins to address testing by discussing it with her grandmother. In the conversation with Grandmè Ifé, Sophie equates testing with humiliation . Her grandmother enquires:

> "Your mother? Did she ever *test* you?"
> "You can call it that."
> "That is what we have always called it."
> "I call it humiliation," I said. "I hate my body. I am *ashamed* to show it to anybody, including my husband. Sometimes I feel like I should be off somewhere by myself. That is why I am here."[49]

In this passage, Sophie explains shame in two ways. First, by referring to testing as "humiliation," she gives the practice the name of an affect (humiliation) which in turn leads to hatred and shame about her body. In Silvan Tomkins' "polar continuum" of affect, humiliation and shame are paired, suggesting a close dynamic between these singular, yet related, affects.[50] In referring to testing as humiliation, Sophie invokes shame as its related meaning, thereby

---

[47] Francis, "'Silences Too Horrific to Disturb'," 84.

[48] *Breath, Eyes, Memory*, 88.

[49] *Breath, Eyes, Memory*, 123. (Latter italics my emphasis.)

[50] Silvan S. Tomkins, *Affect Imagery Consciousness*, vol. 2: *The Negative Affects* (New York: Springer, 1963), paraphrased in Probyn, *Blush: Faces of Shame*, 22.

drawing the effects of testing closer to the actual deed in an effort to make sense, understand, and finally gain control over the destructive affect of sexual shame.

Pointing out the relationship between shame and the body, Probyn remarks that "affects are of the body."[51] Nowhere is this more poignant than in this passage, where Sophie relates her experience of testing to her grandmother. This "negative script" [52] of humiliation writes its shameful text on Sophie's body and leads her to hate her own body. It also triggers her wish to escape "off somewhere" without her husband. This she cites as the reason for her coming to Haiti, and we can therefore read her sexual shame (born of the humiliation of testing and the subsequent hatred of and shame at the body) in its second meaning in this passage as a motive force; one that activates a quite literal transnational movement from the USA to Haiti in the form of her visit. In this instance, shame works as an affective force that motivates action and movement. As debilitated as she is by shame in her marital sex life, Sophie's sexual shame is not entirely subjectivity-dismantling, as it drives her to return to Haiti and begin the process of re-shaping her identity.

In a further discussion with her grandmother, the dimensions of shame are complicated by Grandmè Ifé's account of testing as a method of preventing – rather than constituting a *cause* of – shame. Explaining to Sophie the reasons for testing, her grandmother states:

> "[...] from the time a girl begins to menstruate to the time you turn her over to her husband, the mother is responsible for her purity. If I gave a soiled daughter to the husband, he can *shame* my family, speak evil of me, even bring her back to me."[53]

The fear of being shamed in this passage is yet another example of how shame functions in a circular, self-generating manner. Again, a looming and quite possible consequence of being shamed is a driving force of action. Unfortunately, as the chain of historical continuities would have us understand, at the same time as one form of potential shame is prevented by testing, shame is transferred to the tested subject. In this way, sexual shame ultimately reproduces what it tries to avoid, as its effects reverberate in the identities and actions of those subjected to it. In other words, in shame we can see the simultaneous existence of cause and effect, reason and result. It is therefore no

[51] Probyn, *Blush: Faces of Shame*, 27.

[52] *Blush: Faces of Shame*, 27.

[53] *Breath, Eyes, Memory*, 156. (My emphasis.)

wonder that shame circulates with such power in the narrative, as its self-generating and validating logic is fuelled by everything and everyone that it touches.

Returning from her trip to Haiti, where Sophie re-unites with her mother and finally makes peace with her, Sophie learns that her mother is now pregnant. Having endured rape, persistent nightmares of the traumatic event throughout the years, breast cancer, and her daughter's disgrace in failing testing, Martine's distraught state is amplified by the pregnancy. When she tells Sophie that she is pregnant, shame emerges again in the exchange between mother and daughter:

> "Pregnant?" I stuttered.
> "Marc and I, we have –"
> "You sleep together?"
> She nodded, looking ashamed.[54]

Even as a middle-aged woman, the grandmother of her daughter's child, Martine still experiences shame when her non-marital sexual relationship with Marc, her longtime boyfriend, is revealed to her daughter. It also exposes the double standard of such ideal of sexual 'purity': while attempting to protect her daughter by testing, Martine has at the same time herself been sexually active, as, having been raped in adolescence, she thinks she no longer has anything to lose.

Not long afterwards, Martine commits suicide by stabbing herself in the stomach with a knife. In this act of violence she symbolically and literally kills her shame: by taking the life of herself and her unborn child, she retrospectively attempts to undo the life-long shame inflicted on her by Sophie's birth out of wedlock. At the same time, she makes sure not to experience further shame by again becoming an unwed mother (despite Marc's wish to marry her, which she rejects, perhaps thinking she is beyond redemption). Taking her mother's body to Haiti to be buried in her home village, Sophie, her grandmother, and her aunt conduct their own private wake for Martine, playing cards and singing a funeral song: "*Ring sways to Mother, Ring stays with Mother. Pass it. Pass it along. Pass me. Pass me along.*"[55] Listening to the song, Sophie becomes aware of the larger frame involved in the passing-on of the legacies of her ancestors. The word "pass," repeated as an impera-

---

[54] *Breath, Eyes, Memory,* 189.

[55] *Breath, Eyes, Memory*, 230 (italics in original).

tive, refers in its many senses to the historical continuities discussed in relation to testing and structural sexual violence.

Sophie comes to realize that it is not only a question of her relationship to her mother, but also, as Francis comments, that of "a larger cultural framework that enforces misogynistic patriarchal values."[56] As the request "pass it along" morphs into the form "pass me" and then "pass me along," it signifies not only the need for the deceased to pass along to the other side (i.e. heaven) but also the need for those who stay behind in the land of the living to move along in their lives, to get past the losses that they have experienced. Furthermore, Sophie, the only married woman in the group, uses her wedding ring to be swayed in a thread during the wake song, thus incorporating her own marriage and married status in the ritual. The ring thematicized in the song then also comes to symbolize the passing-on of daughters from mothers and fathers to husbands in the patriarchal marriage institution. In understanding that "we were all daughters of this land," Sophie comes to realize how the land and the nation are made of its histories of oppression, not only its people.[57] After that, her healing can proceed; she comes to understand that she no longer has to pass on the trauma, shame, and pain as heirlooms to her own daughter.

Reworking shame in reading

What does the work of shame in the novel do to the reader? Ahmed writes that shame is experienced as an exposure, where those who experience it are simultaneously turned towards and away from themselves.[58] In shame, subjects feel the need for a hiding place, as they have revealed themselves and/or been exposed to others.[59] That is why, in shame, we turn our heads, cover our eyes or turn away. In the novel, Sophie turns away from herself by separating her mind and body in "doubling" when she is being shamed by testing: "I would close my eyes and imagine all the pleasant things that I had known. The lukewarm noon breeze through our bougainvillea. Tante Atie's gentle voice."[60] Explaining such a need to hide when feeling shame, Ahmed notes: "Shame consumes the subject and burns on the surface of bodies that are

[56] Francis, "'Silences Too Horrific to Disturb'," 85.

[57] *Breath, Eyes, Memory*, 230.

[58] Ahmed, *The Cultural Politics of Emotion*, 103.

[59] *The Cultural Politics of Emotion*, 103.

[60] *Breath, Eyes, Memory*, 155.

presented to others, a burning that exposes the exposure."[61] In shame, we see ourselves through the eyes of another, and this un-covering is followed by our need to hide from ourselves – or from others.[62] Thus, shame shapes the surfaces of our bodies and our orientation towards and away from the surrounding world.[63] Drawing on Silvan Tomkins' theory of shame, Eve Kosofsky Sedgwick and Adam Frank note that shame is activated by "the drawing of a boundary line or barrier," where the dynamics of covering and un-covering that Ahmed discusses are in operation.[64] Placing this idea in the context of *Breath, Eyes, Memory*, I wish to examine the boundary lines or barriers that a reader draws when reading about testing and the shame it generates.

In order to discuss the need to draw boundaries between the text's and the reader's potential affects in reading the shame of testing, I turn to Ahmed's analysis of reading the contingency of pain in accounts of Aboriginal Austra-

---

[61] Ahmed, *The Cultural Politics of Emotion*, 103.

[62] *The Cultural Politics of Emotion*, 106.

[63] *The Cultural Politics of Emotion*, 4.

[64] Eve Kosofsky Sedgwick & Adam Frank, "Shame in the Cybernetic Fold: Reading Silvan Tomkins," in Eve Kosofsky Sedgwick, *Touching Feeling: Affect, Pedagogy, Performativity* (Durham NC & London: Duke UP, 2003): 116. In testing, the hymen is seen as both a symbolic and literal boundary line that defines virginity and thus a woman's marriage value, and, when broken, dismantles it. In cases of patriarchal virginity preservation, the hymen can be seen, after Nina Puren, as "a hegemonic phantasy" and "its own myth" which stays fixed (or unfixed when broken) in the texts on rape and romance that she reads. Puren, "Hymeneal Acts: Interrogating the Hegemony of Rape and Romance," *Australian Feminist Law Journal* 5 (1995): 15–16. Jacques Derrida, for his part, views the hymen as profoundly ambivalent, an undecidable that defies binary logic by simultaneously being a fold in the (vaginal) lining and (made of) that same lining that cannot be smoothed, as there never was an original crease that could or should be smoothed. See Derrida, esp. "The Double Session," in Derrida, *Dissemination*, tr. Barbara Johnson (*La Dissémination*, 1972; tr. 1981; London & New York: Continuum, 2004): 187–316 passim. This ambivalence of the hymen formulated by Derrida as a part of his deconstructive project, can be seen in Danticat's novel in the way in which shame and the hymen do not, despite the efforts of those mothers who test their daughters, in fact become conflated as oppositional – the presence of a hymen does not in fact prevent shame – but as ambivalently co-dependent in that the hymen itself is a hegemonic phantasy that generates shame in all who become interpellated into that phantasy. As Sophie's breaking of her own hymen without male penetration shows, the 'hymeneal' logic of testing is a case of false logic.

lians – the Stolen Generations – abducted and adopted into white families.[65] Ahmed cogently explains why readers should not adopt the texts' affects as their own, because "to hear the other's pain as *my pain*, and to empathise with the other in order to heal the body [...] involves violence."[66] This domination of the other in the form of identification is based on a desire to relate to the other through a process of becoming-like, whereby "in becoming more like you, I seek to take your place."[67] Taking the other's place in feeling shame would generate it into a "wish feeling," a projection of what the subject imagines the other person is feeling.[68] Instead, witnessing shame entails an understanding of the links in historical, socio-cultural, and interpersonal chains that create and trigger shame and which, in turn, are themselves created by shame.

Observing the different forms of shame in the texts enables us to shift position according to each event of feeling shame in order to understand and observe the differences and gaps that they serve to create between women. The shame-preventing (and, indeed, shame-generating) act of testing ultimately produces what it strives to avoid, as it serves to merely instil and shift shame in the tested subject. The dynamic can be described in Foucauldian terms as self-perpetuating: internalized subjection to patriarchal, sexist (and colonialism-derived) power, spurring women to exercise control over each other as did the Macoutes, the dictator's henchmen. Participating in this dynamic by the act of reading, the reader need not pass the shame on to herself by a self-identifying reading. To do so would allow the future continuity of the circulation of shame. Instead, a rejection of shame by the reading subject temporarily breaks the infectious, historical cycle of shame.

The reader's exposure to this intergenerational shame produces not only testimonial witness but also the limits of the interplay of what is shared, and that which creates ruptures, damage, and distrust between women. All the generations of women in the novel had to endure testing: its effects were different for each, but everything was fuelled by fear turning to humiliation and, in turn, to shame. Understanding the mechanisms of shame teaches us about the mortal coil that it produces, and that we, as readers hoping to be affected by our reading, may be able to resist. Woodward states this beautifully when she considers what can be achieved by the desolate, unredeemable scenarios

65 Ahmed, *The Cultural Politics of Emotion*, 34.

66 *The Cultural Politics of Emotion*, 35. (My emphasis.)

67 *The Cultural Politics of Emotion*, 126.

68 *The Cultural Politics of Emotion*, 30.

of shame in *The Bluest Eye*: reading shame can serve as "a touchstone for understanding what we expect to achieve," for, having reflected on the novel's sexual histories, we as readers then orientate our sights toward the future.[69] In Woodward's case, reading Morrison's novel may teach white readers to gain a more refined understanding of the work of racism.[70] In Danticat's case, shame in the novel may motivate its reader to a heightened sensitivity to read, observe, and understand how it draws on the moral insight gained from its traumas. In this way, we not only understand the work of racism, as in the case of Woodward's reading of Morrison's novel, but we also come to understand how sexism, violence, and classism work in the arena of shame.

Although the characters cannot all choose their reactions and responses to shame in a productive way, as Martine Caco does when she commits suicide, the self-reflexive nature of reading grants us, as readers, access to a variety of choices. We may choose to respond to shame, to speak to it and demand that it bend to our political purposes. A close reading of shame gives us access to the contexts in which it arises in each particular shame story, thus giving us the chance to learn from it lest we as readers (whoever we are) be damaged by it. As we recognize the varieties of shame, it ceases to exist as a monolith. Breaking shame down into smaller components is precisely where (in this case, a white) feminist reader's privileged position can be put to work. Utilizing shame through a self-identificatory attempt at feeling the novel's shame is not useful. Rather, adopting a respectful distance in order to witness this traumatic testimony in full is arguably a far more fruitful strategy. We are not to usurp Sophie's, Grandmè Ifé's or Martine's position of shame, but to resist it precisely because of our adopted, affective reader's position. There are times when it is best to be affected by curtailing that very affectivity. The novel's shame needs to be resisted, not in an effort to stand above such confining oppression but, rather, because of the assumption that an affective reader might be 'shame-prone' to its contagiousness.[71] Resistance to the novel's shame produces a reader's preferred observant position from which to witness Sophie's process of freeing herself from sexual shame towards the end of the narrative, ultimately revealing the liberatory potential of Danticat's novel. In addition to this preferred observant position, we need to follow through Sophie's process

[69] Woodward, "Traumatic Shame," 229.

[70] "Traumatic Shame," 212.

[71] Sedgwick, *Touching Feeling*, 36, 37.

in order to understand the novel's message about sexual shame. Examining the liberatory potential of freeing herself from sexual shame becomes the positioning and positioned reader's task in the next chapter.

"Too violent for words": Peppering as a crime against womanhood in *It Begins With Tears*

In Opal Palmer Adisa's *It Begins With Tears*, historical traumas are also projected onto women's bodies.[72] However, shame is evoked quite differently from Danticat's *Breath, Eyes, Memory*. In Adisa's novel, it is the lack of shame by the ex-prostitute, Monica, that strikes the reader as most powerful and interesting for the purposes of reading shame dialogically. Monica becomes the target of extreme sexual violence due to her shamelessness. This section concentrates on the circulation of shame in the relationship between Monica and the three women (Peggy, Grace, and Marva) who punish her with peppering. In the novel, shame again functions as a motivation for sexual violence, but here it is a lack of shame that is cited explicitly by the women as the reason for Monica's peppering. In feeling no shame for her past as a prostitute, her red nails, and her sensual nature, Monica inadvertently invites the three women's condemnation, triggered by a blend of fear and propriety. In other words, the very absence of an affect incites the three women's wrath and the subsequent act of sexual violence. Sara Ahmed discusses the frequent articulation of shame in the Australian 'Sorry Book' phenomenon as a reconciliatory venue for white Australians to express their shame about the treatment of the indigenous Australians by governments both past and present.[73] She writes about the function of the Sorry Book as "a demand to and for the nation to appear ashamed, and to speak the shame on behalf of Australians," and that a failure to express shame before others becomes another form of shame, where the shameless themselves shame the shamed.[74]

Similarly, Monica's shamelessness becomes a shame for which she needs to be punished. From the reader's perspective, what is interesting about the circulation of shame in the novel is the larger community of village women and their response to Monica's peppering. While the narratorial focalization

---

[72] Pin-chia Feng, "Rituals of Rememory: Afro-Caribbean Religions in *Myal* and *It Begins with Tears*," *MELUS* 27.1 (2002): 152.

[73] Ahmed, *The Cultural Politics of Emotion*, 110.

[74] *The Cultural Politics of Emotion*, 110.

shifts to sympathize with Monica's suffering, Adisa the author has her female characters feel Monica's pain in a passage that describes peppering as "too violent for words."[75] As words fail the women who rush to help Monica, the shared affect of pain gives meaning to the severity of Peggy, Marva, and Grace's crime. In the expanded affect of shared pain, their act of attempted shaming then becomes their own shame, a crime against all womanhood – womanhood to which they, too, belong. This implicit judgment contained in the communal suffering catches the reader, and calls on her to join with the benevolent majority of women, who wish to exist in peace, harmony, and sisterhood.

The shameless Monica

Upon Monica's return to Kristoff village, the community is abuzz with rumours about this unusual woman coming back to live there, having left at the age of fourteen to live in Kingston. As a teenager, Monica was forced to abandon her home due to her budding sensuality, which made it impossible for her to flourish within the confines of the strict community (25). Monica is known to have worked as a prostitute for the thirty years that have passed since her departure, and that "no bigger whore than she had ever serviced Kingston or Spanish Town" (26). The condemning communal voice in the passage depicting the rumours and gossip that surround Monica's arrival further describes alleged details of Monica's anatomy, such as the size of her vagina and the youthful appearance of her "tight and high" behind (27).

The first encounter with Monica in the village suggests that little has changed in terms of the disapproving attitude towards her as she gets off the bus from Kingston. Shame is almost instantly articulated in the reactions of the swarming onlookers:

> "Whore!" The wives spat, their grudging admiration fuelling their anger, and pretended they didn't see her.
>
> "Is who have time fi paint them nails?" One said sarcastically.
>
> "Me dear! Hands fah working," another offered.
>
> "And koo de lips. Red like American apple," a toothless old woman added.
>
> *"Shameful woman."*

[75] Adisa, *It Begins With Tears* (Oxford: Heinemann, 1997), 136. Further page references are in the main text.

> Imagine, in her forties with the body of a young woman. Wearing such clothes! Heels, four inches, if not higher, and stepping like she was walking on air rather than the uneven gravel road.
>
> "Is who she think she is?"
>
> "And she barren too. Not a picknie fi bring her water in her old age" (28, italics added).

In this passage, the women cast several affective judgments on Monica, thereby revealing certain things about the dominant mentality on womanhood and sexuality that serve to differentiate Monica from them. Monica's painted nails are a sign that she does something other than the hard menial labour needed from women in the countryside. Her red lips are equally noteworthy, leading to the articulation of shame in the next comment. An elaboration of Monica's shamefulness continues in the further comments regarding the inappropriately youthful body of the middle-aged woman who wears clothes and shoes unsuitable for a woman of her age. The final word of judgment is a comment equating Monica's demeanour with barrenness. Failing at the fundamental task expected of and valued by women, Monica's supposed inability to bear children becomes the final nail in her moral coffin.

Of the women congregating to witness Monica's shameful arrival in her home village, no one does a more rigorous job of condemning her than the three friends Peggy, Grace, and Marva, characterized as "bosom friends, just like their husbands, Trevor, Desmond and Ainsworth" (59). It becomes clear later in this description, however, that their 'friendship' is about the only bosomy feature of this trio, since they are all described as unhappy, bitter, and decidedly unpleasant. Peggy is "tight and mean-spirited," Marva "big like a house," "unhappy," and the mother of five boys, but obsessed with having a baby girl. Desmond's wife Grace is characterized as an anxious woman; uncomfortable in her motherhood and "afraid of most things" (59–61).

It is in Peggy's thoughts that we again encounter shame, as she ponders Monica's arrival in the village. An eager gossip – and the first to remind the villagers of Monica's failure to return for her father's funeral five years earlier – Peggy maintains constant vigil at her window (62). The reader is further informed about Peggy's opinion of Monica when the woman thinks to herself:

> Shame.
>
> Worthless.
>
> [...]
>
> Rumour also had it that Monica was a big-time whore. (62)

In this passage, shame and a woman's value are equated once again; with the absence of one resulting in the presence of the other, and vice versa. We can thus see that the act of determining a woman's worth is clearly affective. The value of a woman's body, in other words, is determined by emotional parameters. Observing Monica from her veranda, Peggy admits to herself that "Monica looked good," and this admission of admiration makes her run her hands over her own body, only to evoke shame again in her thought: "Speak the truth and shame the devil" (62–63). Becoming even more anxious, Peggy quickly proceeds to curse Monica aloud to herself, again reiterating her child-free status to justify her condemnation:

> Monica didn't have any children. Her body hadn't gone through any wear and tear. She was barren. All she did was fuck men, other women's men. Bitch. Whore. Curse her womb and her pussy. (63)

Singling out Monica's reproductive organs, Peggy makes sure to sexualize Monica's sinful, shameful appearance, which nevertheless fascinates her at the same time.

Once Monica begins a relationship with Desmond, Grace's husband, shame escalates into violence as the three women begin to accuse Monica (and everyone associated with her) of the shame that she brings. Suspecting an affair between her husband, Ainsworth, and Monica, Marva becomes jealous and denies the possibility of mere friendship existing between Monica and Ainsworth. She throws shame in her husband's face by shouting at him: "Whe you hear man and woman is friend? Is idiot you tek me fah? You should a shame fuckin de whore" (128). Marva does not know that Monica's sexual appetite is reserved exclusively for Desmond, who begins to stay at Monica's instead of coming home to Grace for dinner. In turn, Grace proceeds to send his dinner over to Monica's house and laments the situation to her friends: "Ah cook him dinner every evening and send it to him, and him and him sweetheart, de one Monica, nyam up me food widout any shame" (129).

Hurt and enraged by Monica's lack of shame, the three women decide to enter Monica's house and her body the following night as punishment. The narration of the act of sexual violence proceeds with no opportunity for anyone to intervene:

> Then they closed in on her and one of them smeared her face with pepper, pushed pepper up her nose. They flung her dress over her head and ripped off her panties. One of them shoved her peppered fingers as deep into her womb as they could reach until the cup of chopped

> peppers was empty and her fingers were on fire. They didn't say anything then. They didn't look at her or one another. They couldn't hear her scream in her head or see her tears sealing her eyes. As they left, they turned off the television and lights and pulled the door shut behind them, leaving her to go silently mad. (131)

The narrative style in which the act of violence is depicted highlights the inevitable, unstoppable nature of the act. First, the night-time isolation and darkness grant the women undetected access to Monica's house. Next, we can see that there is an evident lack of interconnection between the women during the deed: "They didn't say anything then. They didn't look at her or one another. They couldn't hear her scream in her head or see her tears sealing her eyes" (131). The actions of Peggy, Grace, and Marva are almost mechanical and robot-like when they enforce their punishment on Monica ("They flung her dress over her head and ripped off her panties. One of them shoved her peppered fingers as deep into her womb as they could reach until the cup of chopped peppers was empty and her fingers were on fire"). The narrator refrains from naming which of the women entered Monica's vagina with her fingers, simply referring to the aggressor as "one of them" to show how the women work in collusion. This mechanical quality of the narration is further emphasized by the repetitive use of the personal pronoun "they," instead of individuating each woman's role in the crime. The three women have temporarily reached commonality, but without intersubjectivity or social interaction.

This "terrible revenge at the hands of three jealous women" is a punishment for Monica's "indulgence in self-centered pleasure."[76] However, the atmosphere of condemnation turns upside down after this act of sexual violence, which serves as a turning point in the narrative. The violent transgression against Monica's body "goes beyond the limit" and marks a change in how the other women in the village react, and, indeed relate, to Monica.[77] How we can read these new relations between the women (and the reader) is the subject of the next section.

Reading the pain of peppering

Earlier in this chapter, I discussed Sara Ahmed's ideas of responding to pain that you cannot feel in relation to reading shame in Danticat's novel. This idea

[76] Feng, "Rituals of Rememory," 152, 166.

[77] "Rituals of Rememory," 166.

is again relevant to reading the aftermath of Monica's peppering. How are we to read Monica's pain resulting from the sexual violence intended to shame her? Monica survives because of the care that she receives from the other village women sympathetic to her suffering. Their willingness to help endorses their judgment that the punishment was unwarranted, underscored by the collective, sympathizing pain that the women feel while helping Monica. The severity of the crime is captured by the women's inability to voice and articulate it: "The crime was too violent for words."[78] Instead, their collective pain is described as deeply lodged within each woman's body: "They all ached. […] The lips of their vaginas throbbed in sympathy, their wombs ached, and their salty tears left stain marks on their faces" (136). Through this passage, the narrative seems to invite the reader to participate in Monica and the women's pain, and to pass judgment on the violence committed by Peggy, Grace, and Marva, now turning from an individual to a collective offence. However, the way in which a (white) reader is to respond to this pain, I suggest, is a far more complex and subtle process than adopting the pain felt by the novel's women.

I suggest that the reader may witness Monica and the other women's pain by following Sara Ahmed's ideas of the ethics of touch as a way of responding to pain you cannot feel. As mentioned in connection with my reading of Sophie, we know that we cannot feel the pain of the other, but according to Ahmed, we can respond ethically to the pain of the other by opening ourselves to "that which one cannot know or feel."[79] Instead, our task is to learn to be able to respond to pain without claiming it as our own.[80] Ahmed writes:

> Certainly, there is something ungraspable about the other's pain, and this is not just because I do not feel it. But my pain, even when I feel it, is not always so graspable. So in some sense, as I respond to this other's pain, as I touch her cheek, I come to feel that which I cannot know.[81]

Following Ahmed, in reading Monica, one ought not sympathize or identify with the potential textual other of human suffering. Rather, by opening up to the other, and by being touched by her pain in a way that "one ceases to

[78] *It Begins With Tears*, 136.

[79] Ahmed, *The Cultural Politics of Emotion*, 30.

[80] *The Cultural Politics of Emotion*, 35.

[81] *The Cultural Politics of Emotion*, 30.

inhabit the same place," the reading provides a more sustainable way of responding to the other.[82]

Openness to pain that we cannot feel as the key to meaning-production is then supplemented by the idea of impossible hearing as a way of responding to voices you cannot hear. The ethics of touch in being moved, Ahmed contends, has to do with communication. As we know, and as Ahmed argues, each communicative event is laden with traumas and silences of miscommunication, which makes the encounter always "ungraspable and unrealised" in full (156). As readers, it is our task to unravel and to hear those silences. Therefore, we need to be open to the touch of "that which cannot be got across"; being that which "resists pure communication" (158). Pain may be one such expression that resists communication, but which may nevertheless be approached by thinking of hearing (pain) as touch. When we listen to and hear the other, we are also touched by her, and that touch moves us out of our previous habitat (156).

In other words, the ethics of touch and the ethics of hearing come together in communicative ethics which, according to Ahmed, "can deal with, or even better work with, the very impossibility of communication as dialogue, as one voice simply speaking to, and being heard by, another" (156). Full consensus and understanding are impossible, but by listening to the voices that cannot be heard, as Lynette Hunter suggests, we move closer to a more democratic feminist ethics.[83] Thus, listening becomes "a resistant practice" where we can learn from "situated public voices" in reading literature.[84]

Listening as a resistance practice can be practised in reading Monica's pain as a process of being and becoming aware of the limits of one's ability to participate in Monica and the other women's plight. Cognizance of the limits of communication is therefore crucial to meaning-production. The drawing of one's personal boundaries is not an act of dismissal; rather, it prevents harmful self-identification, where the white Western reading subject does her personal identity-work at the expense of the suffering of the Other. At the same time, of course, the potential (and, given the statistics, likely) personal experiences resulting in sexual damage to the reader need to be acknowledged in order to differentiate between one's own pain and the pain of the other.

---

[82] Ahmed, *Strange Encounters*, 156. Further page references are in the main text.

[83] Lynette Hunter, "Listening to Situated Textuality: Working on Differentiated Public Voices," *Feminist Theory* 2.2 (2001): 206.

[84] Hunter, "Listening to Situated Textuality," 212.

The reader's own pain may also be felt because of "the potential risk and trauma of reading."[85] By this, Pearce refers to the ghostly role of the reader in the reading-event: she cannot change the course of events or make herself heard. As Pearce writes in her reading diary on the experience of reading a novel,

> As a reader I am a ghost not only because I return, but because I am returning to a text. As a reader I am a voyeur of action in which I cannot participate or intervene. And this is sometimes experienced as a deep pain.[86]

In the context of reading Monica's pain, Pearce's realization proves helpful in differentiating between the pain of the other and the reader's potential own pain in the face of Monica's violation. Cutting oneself off from the pain of the other does not mean that we are oblivious to injustice. Rather, we may feel pain for not being able to intervene. We are trapped in our ghostly status as readers who are perforce helpless bystanders when Peggy, Grace, and Marva mete out sexual violence to Monica.

Differentiating between the pain of the other and the witness's pain of helplessness might prove advantageous, as it shows the reader the limits of one's own experience and obviates the possibility that one's pain will be pushed into a context where it does not necessarily fit. In this scenario, then, what becomes important is not the reader's observance of any and all affective experiences in reading but, rather, her becoming aware of the limits of her own understanding through the conscious, contrastive activity of differentiation. In other words, as affects (here: shame) serve to create differences between subjects, the production of differences in the reading process can be put to good use. This need not be imposed by force at the level of the text; rather, shame can be put to good use through the affective text–reader relationship in constant interaction.

The whisper circle: Shame, blood, and taboo in Brodber

As indicated earlier, the Puerto Rican scholar and educator Lizabeth Paravisini–Gebert criticizes white Western readings of the representation of Caribbean women's bodies for their tendency to see the body solely as a symbolic

[85] Pearce, *Feminism and the Politics of Reading*, 2.

[86] *Feminism and the Politics of Reading*, 2.

construct, and for failing to account for its materiality, its "flesh-and-blood quality."[87] Paying heed to Paravisini–Gebert's stricture, the following section explores the connections between shame and menstrual taboo in two works by Erna Brodber. In Brodber's works, there is a continuing theme of separation of (female) mind from (female) body as a consequence of trauma caused by colonial and/or patriarchal pressure. In *Jane and Louisa Will Soon Come Home*, the protagonist Nellie Richmond experiences a traumatizing loss of self at the onset of puberty and menarche due to attitudes of shame and concealment on the part of the surrounding community, her mother, and her Aunt Becca. In Brodber's story "Sleeping's Beauty and the Prince Charming," the female protagonist Sleeping's Beauty's menstrual cramps lead her new-found partner, Prince Charming, to take off into the horizon. In this story as in *Jane and Louisa*, voice plays a central role in contributing to taboo and loss – whether loss of self or loss of love.

Taboo in its sense of the unnamed or forbidden, or that which is left unvoiced, becomes destructive for the female mind and body, whose reintegration fails to take place. But what happens to the reader in this case when the voice is detached from the body, a disembodied voice or an echo? How is a reader affected by these texts, where the voice is reduced to a whisper, a whisper that fails to articulate that which is taboo – the female body? The foregrounding of voice in Brodber recalls Adriana Cavarero's philosophy of vocal expression and its role in subject-formation.[88] Reading the concept of voice in connection with sexual shame shows that vocality and subjectivity are vital for each other in the context of an orality-based Caribbean narrative on female sexual taboos. The "whisper circle" referred to by Nellie in *Jane and Louisa* refers to such gendered sexual taboos, which need to be voiced in (and by) reading before beginning to contemplate possible liberatory processes.

Nellie's whispering shame in puberty

In Brodber's *Jane and Louisa Will Soon Come Home*, Nellie learns as a young girl that sexuality is something shameful and mysterious. Consider the passage when thc eleven-year-old Nellie's mother summons her to her room

[87] Paravisini–Gebert, "Women Against the Grain," 164.

[88] Adriana Cavarero, *For More than One Voice: Toward a Philosophy of Vocal Expression,* tr. Paul A. Kottman (*A più voci: Per una filosofia dell'espressione vocale*, 2003; Stanford CA: Stanford UP, 2005).

to discuss puberty and menstruation. Nellie cannot locate the tone of her mother's voice; she is confused by it and immediately responds with a feeling of shame.

> My mother, in her dead-pan voice that I cannot figure calls out to me. It is not her scolding voice, it is not her praising voice. So what is it. No eye contact and she is pretending to sew. My God. I'm hardly eleven. What shame have you to hide from me? (23)

In the passage, Nellie is unable to read the message conveyed by her mother's voice. In Adriana Cavarero's model of vocal subjectivity, the voice plays the role of a signifier by its "revelatory function," where the voice communicates due to a vocal uniqueness often neglected by theorizations of the "voice in general."[89] The uniqueness of Nellie's mother's voice communicates to Nellie, but she is unclear as to what exactly its (affective) meaning is. As attested by Pearce, "*the tone of voice* we use in our address always supplements its semantic communication in some way," and it is in fact the speaker's tone or intonation that typically reveals the speaker's attitude or affective mood.[90] Nellie does not find the familiar tones of reprimand and approval, the two affective meanings most heard by Nellie in her communication with her mother. This uncertainty leads her to interpret her mother's voice as that of concealment, which evokes in turn the affect of shame as central to the message. In her confusion, Nellie does recognize something, even if that something is not her mother's intended message. Nellie gathers the affective meaning of subconscious shame from her mother's tone as if anticipating what her mother is about to say.

Nellie's mother has summoned her daughter to be educated about puberty, but the ensuing conversation becomes a dialogue loaded with silence.

> Silence.
> – You are eleven now and soon something strange will happen to you
> –
> Silence; still no eye contact.
> – Well when it does, make sure you tell your aunt –
> Period. End of sentence. I presume I am dismissed. (23)

The word-play with the word period, the full stop, links Nellie's oncoming puberty to an end, not to a new beginning of budding womanhood, as one

---

[89] Cavarero, *For More than One Voice*, 5, 9.

[90] Pearce, *Reading Dialogics*, 4.

might imagine. The mother's lack of eye-contact contributes to Nellie's shame and her feeling mystified by female sexuality. In other words, it is not only voice but also vision that mortifies Nellie when her gaze is not met. Communication fails as it ends, with her mother delegating responsibility for Nellie's sexual education to her stern and religious Aunt Becca.

For Nellie, her mother's dismissal constructs her womanhood as a mystery, leading to uncertainty and distress about growing up. Sylvia Burrow discusses the frequent dismissal of feminist expressions of anger: "dismissal silences one's political voice and, at the same time, compromises a valuable source of self-worth and self-trust."[91] According to Burrow, "dismissal is itself a form of emotional abuse."[92] Simone A. James Alexander also discusses the complex relationship between mothers and daughters in Caribbean women's writing by remarking that the biological mother "is often seen as an 'other' mother, an enemy to her daughter, particularly when she appears to advocate colonial habits and mannerisms."[93] In Brodber's novel, Nellie's mother is one such example of the mother as "other" instead of a nurturing, positive influence. The mother's attitude towards her daughter's oncoming puberty can be seen to parallel the values of "Victorian prudery" inherited from colonialist sexual culture.[94] Tellingly, other modes of communications between Nellie and her mother are virtually absent from the novel.

There is another sense the term "the othermother," which also refers to the role of women as substitute nurturers of children other than their biological offspring.[95] Nellie has two such figures in her life; Aunt Alice and Aunt Becca. Of the two, Aunt Becca – appointed by the young girl's mother as the guardian of Nellie's sense of morality – further contributes to Nellie's shaming. In turn, Aunt Alice, the free spirit (in senses both literal and metaphorical), helps Nellie to find her voice and, in turn, to heal. Shame is strongly evoked in passages where Nellie is in contact with Aunt Becca, her father's eldest siste, and Nellie's repeated iteration of the word shame signals the magnitude of Aunt Becca's affect:

---

[91] Burrow, "The Political Structure of Emotion," 27.

[92] "The Political Structure of Emotion," 28.

[93] Simone A. James Alexander, *Mother Imagery in the Novels of Afro-Caribbean Women* (Columbia: U of Missouri P, 2001): 7.

[94] See Narain, "Standing in the Place of Love," 336.

[95] Alexander, *Mother Imagery in the Novels of Afro-Caribbean Women*, 7.

> Aunt Becca is a lady. Aunt Becca is a lady who feels shame. Plenty of shame. But mostly for her family. Aunt Alice shames her. Aunt Alice has no husband. Aunt Alice works nowhere. She never seems to make a living. She plants nothing. She reaps nothing but only helps us now and again, helps out Aunt Becca now and again and smiles. Aunt Alice in Wonderland. Aunt Alice is so nice.
>
> I have shamed Aunt Becca and I will shame Aunt Becca. My mother has so many children. [...] Aunt Becca is ashamed that I will fail the parish scholarship. Aunt Becca wishes that I would follow Egbert around less. It shames Aunt Becca that I sit with him while he cooks the hog's food. It shames her past all understanding to know that I eat the cooked breadfruit hearts meant for his hog. [...]
>
> Aunt Becca's shaming eye ruled the roost. [...] Aunt Becca's fish eyes shamed everyone into unworthiness. (92–93)

Repeated ten times in this excerpt, shame is Aunt Becca's primary affect and value judgment. As Gay Wilentz notes, the "assimilated, psychically disturbed" Aunt Becca further contributes to Nellie's confusion, as "her sexuality is twisted into horror by Becca's repressive Anglican values."[96] Religion, middle-class aspirations, and a keen eye to the adolescents' sexual chastity are contrasted with Aunt Alice's smiles and lack of socio-economic aspirations. Yet, when coupled with Nellie's mother's shameful secrecy about her daughter's sexuality, Becca's shame is powerful enough to damage Nellie's shrivelling sense of self.

Nellie's relationship to her mother and Aunt Becca shows how the concept of shame is intimately connected with language, as it is something that cannot be spoken, expressed aloud. Anita Haya Patterson remarks that shame is what cannot be spoken, and is thus "language-destroying";[97] shame results from "a failure to live up to conventional [...] self-contradictory cultural norms."[98] Nellie internalizes these contradictory norms of sexuality as a child, thanks to her mother's evasive approach to her daughter's oncoming puberty. This is when she comments: "I was strange and everybody knew it" and "It was a hidey-hidey thing! It made you a whisper" (120). Whisper, the muted utterance, has an important role here: 'it', referring to menstruation, is something

[96] Gay Alden Wilentz, *Healing Narratives: Women Writers Curing Cultural Disease* (New Brunswick NJ: Rutgers UP, 2000): 38–39.

[97] Patterson, "Contingencies of Pleasure and Shame," 269.

[98] "Contingencies of Pleasure and Shame," 270.

that is only talked about in secrecy, only among women, by whispering. When 'it' as a hidey-hidey thing makes Nellie "a whisper," as she describes herself, the developing and changing self is then transformed into language – into an utterance that contributes to the mortification of the self.

Nellie's three cousins, each of whom has cast off her unwanted offspring, provide warning examples of the shamefulness of sexuality. They, too, are reduced to whispers. The women who have thrown away their babies were, in Nellie's words "whispers and echoes" and "you heard from them, you heard of them. At times they were nothing but rumours" (120). Nellie finds out that in fact each woman who has "it" is made a whisper by other women, which shows us the reciprocal, self-generative nature of silenced sexuality. Nellie discusses what she, Jane, and Louisa discover about the secretive women: "We knew that when they sat down and made themselves whispers one to the other, they were talking about 'it'" (120). Unable to differentiate between 'it' (the shorthand for menstruation and female sexuality) and the negative values attributed to it, Nellie links sexuality directly with negative affect. A sense of alienation also becomes inherent to the life of a woman, for "'it' cut them off from everybody" (120). Nellie feels a sense of alienation and separation from her usual life, as she is no longer allowed to play with boys and has to settle instead into a segregated adolescence. The boys no longer acknowledge Nellie, and when they do, "they looked at me strangely" (121). Nellie's frustration grows when she is split off from the life that she is used to living.

The form of the circle associated with women's modes of writing and thinking, as distinct from the linear patriarchal mode, becomes important in the silent voice of taboo. Nellie speaks of "the whisper circle" when she describes the rumours that circulate about her cousins' shameful, unwanted pregnancies. The novel, which itself disrupts linear logic with its narrative structure, also shows the pitfalls of exclusion in a suffocating, women-only circle.[99] Nellie finds solace with her Aunt Alice, who "could not make the whisper circle. She had never been like Baba's mother, Cousin B, the whisper circle, like the women. She had no need to push us away. She stayed with us" (120). The sense of connection offered by Alice's presence to the growing girls becomes integral to their escape from the destructive whisper circle. The latter is a sexual affect which shows how the relationship between sexuality and emotions in this instance is a decidedly negative and destructive one. That which cannot be voiced aloud, the taboo of sexuality, must be whispered. A

[99] Wilentz, *Healing Narratives*, 35.

clear connection between a whispered mode of utterance and affect can be seen in the case of the whisper circle.

Associating the whisper circle with womanhood, Nellie further describes the repercussions of "it" thus:

> A chute without dimension, a hollow without name or face, a hollow that pulled innocent girls in, an instrument as hollow and one-sided as a drum, and like a drum, its message reverberated loud and very clear but it carried no physical form nor even image of one. That is you. That's what 'it' makes you. (120)

In this passage, Nellie equates herself with an empty, faceless, and nameless non-being that "it" makes her. In the whisper circle, the woman who has "it" fades into nothingness. At the same time, paradoxically, Nellie hears the message transmitted by "it" loud and clear. She is to downplay and remain quiet about her bodily materiality, Paravisini–Gebert's "flesh-and-blood quality."[100] If whispering as a silenced voice refuses or fails to speak out, so too, do echo and rumour. The echo that traps Anancy the spider in the forest is reminiscent of the sound of a hollow drum evoked by Nellie as a consequence of "it" (36–38). Just like the noise of a one-sided drum, echo is a disembodied voice that reverberates from an inanimate surface and eventually dies out. Similarly, rumours about the women's sexuality are the community's echoes, the unproductive voices referred to as possessing "no physical form" (120). As the community's deadly (or dying) voices, rumours serve to ruin the fallen women's reputations and lead to their destruction.

The shame of negative sexuality leads Nellie to escape from the enclosure of the whisper circle into another enclosed space, the kumbla: "The circle narrowed, the distance was complete. Go eena kumbla for you need to be cleaned and preserved like peppers in a kilner jar. Go eena kumbla" (122). For Nellie, as O'Callaghan notes, "confusion and guilt associated with varying models of female sexuality lead toward mental breakdown."[101] As a sexual affect, the whisper circle, like Nellie's mother and Aunt Becca, dismisses sexuality and renders it negative. In the text discussed next, Brodber further foregrounds the distress of female sexuality in a dismissive sexist environment.

---

[100] Paravisini–Gebert, "Women Against the Grain," 164.

[101] O'Callaghan, "Interior Schisms Dramatised," 99.

Blood and shame in "Sleeping's Beauty and the Prince Charming"

The authors of the now feminist classic *The Curse*: *A Cultural History of Menstruation* hypothesize that the word 'taboo' may originate in the Polynesian word for menstruation, *tupua*.[102] In mapping the cultural history of menstruation, they also read menstrual imagery in literature, including fairytales. According to the authors, the allusion to menstruation in the Sleeping Beauty fairytale is obvious: the girl-child is cursed at birth by a fairy who foretells that on her fifteenth birthday, Sleeping Beauty will hurt herself on a spindle and bleed. The authors remark that blood is a crucial component of the fairytale's plot development.[103] The connection between blood, seclusion (Sleeping Beauty slept for a hundred years desolate in her castle), and taboo underlines Brodber's story from its very beginning, too. The short story is a rather depressing example of the body/mind split that we can observe in Brodber's writing. Brodber's narrative reveals the erasure of black female corporeality in the European textual and ideological framework of the parable. This results in the failure of the black diasporic project of emancipation and return to Africa, whether understood as a spiritual or as a physical enterprise.

In the story, the role of voice is integral to establishing and maintaining the mind/body split. When Sleeping's Beauty first meets Prince Charming, it is only her disembodied voice that engages in conversation with him as Sleeping's who, as a young burnt-out writer, has fallen into a deep sleep that separates her mind from her body. The narrator tells us:

> The doctors ordered an antidote and gave her a shot of I don't know what that split the body from the soul. Her muscles went limp, her head fell back, a black Ophelia sleeping for seven years. But while her body was sleeping, her soul was having a ball.[104]

As Sleeping and Charming get to know each other, they begin to plan a repatriation of their people to Africa, the typically Rastafarian spiritual as well as physical enterprise.

However, their plans for repatriation require the Fairy Godmother to return Sleeping into a corporeal being, which also entails getting her period. As

[102] Janice Delaney, Mary Jane Lupton & Emily Toth, *The Curse: A Cultural History of Menstruation* (1976; Urbana & Chicago: U of Illinois P, 1988).

[103] Delaney, Lupton & Toth, *The Curse*, 162.

[104] Brodber, "Sleeping's Beauty and the Prince Charming," 1.

delighted as Charming is to finally be able to see her, he cannot bear Sleeping's painful cramps:

> And he left her to be a woman alone and that is why black people have to wait another four hundred years before King Alpha and Queen Omega will appear to settle them in their kingdom in the promised land. For Sleeping's beauty is still only half awake, drugged in its woman's pain and she cannot properly put body and soul together for that needs the help of Charming.
> Rastafari me nuh chose none. (4)

According to the Jamaican-born (but now international) Rastafarian religion, black people are the descendants of the people of Egypt in the Old Testament, who in slavery had to give up their promised land, Zion, and were forced to live in the land of Babylon, the white colonial world (of vice, the Catholic church, and the police – the main objects of disapproval in Rastafari). Barry Chevannes sees Ethiopianist Rastafari thought as based on the experience of slavery, revivalism, African religions and folklore, and highly selective interpretations of the Bible, as well as on the nostalgic remembrance of the lost home in Africa as a kind of Pan-African mosaic.[105]

In the above passage from Brodber's story, King Alpha and Queen Omega refer to the Rastafari God, Jah, the Ethiopian emperor Haile Selassie I, and his wife, Empress Mennen. But King Alpha and Queen Omega are also used to refer to Rastaman and his woman; implying, as in Brodber's story, that the sexes are complementary and unable to function without one another. The story thus makes a strong comment on the gendered practice of Rastafari religion where the inability of the black man to deal with the female body (specifically, the menstruation taboo) causes emancipatory attempts to fail, as Prince Charming cannot deal with Sleeping's corporeality and he takes off into the horizon, leaving "her to be a woman alone."[106] The narrator remarks that Sleeping is unable to reintegrate mind and body without the help of Charming and so remains asleep, and since neither Sleeping nor Charming can operate alone, Charming is also unable to resettle their people in the promised land, back in Africa.

The story's cryptic concluding phrase, "Rastafari me nuh chose none," is a clue for the reader to the context in and from which Brodber transmits her

---

[105] Barry Chevannes, *Rastafari: Roots and Ideology* (Syracuse NY: Syracuse UP, 1994): 34.

[106] "Sleeping's Beauty and the Prince Charming," 4.

feminist message. The phrase is a variation of the formulaic ending of Anancy stories, the Caribbean trickster tales, where 'Jack Mandora' is replaced by 'Rastafari'. Originally in Anancy stories, Jack Mandora is the doorman at Heaven's gates; fearful of him, the narrator has to distance him/herself from the story's events by saying 'me nuh chose none', meaning that Anancy's trickery is not the narrator's responsibility. With the revised formulaic ending, the narrator can be thought to address the Rastafari religion, or the Rastaman (the word can refer to both), as one of the original functions of the concluding phrase in Anancy stories is to mark a completion point and a shift of narrative turn. Thus, at the same time as the phrase with its Rastafari reference ties the story into a Rastafarian context, it also evokes a trickster ethos. Anancy stories traditionally depict the spider's ability to negotiate problematic situations through humour and trickery, and thus survive and prevail.

Helen Tiffin suggests that with this phrase Brodber "rewrites the European script [the Sleeping Beauty fairytale] in a Caribbean narrative mode.[107] It could also be that the Western fairytale of Sleeping Beauty provides a strategic device by which Anancy politics (the breaking of taboos such as talking openly about menstruation) becomes possible in the tight frame of Rastafari's sexist religious practice. There, women's sexuality and menstruation in particular are seen to interfere with 'reasoning', the Rasta practice of meditating and interpreting the Old Testament. For example, among the Bobo Dread, one of the most fundamentalist of Rastafarian sects, women are secluded from the community for sixteen days of the twenty-eight-day cycle so as not to contaminate the male members and break their concentration in reasoning. However, as Chevannes remarks, adherence to the strict practice leads some Bobo men to engage with non-Bobo women in "what would appear to be less than divine reasoning."[108] But the menstrual taboo is not restricted to the Bobo Dread.[109] Chevannes notes that views on menstruation are quite uniform, in that women are seen as possessing dangerous supernatural powers

[107] Helen Tiffin, "Cold Hearts and (Foreign) Tongues: Recitation and the Reclamation of the Female Body in the Works of Erna Brodber and Jamaica Kincaid," *Callaloo* 16.4 (Autumn 1993): 911.

[108] Chevannes, *Rastafari: Roots and Ideology*, 178.

[109] Such seclusion of women during menstruation is not an exceptional practice; it is so common among 'traditional' societies worldwide, including the sub-Saharan and Ethiopian 'catchment areas' of Rastafari, as to require no documentation here.

when they have their period, and that their presence may therefore hinder a boy child's growth, or produce a scarce crop.

Finally, then, it is the trope of the trickster that serves as our guide in navigating the story. Henry Louis Gates Jr. characterizes the Yorùbá trickster figure, Esù, as the African counterpart of the Greek Hermes, messenger of the gods, and after whom hermeneutics, the original study of interpretation, was named.[110] According to Gates, Esù is in effect the African literary critic, the indigenous interpreter. The Yorùbá verbs for what Esù does are *itumo,* which means "to untie or unknot knowledge," and *iyipada*, which literally means "to turn around or to translate."[111] This idea of turning around can be paralleled with the act of cross-cultural reading, in that it involves a transfer of signification, where a meaning is 'turned around' or translated into a different context. The story of Sleeping's Beauty and Prince Charming does not have a happy ending, but it does something more important in voicing the menstrual taboo in the form of the parable. As in *Jane and Louisa*, Brodber shows how woman cannot be defined in an environment that shuns her corporeality. How these non-defined women can be read in and by a reparative reader is the topic of the next section.

Voicing the whisper circle in reading

In *Jane and Louisa*, the protagonist Nellie, troubled by the "whisper circle" of destructive sexuality, ultimately experiences a mental and physical breakdown (120). This negative aspect of polyphony refers to the whispers and echoes Nellie hears about the women of her community. The mystification of women's sexuality leads to Nellie's uncertainty about her corporeal subjectivity. Evelyn O'Callaghan discusses how, in accounts of mental illness in Caribbean women's writing, an ontologically insecure person experiences her/his body as detached from the mind, feeling no integration between the two.[112] In "Sleeping's Beauty and the Prince Charming," the female protagonist stays trapped in a disembodied state as her prince cannot cope with her menstruating body. Similarly, Nellie's dissociation of her body from her mind begins at the onset of menstruation in puberty, when she refers to her body as a rotting banana tree, thereby disconnecting her body from human existence

---

[110] Gates, *The Signifying Monkey*, 8.

[111] *The Signifying Monkey*, 11.

[112] O'Callaghan, "Interior Schisms Dramatised," 92.

and linking it to something which, dying, is unable to function anymore (119). For Nellie, this feeling arises from the mystification (by people around her) of what happens to the body in puberty. For Sleeping's Beauty, the dissociation of the mind from the body results from the irreconcilable discrepancy between the celebratory complementarity of the sexes and the menstruation taboo that exists in Rastafarian thought.

Using the metaphor of the whisper circle to depict the two women, Nellie and Sleeping's Beauty, in their voiceless, disembodied or disassociated states, I argue here that their whisper circles need to be broken by reading before discussing their healing and liberatory processes. Voice in feminist theorizing has been seen as integral to subjectivity. Similarly, the struggle for voice has been one of the driving forces of the feminist movement throughout its history. This is seen, for instance, in the first-wave struggle for suffrage in languages where the words for 'vote' and 'voice' are homonyms: *ääni* in Finnish, *röst* in Swedish, *voix* in French, *Stimme* in German. Quite literally, as well as metaphorically, having one's voice heard and being able to articulate oneself freely are indispensable for emancipation. In the context of Caribbean women's writing, the metaphor of voice can be seen used to describe the tradition that is increasingly getting its collective voice heard in the global literary market.[113] There is no longer a whisper circle as far as Caribbean women writers are concerned, as Newson and Strong–Leek explain: "what began as a whisper years ago in the Caribbean is now a loud reverberating shout! A shout to be heard – a shout to be reckoned with – a shout, a scream for acknowledgement."[114]

However, it would be too simple in a reparative reading to view the deconstruction of voice(lessness) as a process of emancipation. The idea of moving from silence or whisper to a voiced subjectivity would be precisely the kind of teleological reading that Sedgwick rejects in her quest for reparative readings existing beside, rather than beyond. Sara Ahmed notes that the question of who speaks has always been central to postcolonial feminist thought, par-

[113] On postcolonial literature as an industry, see Brouillette, *Postcolonial Writers in the Global Literary Marketplace*, ch. 2.

[114] Adele S. Newson & Linda Strong–Leek, "Introduction" to *Winds of Change: The Transforming Voices of Caribbean Women Writers and Scholars*, ed. Newson & Strong–Leek (New York: Peter Lang, 1998): 5.

ticularly in Gayatri Spivak's famous question "Can the subaltern speak?"[115] However, the agency of speech, to all intents and purposes, does not guarantee change, action or audience: "who hears?" (let alone 'who is listening'?) thus becomes another question yet to be answered.[116]

Ien Ang remarks that the feminist establishment relies heavily on its "(limitless?) capacity not only to speak, but, more importantly, to listen and hear."[117] When deconstructing white Western feminist praxis and examining critical voices raised by Third-World women, Haggis and Schech list "I want to hear your pain" as a typical white women's response to the "vocality of the Other."[118] As discussed in relation to Monica and Sophie's pains, wanting to hear the other woman's pain is one of the select few ways in which Western feminists allow Third-World women to speak.[119] Witnessing and hearing the pain of the other raises the white woman to a martyr's position as she takes on the burden of pain and anger from the other woman.[120] Here, the Third-World woman's pain – heard (and thus adopted) by the Western feminist – becomes a vehicle for the improvement, not of the Third-World woman's living conditions but, rather, of the Western feminist's conscience. This is why the whisper circle of female sexuality should not be broken by forcible (and forced) Western readings.

In "Sleeping's Beauty," the inability or unwillingness of the prince to hear his princess' pain has catastrophic consequences, as the Alpha and the Omega (the Rastaman and woman) are unable to function without one another and their larger plans for emancipation and repatriation fail. In fact, the prince adopts Sleepings's pain as he bids her farewell "through lips frozen with pain."[121] Unethical in the way he allows himself to feel the pain of the other, he flees. The narrator makes it clear that the ability to live with the pain of the other (without appropriating it) would have been integral to the construction of a collective subjectivity celebrated by Rastafari in principle but not in prac-

---

[115] Gayatri Chakravorty Spivak, "Can the Subaltern Speak?" in *Marxism and the Interpretation of Culture*, ed. Cary Nelson & Lawrence Greenberg (Basingstoke: Macmillan Education, 1988): 271–313, cited by Ahmed, *Strange Encounters*, 60.

[116] *Strange Encounters*, 61.

[117] Ang, *On Not Speaking Chinese*, 179.

[118] Haggis & Schech, "Meaning Well and Global Good Manners," 391.

[119] "Meaning Well and Global Good Manners," 391.

[120] "Meaning Well and Global Good Manners," 394.

[121] "Sleeping's Beauty and the Prince Charming," 4.

tice. As allegorical as the story is, responses to Sleeping's Beauty's pain may serve as a guide to reading the whisper circle. Here again, differentiation between the pain of the other and the reader's own potential pain is important. The whisper circle involves Brodber's sexually damaged women, whose trauma is deeply embedded in Jamaica's histories of colonial exploitation, and without an understanding of these strands of oppression, the whisper circle remains intact and unbroken.

Brodber herself makes it difficult – if not impossible – to ignore the inherent legacy of slavery in both Jamaican and Euro-American societies. There is an illustration in *Jane and Louisa* of the ways in which the text itself sometimes drops hints at the reader of the manifold power structures at play in each embodied, affective experience. In this instance, the forces at play are decidedly sexual in nature. In a passage where Nellie has a sexual experience in the cinema when she is a student in the USA, oral sex and sugarcane are linked metaphorically where the humiliating nature of the scene is expressed through an evocation of sugar in the organization of Jamaican society, and in the exploitation of the Jamaican people. Taylor characterizes Jamaican society as a plantation society, where sugar and plantation slavery were the main elements of the social order, of which "the modus operandi was exploitation not development."[122] In *Jane and Louisa*, a boy takes Nellie to the cinema and she feels she has to return the favour. She recounts:

> The first root of cane you've ever popped out. [...] Premature but this is your effort so you eat it like it is sweet. [...] You want to be a woman; now you have a man, you'll be like everybody else. You're normal now! Vomit and bear it! (28)

The sucking and chewing of a piece of sugarcane serves as a metaphor for oral sex in the scene. The colonial histories of forced labour and sexual exploitation are linked in the passage, making the play with double meanings obvious: in order for her to be a 'normal' woman, Nellie feels obligated to continue the tradition of sucking the masculine sugarcane. The power difference in the awkward situation is highlighted by telling the incident through sugarcane imagery, but it is the obvious irony of giving the boy a "little sugar" that lends the passage its gendered and sexualized nature. The lack of reciprocation in the act of oral sex makes the unhappy incident resonate even

---

[122] Orville Taylor, "Cultural Considerations for Social Workers in the Jamaican Inner City: A Sociological Perspective," *Caribbean Journal of Social Work* 1 (March 2002): 68.

to those who fail to catch the historical undertones of the polysemous metaphor. The white feminist reader, too, is bound to recognize Nellie's struggles to 'normalize' her distorted womanhood by engaging in the unreciprocated act of giving oral sex to her date.

Reading this scene, in which female sexuality is again performed according to the logic of the whisper circle, may help to embody the whispers and echoes that haunt Nellie. Here, she herself has become an active agent of the shame that was instilled in her as a girl. Later on in life, Nellie begins to understand the reasons for her shame, as she makes sense of the whispers and rumours about her Aunt Becca. Breaking her whisper circle, Nellie learns that Aunt Becca had created for herself a protective kumbla out of the denial that she adopted after the birth of her illegitimate child, who was given away. Suddenly, the rumours that she had heard about Aunt Becca begin to make sense, and Nellie's Aunt Alice guides her through a process of reconnection by showing her slides that record the Richmond family history (131–33). Aunt Becca, as Alice explains, "is barren. Threw away Tanny's child and made herself a mule" (133). Alice appeal to Nellie:

> "So who is going to call her out of her cocoon and put back her heart and her body together and her baby in her arms? Wake up Nellie. She tried. It's your time now and I can take you no further." (133)

Alice urges Nellie to consider her own situation, and to learn from Aunt Becca's trauma.

The process by which Nellie discovers and, indeed, *un*covers family traumas is read by Wilentz as the novel's liberation – the narrative

> develops from Nellie's disjointed narrative from her breakdown to a curative process that uncovers her own, her family's, and her nation's trauma of separation from their African heritage and its healing traditions.[123]

However, voicing the whisper circle in and by reading does not automatically mean the completion of one's healing process. In a paranoid reading, the deconstructive practice of uncovering oppression might suffice, but it needs to be recognized that, in a reparative reading, still more is needed. Inasmuch as Brodber's "Sleeping's Beauty" does not permit a reading that furthers the discussion of sexual emancipation, its female protagonist's story ends here with my paranoid uncovering of its cunningly veiled comment, "Rastafari me nuh

[123] Wilentz, *Healing Narratives*, 29.

chose none" on the sexism of Rastafari thought and practice. However, Nellie's journey continues in the following chapter, in which I consider ways to move forward by reading Nellie's, Monica's, and Sophie's processes of healing and liberation.

⌘

4
Communities That Heal – Reading Sexual Healing

Edwidge Danticat, Opal Palmer Adisa, Erna Brodber, and Shani Mootoo

TO JUDGE FROM THE EMPHASIS of my discussion so far, it would be easy to think of negative affect as dominating this selection of anglophone Caribbean women's writing. To be sure, many authors do depict sexuality and its associated emotions in negative terms, where sex and sexuality inevitably lead to self-destruction. However, most novels in this tradition are also deeply committed to narrative processes leading from pain and suffering through to healing and emancipation. This chapter is concerned with the possibilities arising from reading such feelings of sexual healing. My main question here is how we should read these feelings, but this can only be broached by first examining the women's relationships in the novels, as healing feelings serve not only to describe these relationships but also serve to position the reader in a framework that calls for a reconsideration of empathy and collectivity. My ultimate concern is how a feminist reader should, or could, participate in such emancipations.

Witnessing the novels' liberations is bound to evoke the affective reader's emotional investment in feminism – the feminist attachment[1] that figures prominently in cross-cultural feminist work, where empathy is central to the investment that Western feminists have in the Other woman. As Schech and Haggis show, empathy in the form of general benevolence and goodwill has its roots in the violence of Western colonialism – particularly in the Christian mission disguised as altruistic love, where the well-meaning 'good white

---

[1] Ahmed, *The Cultural Politics of Emotion*, 171.

woman' does what she thinks is best for her colonized sisters without deconstructing her own position.[2]

Interrogating the healing of the sexual, textual female body calls attention to the reading processes at play in these liberatory quests. I view the white reader's feminist attachment as a potential textual other, characterized by Pearce as the reader's love object,[3] whose mechanisms need to be scrutinized in a reading that wishes to stay open to the affective responses of reading, but that does not perpetuate their potentially harmful effect as epistemic violence. This requires each of the texts examined here to be read with cognizance of the regulated nature of their liberties. The reader should resist any impulse to interpret the texts' recoveries and emancipations according to the "inherently redemptive" form and ideology of the European novel.[4] Instead, there may be more subtle, 'minor' redemptions that escape the eye of the outsider reader.[5] Nurturing an illusory quest of full emancipation as a textual other may turn into a violent misreading. Instead, the interplay of the paranoid–reparative axis as formulated by Eve Kosofsky Sedgwick helps to balance the reader's options of interpreting emancipation with cautious optimism.

The affective potential of feminist attachment as the reader's textual other may, despite its risks, serve to highlight and reinforce communities based on the premise of difference, rather than sameness. Such partial politics in an ethics of empathy may also be seen in Ahmed's notion of "withness" as a way of forming agency. For Ahmed, "withness" is a reparative act of self-formation through participation in the emotional responses of others. In writing about the neglect of the grief of gay and lesbian families who lost family members in the 9/11 tragedy, Ahmed conceives of 'withness' as an ethical response to the pain and grief of the Other. In withness,

> others exist within me and apart from me at the same time. Taking you in will not necessarily be 'becoming like you', or 'making you like me', as other others have also impressed upon me, shaping my surfaces in this way and that.[6]

---

[2] Haggis & Schech, "Meaning Well and Global Good Manners," 387.

[3] Pearce, *Feminism and the Politics of Reading*, 17.

[4] Lynne Pearce, "Beyond Redemption? Mobilizing Affect in Feminist Reading," in *Working with Affect in Feminist Readings: Disturbing Differences* ed. Marianne Liljeström & Susanna Paasonen (London & New York: Routledge, 2010): 151.

[5] Pearce, "Beyond Redemption? Mobilizing Affect in Feminist Reading," 162.

[6] Ahmed, *The Cultural Politics of Emotion*, 160.

This affective process of 'withness' becomes a way of conceptualizing a dimension of Caribbean feminist emancipations and the text–reader relationships in which they materialize.

In the cases of the two violated women, Sophie and Monica (in Danticat and Adisa, respectively), the collective act of naming their wrongdoers in a women's ritual serves to catalyze the healing process. In the ritual, the individual and the collective healing women's subjectivity exist side by side without merging. Naming isolates the victim–perpetrator relationship so that it can be deconstructed – from which the victim can reconstruct and heal her relationship with her self, and also with the surrounding world. In the rituals Sophie and Monica undergo, the participating women's voices chant reaffirming mantras – both in unison, and in a call-and-response style. This reflects the polyphony of the black women's community and highlights subjectivity as plural and heteroglossic, thereby inviting dialogic reading strategies to account for the multiple relationships between the novels' women and the reader/text nexus.

In the case of Brodber's *Jane and Louisa*, the importance of kinship and connection with one's own tradition helps Nellie to reconcile her troubled sexual past – as aided by her Aunt Alice, who shows Nellie the importance of her family history and roots. Another important figure is the Rastafarian Baba, who nurtures Nellie after her breakdown. The novel's concluding phrase, "we are getting ready," provides a key to the story's communal politics of sexual healing. In reading Nellie's healing process, the reader needs to question her own belonging to and participation in the "we" who are "getting ready," expressed by Nellie in the present-progressive form to signal the ongoing process of healing, instead of an absolute completion of self.

The affects and effects of naming as a collective experience: Sophie and Monica

Both *Breath, Eyes, Memory* and *It Begins With Tears* end with a healing process that takes place in a ritualized social setting, implying that individual traumas may only be overcome by comprehending the weight of historical sexual violation that each traumatized black woman carries within herself. The social nature of Afro-Caribbean trauma and emancipation highlights the historical links at play in Monica and Sophie's individual stories. Read in terms of this sensibility, the novels remind us of how deeply grounded the

Afro-Caribbean diasporic identity is in the trauma of the Middle Passage.[7] We cannot draw a direct causal link from slavery to the specific acts of violence experienced by either Sophie or Monica, as these are firmly rooted in prevailing power-structures within their immediate communities. Still, the history of colonialism and slavery underlies the lives of Caribbean women. Simultaneously, these survivalist histories also carry with them the tools for emancipation and healing, as demonstrated by the African-derived ritual practices represented– such as the healing ceremony in river water in *It Begins With Tears,* and the aforementioned call-and-response-style healing ritual in *Breath, Eyes, Memory*.

The act of reading brings the feminist affective turn together with a feminist version of African-derived ego-critical philosophy, and this hybrid formation can be seen at work in the novels' healing quests. Reading is the place in which this unique coexistence of the individual and the collective in the form of the spiritual rituals takes place. At the same time as we note the importance of the social nature of Afro-Caribbean trauma and emancipation, it is also important to understand the significance of identifying a direct victim–violator relationship through the ritualized act of naming. In naming, after the act of violence has been given identified agency, the very relationship born of the act of naming can be deconstructed, and the victim becomes a survivor.

Sophie's healing process: burning the bridges of trauma

Helen Scott remarks that Haiti is "a land long dominated by the legacy of forced labour, dictatorial domestic rule, external domination, revolutionary struggle and the ever present sugarcane."[8] This legacy of domination also gives rise to the virginity cult known as testing, as seen in Danticat's novel.[9] Furthermore, as Chancy observes and as indicated earlier, Duvalier's military used rape as a "means of domination" and is thus "clearly patriarchal in structure."[10] This is referred to by Donette A. Francis as "politically motivated rape," an act of sexual violence perpetrated by Duvalier's goons to gain state

[7] Feng, "Rituals of Rememory," 149.

[8] Scott, "Ou Libéré?," 463.

[9] "Ou Libéré?," 467.

[10] Chancy, "'No Giraffes in Haiti'," 318.

control over Haiti's countryside villages and its people.[11] To understand Sophie's sexual shame at the violation of testing thus involves seeing the practice as a part of a larger framework of domination in the country. Sophie is unable to understand this fact until later in life – on account of her mother's failure to come to terms with her trauma of having been raped by a Macoute amidst the ubiquitous sugarcane.[12]

After returning from her trip to Haiti with her baby daughter, Sophie takes part in a group-therapy session with two other women who have been subjected to sexual violence: Buki, an Ethiopian college student who has undergone female genital mutilation, and Davina, a middle-aged Chicana woman raped as a child by her grandfather, join with Sophie in a spiritual ritual in which they pray for each other and chant a call-and-response mantra. Francis remarks that Danticat introduces a larger postcolonial perspective by showing how "sexual traumas are a collective plight" shared by women of colour.[13] Drawing on the African-derived spiritual practice of call-and-response, the three women express their 'withness' in an effort to heal their selves.

The Chicana woman, Davina, hosts the group in her home, where she has a room dedicated to the therapy meetings. She begins the ceremony thus:

> "I am a beautiful woman with a strong body," Davina led the affirmations.
>
> "We are beautiful women with strong bodies." We echoed her uncertain voice.
>
> "Because of my distress, I am able to understand when others are in deep pain."
>
> "Because of our distress, we are able to understand when others are in deep pain."
>
> I heard my voice rise above the others.
>
> "Since I have survived this, I can survive anything."[14]

In the affirmations, Davina's "uncertain voice" begins the call and response by stating her own first-person-singular call to healing. In the response, Buki and Sophie affirm her call with their first-person plural, so morphing each woman's individual experience of suffering into a shared one. This voicing of pain and shame serves to communicate the women's will to heal, and is a

[11] Francis, "'Silences Too Horrific to Disturb'," 78.

[12] See "'Silences Too Horrific to Disturb'," 86.

[13] "'Silences Too Horrific to Disturb'," 85.

[14] *Breath, Eyes, Memory*, 202.

reparative act. The declaration of individual distress leading to an understanding of the pain of the other is an expression of 'withness' where the pain of the self results in an identification and appreciation of the pain of the other.

As Sophie's voice rises above the others when she hears herself uttering the words of affirmation, the individuality of her voice remains audible. The ritual, as performed in a collective voice, does not entail the appropriation or abuse of the other person's subject-position. Rather, it refers to the drawing of strength from the courage of the other two women, each working to "confront and move beyond their histories of silence, shame and trauma."[15] As the notion of 'withness' is a process of simultaneous existence of the others "within" and "apart from" the self, [16] Sophie is thus able to find solace by relating to a group of women who have undergone similar experiences – and yet each woman expresses the shared mantra in her own voice.

Sophie's experience parallels Nellie's shame in Brodber's *Jane and Louisa,* when she becomes confused trying to interpret the affective tone that she hears in her mother's voice. Cavarero points out that the communication of a voice entails a reciprocal relation "with another unique existent."[17] By this, Cavarero refers to the act of listening as integral to the constitution of voice. She contends that being able to communicate the uniqueness of each voice "takes at least a duet, a calling and a responding – or, better, a reciprocal intention to listen, one that is already active in the vocal emission, and that reveals and communicates everyone to the other."[18] This means that, from the perspective of voice, the women's shared exchange of affirmations is also an act of listening: an act of placing emphasis on what is heard, and not simply on what is said. As the women voice their healing quests together, they also hear and heal each other. The performative act of call and response serves to re-shape the women's subjectivities in this act of wit(h)ness, where past and present strengths are spoken aloud collectively, and heard by each individual woman.

As mentioned in the case of Nellie's whisper circle, Danticat's voicing of the women's traumas in the act of ritual does not depict a unilateral movement from silence to voice. As denoted by the criticism directed at consciousness-raising practiced by feminists in the 1960s and the '70s, speaking about

---

[15] Francis, "'Silences Too Horrific to Disturb'," 85.

[16] Ahmed, *The Cultural Politics of Emotion*, 160.

[17] Cavarero, *For More than One Voice*, 5.

[18] *For More than One Voice*, 5.

oppression does not automatically lead to liberation. Here Sophie, Buki, and Davina's naming ritual functions as another step in the healing. After the polyphonic choir affirms the women's suffering and will to survival, they name their evildoers in writing:

> We each wrote the name of our abusers in a piece of paper, raised it over a candle, and watched as the flames consumed it. Buki blew up a green balloon. We went to Davina's backyard and watched as she released it in the dark. It was hard to see where the balloon went, but at least it had floated out of our hands.[19]

In the ritual of naming, the responsibility of the act of violence is relocated to its named agent. This radical act of hailing differs from the shame discussed in the previous chapter, where the victim herself assumed responsibility for the abuse and violence to which she was subjected. As Jordan Stump remarks, on the relationship between naming and power in his reading of the function of naming in the novels of Raymond Queneau,

> There are no anonymous presidents, and certainly no anonymous dictators; no nameless laws, and certainly no nameless wars. Wars require enemies, and enemies require names.[20]

Naming, in other words, is an act of power. The performative, individuating power of naming in Caribbean feminist literature has also been analysed by Sara Eeva in her reading of the novels of Jean Rhys, where naming functions as a controlling device for social (and racially sexualized) differentiation.[21] Contrary to this harmful example of naming as an act of domination, such a process of interpellation in fact becomes applied to a process of liberation in Danticat's novel.

Furthermore, the active destruction of the names by burning the piece of paper on which they are written is a synecdochal dismantling of the destruc-

---

[19] *Breath, Eyes, Memory*, 203.

[20] Jordan Stump, *Naming and Unnaming: On Raymond Queneau* (Lincoln: Nebraska UP, 1998): 121.

[21] Sara Eeva, "Kreolinaisen heteroseksuaalisuuden 'pakollinen' ja melankolinen rakentuminen Jean Rhysin romaaneissa *Voyage in the Dark* ja *Siintää Sargassomeri*" [The 'compulsory' and melancholy construction of Creole female heterosexuality in Jean Rhys's *Voyage in the Dark* and *Wide Sargasso Sea*], in *Pervot pidot: Homo-, lesbo- ja queer-näkökulmia kirjallisuudentutkimukseen* [Queer feast: Perspectives on gay, lesbian, and queer literary studies] ed. Lasse Kekki & Kaisa Ilmonen (Helsinki: Like, 2004): 326.

tive relationships that these healing women had with their perpetrators. As the burning of the name symbolizes Sophie's deconstruction of her relationship with her mother, it also creates a metaphoric chain across the generations of women who were forced to endure testing. In contrast, as will be seen in my discussion of Adisa's *It Begins With Tears* presently, naming serves to create a link between the village women; each traumatized by her respective moments of sexual shaming. Even if the victim and the reader know the identity of the violator, the deed remains anonymous until it has been named. The empowering act of naming thus enables the victim to confront her trauma, and she is then able to dissociate herself from it by calling her violator by name; thereby gaining control over her suffering. The burning of that name is the ultimate act of rebellion and liberation from the constraints of the abusive relationship.

The reader's dialogic participation in Sophie's healing

Caribbean women writers such as Erna Brodber, Olive Senior, and Merle Hodge "imply in their texts that positive individual identities can only be realized via a more collectively mobilized notion of identity."[22] Forbes confirms this statement in her article on more individualist literary accounts of Caribbean identity, remarking that "Caribbean literary discourse has always been a narrative of community" and that there is a decidedly "communal commitment" omnipresent in the literary tradition.[23] Furthermore, this paradigm is emphasized and privileged in reading.[24] This privileging of the communal in Caribbean fiction by women could, then, be interpreted as the novels' tendency to surrender the individual in favour of the collective. However, neither in Danticat's novel nor in the others featured in this selection does collective identity emerge at the expense of the individual. As shown in the previous section, the interplay of the collective and the individual in the plurality of voices in Danticat's narrative places emphasis on a polyphonic black female identity engaged in intergenerational and inter-ethnic dialogue.[25]

[22] Narain, "Standing in the Place of Love," 335.

[23] Forbes, "Fracturing Subjectivities," 16.

[24] "Fracturing Subjectivities," 18.

[25] See Scott, *Caribbean Women Writers and Globalization*, 30.

Foregrounding the plurality of voices in black women's writing at large, Mae Henderson suggests that black women's discourse is dialogic. Through her reading of two African-American novels, Zora Neale Hurston's *Their Eyes Were Watching God* and Toni Morrison's *Sula*, Henderson discusses black women's discourse as interlocutory; reflecting on the plural nature of the self containing various othernesses (here referring to the intersectional nature of differences at play in the lives of black women).[26] Henderson accordingly claims that black female subjectivity is forged by language as the medium of consciousness, in which speech and writing are simultaneously in dialogue with both the self and the society, and also with the self and the psyche.[27] Dialogism serves to highlight the ways in which black women have used literature as a means to negotiate different centres within the self.[28] This stress on the simultaneity of collectivity and individuality serves to avoid the essentializing view of African-based female identity as a monolith.

Henderson's account of the dialogic nature of African-American women's discourse clarifies the relationship between the communal and the individual wherein polyphony creates subjectivity as plural, thereby enabling black women to have coinciding "dialectics/dialogics of identity and difference."[29] Henderson concludes by suggesting that black feminist critics should be in charge of interpreting this heteroglossic discourse. However, a dialogic reader "expressing engagement with the social aspects of self ('the other[s] in ourselves')"[30] may also be differently positioned, since this approach is premised on the continuous interplay of difference as constitutive of identity and meaning.

Turning from polyphonic black women's dialogic textual strategies to a dialogic model of reading, we can see how the reader's presence in the utter-

---

[26] Mae Gwendolyn Henderson, "Speaking in Tongues: Dialogics, Dialectics, and the Black Woman Writer's Literary Tradition," in *Changing Our Own Words: Essays on Criticism, Theory, and Writing by Black Women*, ed. Cheryl A. Wall (New Brunswick NJ: Rutgers UP, 1989): 17–18.

[27] Henderson, "Speaking in Tongues," 19.

[28] Pirjo Ahokas & Eila Rantonen, "Feminismin muukalaiset: Rodun ja etnisyyden haasteet" [The strangers of feminism: The challenges of race and ethnicity], in *Naissubjekti ja Postmoderni* [The female subject and the postmodern], ed. Päivi Kosonen (Tampere: Gaudeamus, 1996): 78.

[29] Henderson, "Speaking in Tongues," 37.

[30] "Speaking in Tongues," 37.

ance event constitutes the narrative. The ability of the self to articulate and to realize itself depends on the "enabling role of the dialogic 'other'."[31] The dialogic 'other' refers to the Self, the Other, and their relationship as the prerequisite of the dialogic condition. To echo Lea Rojola's formulation of the dialogic principle in reading, the (implicit or explicit) presence of an intended recipient in a text provides the foundation upon which readership becomes constructed.[32] Relying on this dialogic principle, testimonial stories of suffering and liberation become particularly interesting, as their signifying power relies on their audiences' willingness to react to the texts that they read.

I suggest that the recovery from suffering in Danticat's novel, which takes place with the support of a community of women with similar experiences, should not be read as de-individualization of trauma, or as the insignificance or crumbling of individual subjectivity. Rather, the communal aspect of healing can be seen as fortifying a kind of collective subjectivity that follows Afro-Caribbean spiritual cosmologies, in which the self in the other and the other in the self are seen to nurture and sustain each other. These healing processes are examples of affective ethics based on the premise of withness as a reparative orientation toward trauma. The white feminist reader, too, may exercise withness with regard to the narrative, even if she cannot claim the communality of ritualistic agency created by the collective voices of Sophie, Buki, and Davina.

It is therefore crucial to consider the kinds of communities that we perceive to be born of each literary and textual encounter, and the kind of presence in which a reader finds herself in the multiple liberations witnessed in these novels. Adriana Cavarero's views on voice resonate with the idea of reading as interactive or dialogic; one that is always dependent on the enabling role of the dialogic Other. Cavarero's model also presupposes a listener: "The sense of hearing [...] has its natural referent in a voice that also comes from internal passageways: the mouth, the throat, the network of the lungs."[33] As Sophie, Buki, and Davina hear each others' voices in the ritual, the reader, too, becomes positioned in this reparative discourse. As the act of reading is premised on the construction of a community or communities of readers, she may learn to see difference in the collective, and, indeed, collectivity in difference.

---

[31] Pearce, *The Rhetorics of Feminism*, 10.

[32] Rojola, "Speaking about *it*," 484.

[33] Cavarero, *For More than One Voice*, 4.

Staking a claim in the dialogic act of reading is the task of the reader, and, just as Danticat's writing of Sophie's healing process can be deemed an act of withness, so, too, can the reading of the text be deemed such. As Ahmed recounts in relation to her mother's chronic illness and pain, witnessing and co-existing with the pain of the other give it "the status of an event" that may serve to bring subjects together.[34] Practising withness in reading as an approach to the pain of the other ultimately shapes the bodies of those who witness that pain. This is how reading as a ritualized testimonial wit(h)ness brings about change in the reading subject. In the context of the novel, the post-trauma healing processes serve as "calls for recognition" and reading them serves as "forms of recognition" which calls into question historical "truths."[35] The act of recognition in reading can be seen as the white feminist reader's position of being "beside" in the ritual.

After the ritual, Sophie is fatigued from the ordeal, yet she feels that she has taken a step towards recovery:

> I felt broken at the end of the meeting, but a little closer to being free. I didn't feel guilty about burning my mother's name anymore. I knew my hurt and hers were linked in a long chain and if she hurt me, it was because she was hurt, too.
>
> It was up to me to avoid my turn in the fire. It was up to me to make sure that my daughter never slept with ghosts, never lived with nightmares, and never had *her* name burnt in the flames.[36]

Feeling "a little closer to being free," Sophie recognizes the ongoing nature of her recovery process in which she has now advanced to break the intergenerational cycle of testing. Having reconciled with her mother, she now shifts her position from that of daughter to that of a mother herself. She realizes that it is in her power to protect her own daughter from the traumatizing sexual violence to which she, her mother, and previous generations of women were subjected. Francis suggests that this is the turning point for Sophie to "reclaim her body and to experience it whole, inviolate, and pleasurable, rather than as an extension of her mother's control or defilement."[37] Despite the deep-rootedness of the histories of violence against women in Haiti, unlearning those legacies becomes possible through a ritualized process of recovery.

---

[34] Ahmed, *The Cultural Politics of Emotion*, 30.

[35] *The Cultural Politics of Emotion*, 200.

[36] *Breath, Eyes, Memory*, 203.

[37] Francis, "'Silences Too Horrific to Disturb'," 85.

Martine's life ends with her suicide by stabbing herself in the stomach, thereby also killing her unborn baby. Sophie takes her mother's body to be buried in Haiti, and returns to the cane fields after the funeral to confront the site of trauma for a long history of women in the Caco family.[38] This "willful re-membering," wherein Sophie beats down and destroys cane stalks in a symbolic act of resistance, serves as the final act of ceremonial healing.[39] In the cane field, Sophie has another ritualistic call-and-response exchange, this time with her grandmother and her Tante Atie. The narrative process of healing comes full circle, as Sophie hears her grandmother's voice calling the traditional Haitian market women's call, "Ou libéré?" (are you free?).[40] Her Tante Atie joins in the polyphonic call and response of the Caco women; sobbing the expression aloud. As a dynamic event, this act of co-voicing symbolizes "the ongoing hope for freedom" present in the novel.[41] Reading these struggles for liberation from the peripheral position of 'beside', the white reader may, through vicarious reparative participation in the form of wit(h)ness, help realize the significatory potential of such powerful voices.

Monica's healing at the river: Naming and black women's polyphony

In Adisa's *It Begins With Tears*, the three jealous women punish and attempt to destroy Monica's sexuality through the act of peppering. This traumatic event calls for healing and purification by another community of women who, in turn, help Monica to rebuild herself. A group of village women led by Miss Cotton (a spiritual elder, and Monica's aunt, who also raised her) gather at Monica's house when the news of her plight reaches them. Aunty Olive, Miss Velma, Miss Dahlia, and Arnella – all of whom are related and are described in the novel's character list as "mediator," "enigma," "high priestess," and "priestess in training" respectively – are affiliated with healing obeah. Joining the women are Beryl and Angel, a mother and daughter who are unaware of their blood connection. All of these women rush to Monica's side to give first aid, and to ease her pain.

---

38 Francis, "'Silences Too Horrific to Disturb'," 87.

39 "'Silences Too Horrific to Disturb'," 87.

40 *Breath, Eyes, Memory*, 233.

41 Scott, "Ou Libéré?," 477.

In the midst of the herbal medicating process, while bathing and cleaning the victim, the women feel Monica's pain in sympathy with her suffering, which highlights the severity of the crime: "They all ached. [...] The lips of their vaginas throbbed in sympathy, their wombs ached, and their salty tears left stain marks on their faces."[42] As mentioned in the previous chapter, the women's sympathizing pain serves as a catalyst for the women to take action. Here, in fact, sympathy (adopting the pain of the other) serves a redeeming function, prompting the other women respond to the act of violence to which Monica has been subjected. For the women in the village, the feeling of pain is a message: the crime cannot be ignored, and a healing ritual is required in which the offence receives proper treatment.

On Sunday morning, the village community withdraws into gendered groups to perform their respective rituals. The men go hunting and the women set off for the river to conduct a healing ceremony, where they employ water as a Christian and African symbol of purification, and summon their collective power to overcome the suffering that they have experienced.[43] This scene in which the women take Monica to the river reveals how a ritual, spiritual act can help treat trauma.[44] Donna Weir–Soley comments that the river has "a specific significance in women's culture in traditional peasant communities of the Caribbean," where it is connected to "sexuality, spirituality, healing, sustenance, life-giving water, and cleansing of the body and garments."[45] The women begin the ritual by undressing and wading into the river. Naked, the women display liberation from the shame that has previously characterized their lives. This is in stark contrast to those village women who, upon Monica's return, condemned her as a shameful woman due to her very lack of shame. Instead, this group of women act in solidarity by baring their bodies and sharing their nudity in order to purify themselves together.

The river water as the healing element evokes maternal connections to the 'Rivermumma', the spirit of the river in the African Oshun tradition that survives in hybridized Jamaican folklore.[46] The narrator depicts the scene at and in the river:

---

[42] *It Begins With Tears*, 136.

[43] Feng, "Rituals of Rememory," 166.

[44] "Rituals of Rememory," 152.

[45] Weir–Soley, *Eroticism, Spirituality, and Resistance*, 176.

[46] *Eroticism, Spirituality, and Resistance*, 176.

> The water was warm and milky. The air was still and the rays of the sun cast golden sheaths on the river. Arnella cupped a handful of water to her mouth and drank. Each woman found her own space and splashed around. [...] Angel immersed her entire body, imagining she was baptising herself. [...] Suddenly she was overcome with a desire to know her real mother; she could taste her salty tears mingling with the warm, sweet, breast milk that was the river water, and she allowed herself to surrender, feeling very close to the mother she never knew. (214)

Each woman who wades into the river has a unique relationship with the female, maternal river that cleanses and nurtures her. The warmth and milkiness of the river water that Arnella drinks recalls a mother's breast milk. Drawing on Christian religious connections, Angel baptizes herself in the maternal water, thus bringing together the idea of maternality and religiosity that amalgamate in the Rivermumma. Angel has a bodily affective response in the form of tears, which dissolve in the water and enable her to let go of her sense of orphanhood from having grown up without a mother. Here, the river as a nurturing, healing, maternal woman performs the function of merging the women's consciousnesses in an intersubjective, communal black female subjectivity.[47]

The flowing maternal river is evocative of sensory and sensual phenomena in the women who participate in the ritual. In fact, it enables the women's "complexly erotic" bonding.[48] The river is thus not only the physical place of the ritual, it is also a healer and a spiritual character personified by the Rivermumma. Having washed Monica and each other in the river, the women gather in a circle and, with Arnella's encouragement, the punitive, yet emancipatory, naming ceremony can begin.

> Then Miss Cotton and Arnella stood either side of Monica again, and tossed her back and forth with open hands. Monica's body was like a weightless sponge, and each time Miss Cotton and Arnella tossed her, water spewed from her body, and she screamed, 'Ah gwane name dem. Mamma came to me afta Miss Madge funeral and say she forgive me. Ah gwane name dem out for Althea say she no hate me. Ah name dem for ah forgive meself'.
>
> 'Name dem', Arnella demanded.

---

[47] Weir–Soley, *Eroticism, Spirituality, and Resistance*, 177.

[48] *Eroticism, Spirituality, and Resistance*, 178.

> Monica began to weep anew, leaning forward, hugging her stomach. Miss Cotton put her arms around her. 'You have to name dem me child. Dem must face dem punishment'. (216–17)

Like Sophie's healing ritual in her therapy group, Monica's ritual involves a ceremony in which the act of naming is a catalyst for healing, and incites an emancipatory desire in each woman. After Monica hands herself over to the sustaining community of women worth her trust, she begins to name her violators. Monica recounts the traumatizing event in detail, singling out Marva as the instigator of the violent act of peppering and Peggy and Grace as her accomplices (217). The graphic description serves the purpose of testimony in the presence of an audience, after which Monica is passed around the circle of women, who rinse her body with water as she floats in the circle.[49]

In testimonial naming, the violent act receives an agent and is no longer an anonymous deed. Naming empowers the victim to face the trauma and break away from it as she incorporates her perpetrator in her discourse of reparation. The act of violence acquires a subject when the power of the word is used, as the women work to create "ways in which these traumas can be described and de-scribed."[50] It is the ritual that serves to sustain the women's community, and shows how women's sexuality and kinship are tied to that community; itself formed by the women's shared experiences and sisterhood.

As a social practice, the ritual also helps the other participating women to cleanse themselves of their traumas. Althea, Grace and Desmond's teenage daughter, was beaten by her mother after revealing that she was pregnant. In a scene prior to the ritual on the river, the sexually ignorant Althea discusses her pregnancy with Monica and vehemently denies sleeping with the baby's father. According to Althea, they only went to the river and "we did lean up against a tree. Him tell me ah couldn't get pregnant if we no lay down" (205). By participating in the ritual, however, Althea begins to understand the meaning of the life that she carries inside her. Monica's body also serves an emancipatory purpose for Althea when she encounters Monica's naked body when it is her turn to rinse the latter during the ritual. In a reparative moment, and through her encounter with Monica, Althea assumes responsibility by asking forgiveness for her mother's deeds. She is sufficiently encouraged to look Monica in the eye and ask for her help in raising the baby she is expecting

---

[49] On testimony and recognition, see Ahmed, *The Cultural Politics of Emotion*, 200.

[50] Feng, "Rituals of Rememory," 152.

(219). By drawing strength from Monica's corporeality, Althea gains confidence in her own.

Similarly, Beryl, one of the village's unmarried women, finally finds the voice to speak out about her rape by a white male tourist when she was a young hotel maid. The rape resulted in pregnancy and the birth of a girl-child that she could not love until later in life, when her kinship with Angel – her long-lost daughter – is revealed. To finally be able to speak aloud of this violent act makes the trauma nameable, and thus enables recuperation and liberation in a safe community of women who support and sustain each other. The end of the novel depicts Monica's body as the site of empowerment for other women besides herself – her body is transformed from an object previously reserved for the sexual (ab)use of men to a positive agent functioning for the good of the community of women; all healing from their traumas.

Naming enables the victim and her healing community to take control of their respective traumas, and to forge links and alliances between one another through seeing larger oppressive structures and shared experiences of injustice. The novel positions the individual suffering subject, Monica, in a polyphonic relationship with each healing woman. 'Healing women' thus involves both an adjective and a transitive verb, capturing the way in which the women help each other to heal and to simultaneously heal themselves. Thus, naming in itself is not emancipation; rather, it serves a larger function as a shared rite of passage that mobilizes the healing aspect of polyphony. The revelatory act of naming is echoed in a recurring phrase that is the title of the novel's penultimate chapter: "Deeds done in darkness shine bright in daylight" (228). Bringing the violators' names into the open also brings the act of violence into the metaphorical daylight, in which it is exposed for the whole community to see and to react to. As a community of voices, the polyphonic women's choir incites a discourse of reparation by their acts of exposure. Witnessing this ritual act enables the reader, too, negotiate access to the healing community.

The ghostly voice of the reader in polyphony

Adisa's novel has a polyphonic structure in which certain characters serve to highlight the traditional aspects of the village life and certain characters incite change.[51] However, as Weir–Soley observes, in the novel

[51] Weir–Soley, *Eroticism, Spirituality, and Resistance*, 143.

> all the characters make up a seamless whole. Separately, they maintain their own individuality, but the many voices in the text delineate the structure of village life: a community made up of distinct individuals who need each other in order to survive as individuals and as a group.[52]

This condition of intersubjectivity in the novel means that the reader is required to abandon "conditioned expectations and enter the text prepared to deal with the radically unsettling potential of difference."[53] Weir-Soley remains implicit about the reading strategies employed by such a reader, but her injunction to discard readerly anticipations closely resembles the idea of reading in an affective, reparative manner. There, the reader is open to the dialogic dimension at play in the reading-event itself. Next, I consider what it might mean to read the polyphonic women's ritual as an affected reader participating in the novel's liberatory quest, while remaining cognizant all the while of the limited nature of such participation.

As stated in the last chapter with regard to Monica's suffering, the feelings of sympathy shared by the community's women who feel Monica's pain are not reserved for the reading subject. Instead, she must pay heed to her ghostly role in romancing her potential textual other – empathy. The reader must stay beside the text, and not move beyond her realm of experience to appropriate feelings that do not belong to her. As Pearce notes, the metaphor of ghostly reading helps us understand how readers can "enter texts from which they are notionally excluded."[54] As ghostly readers, we are able to move in and out of the texts that we read, but we are, of course, unable to intervene or change the characters and the events, which remain frozen in their fictional time and place. The ghostly ability of returning means that we, as readers, sometimes wander about texts long after the reading event.[55]

Although Pearce writes that, for her, it is evidently the readers who haunt texts and not vice versa, in my view texts do also haunt readers. This could be best characterized by borrowing a term from music which refers to the endless return of songs in their listeners' minds: an 'ear worm' is a loan translation from the German equivalent to referring to a melody, refrain, or phrase from a song that is repeated in the mind – often to the frustration of the person whom

---

52 Weir–Soley, *Eroticism, Spirituality, and Resistance*, 144.

53 *Eroticism, Spirituality, and Resistance*, 148.

54 Pearce, *Feminism and the Politics of Reading*, 96.

55 *Feminism and the Politics of Reading*, 2.

it affects. Reading can also be characterized by this potential of return, where certain words, sentences or scenes haunt us. We can see the interactive nature of this kind of haunting, comparable to Ahmed's idea of signs that are "sticky,"[56] and thus view it as useful for our readerly strategies of participating in Monica's ritual.

The way in which the reader can participate in the commonality of the ritual, I suggest, is by joining the ritualistic women's choir as a ghostly voice. Before Monica names her perpetrators, she is encouraged by the chorus, which urges her to speak out about the crime that she had to endure.

> After more than half an hour soaking in the warm water that was like expert hands massaging their bodies, Miss Cotton called the women together. They formed a circle and Dahlia and Velma raised the song, 'Dere is a meeting here today, come along now…' Olive and Valrie pulled Monica to the centre of the circle and immediately all the women splashed water on her. Through the crystal sheet of water they created, Monica looked like a torso in the centre of a glass sculpture.
>
> Arnella's firm voice broke through the spraying water.
>
> 'Call dem out. Name dose who peppa you. Name dem; dem not you sistas.'
>
> The other women echoed Arnella's words, until their collective voices were a mantra for retribution. All the women cleared their throats and spat in the water. Even Baby-Girl appeared to join the women voices when she began bawling, as if to shout too, 'Name dem'. Everyone except Althea and Monica was shouting, 'Name dem; dem is not you sistas. Call dem out'. (215–16)

The chant, which begins with Dahlia and Velma's duet, continues with the polyphonic choir of women demanding atonement. Everybody, including the newborn Baby-Girl, participates in voicing their need for Monica's retribution. This seems to suggest a replacement of the individual with the communal. However, the act of reading as an affective task may be here seen as the kind of politicization of affect which "reanimates the relation between the subject and a collective,"[57] for it is through the circulation of affects that we get to understand relationships between women as continua, and as political communities.

If we envisage the reader as a ghost, entering the story but not attempting to monopolize it, we may also further imagine this ghost as having a quiet

---

[56] Ahmed, *The Cultural Politics of Emotion*, 91.

[57] *The Cultural Politics of Emotion*, 171.

voice that joins this polyphonic choir of collective voices. If the ear worm is an Ahmedian sticky sign, then the reader's ghostly voice in polyphony is a way of reading that sings along to the reparative tune she hears in the healing women's voices. And yet, the reader's voice differs from those of the women calling for Monica to name her perpetrators. The ghostly voice of the reader, coupled with the women's voices in the choir, serves to create a "plurality of voices"[58] in the reading event, which together form a symphony. Thus, we need not assume that the community's collective voice means that a vocality of sameness would be the only way to participate in this ritual.

The constructed presence of a reading subject is integral to the texts for their meaning-potential to materialize. The presence of the dialogic Other is particularly important in a testimonial narrative that requires a witness for it to trigger political reactions. In fact, Sara Ahmed contends that "a politics which acts without reaction is impossible."[59] Literary texts with an emancipatory function apply to Ahmed's view of politics, as their potentials cannot be materialized without their readers; readers are vital for the survival of these testimonies and quests for liberation. Feng notes that the writing of literary accounts of healing is itself a ritual, and so is their reading.[60]

As the reader becomes increasingly aware of this interplay of individuality and collectivity by participating in Monica's ritual, she also needs to be aware of the ontological history of the women's collective energy. Much like Sophie's healing ceremony in Danticat's *Breath, Eyes, Memory*, the shared experience of the ritual marks a feminist endorsement of African ego-critical world-views. As Paget Henry writes in his account of traditional African philosophy, there is an ongoing "critique of egoism that resolves the contradictions of the latter in the idealism of religious spirituality."[61] Thus, the ego cannot create itself without being grounded in spirituality.[62] In the form of the ritual, this serves to fortify the Afro-Caribbean diaspora as what Gourdine calls "sistered kinship."[63] The sisterhood created by the women's community in *It Begins With Tears* shows how the women "propose a kinship system that

[58] Cavarero, *For More than One Voice*, 11.

[59] Ahmed, *The Cultural Politics of Emotion*, 174.

[60] Feng, "Rituals of Rememory," 157.

[61] Paget Henry, *Caliban's Reason: Introducing Afro-Caribbean Philosophy* (London & New York: Routledge, 2002): 62.

[62] Henry, *Caliban's Reason*, 63.

[63] Gourdine, *The Difference Place Makes*, 17.

recognizes the intellectual, social and (re)productive values of all its members."[64] The outcome of the ritual on the river attests to a defiance of peppering as a damaging tradition, in favor of an Afro-Caribbean woman-centred commitment to an embodied, corporeal energy, drawing its strength from a shared process of recovery from various oppressions and histories of violence.

According to Weir–Soley, Monica functions in the narrative as "a catalyst compelling the community to resolve some of its internal issues and possibly redefine itself."[65] Monica herself comes to "reassess her actions, her relationship to the community, and her role within Kristoff Village."[66] Through these re-negotiations, the reader is better educated about the communal relations striving for harmony in the story's frame. At the same time, the power of the erotic as called for by Audre Lorde is put to work to signal the vitality of sexuality in healing.[67] Readers, too, are asked to open themselves to being affected by these sexual healings through an intimate reading of the ritual in which she participates as an affective, ghostly voice.

No longer a stranger: Nellie and the first-person plural

As discussed in the previous chapter, Brodber's *Jane and Louisa* moves along with Nellie's life from her home village in Jamaica to the university in the USA, and then back to Jamaica. The metaphorical gardens of sexuality she discovers on the cyclical journey are not always pleasant and are, at times, destructive and damaging. However, after her breakdown and the help of her Aunt Alice and her male friend, Baba, Nellie comes to the realization that her healing process is well under way. However, the cleansing and "getting ready" is ongoing.[68] As Pearce remarks, the use of the first-person-plural pronoun has its consequences for the addressee,[69] and it is my task in this section to negotiate how the white feminist reader may participate in Nellie's communal healing process with Baba, Alice, Jane, and Louisa.

[64] Gourdine, *The Difference Place Makes*, 102.

[65] Weir–Soley, *Eroticism, Spirituality, and Resistance*, 151.

[66] Soley, *Eroticism, Spirituality, and Resistance*, 150.

[67] *Eroticism, Spirituality, and Resistance*, 153.

[68] *Jane and Louisa Will Soon Come Home*, 147.

[69] Pearce, *The Rhetorics of Feminism*, 22.

Nellie's healing process

In *Jane and Louisa,* shamed by her Aunt Becca and drawn into the whisper circle by the women's rumours and echoes about destructive sexuality, Nellie retreats into a kumbla and experiences a breakdown after her Marxist political group fails to gather impetus.

When Nellie enters her healing process, another important figure besides her childhood friend, Baba (who is discussed at length in the next chapter), is her Aunt Alice, who shows Nellie the importance of her family history and roots by telling and showing her stories about her ancestors. Serving as an antidote to Nellie's illness, Nellie's long-deceased favorite aunt visits her as a healing mediator.[70] In the return of Aunt Alice as a ghost we can again see the ways in which the living and the dead interact in Brodber's fiction, which helps in the negotiation of new paradigms of reality.[71] What is remarkable about the stories that Alice tells Nellie is that they are told through visual devices. With this multi-sensory method of healing, Brodber seems to suggest that finding one's voice in terms of language is not sufficient. Instead, a closer look at the ground conditions, the histories, on which voice(lessness) is constructed provides a way for Nellie to begin negotiating her identity. As Saunders remarks, this means that "the category of history is no longer a site of dormancy but an occasion for the growth of the subject's consciousness."[72] Aunt Alice helps breathe life into the silenced family histories previously invisible to Nellie.

In the chapters entitled "Spying glass" and "Moving camera," Nellie *sees* into the social history of her family, and with the help of these metaphorical devices, she is able to view her situation more accurately after emerging from the kumbla:

> Now the spying glass is a totally different affair. You can get in and out of it at will. You see and feel everything twice as acutely. Consider the bind for my tender flesh and eyes after nearly quarter of a century in my kumbla. (131)

The spying glass and the moving camera operated by Nellie's Aunt Alice give Nellie an insight into her family:

---

[70] Wilentz, *Healing Narratives*, 45.

[71] Saunders, "The Project of Becoming for Marlene Nourbese Philip and Erna Brodber," 150.

[72] "The Project of Becoming for Marlene Nourbese Philip and Erna Brodber," 142.

> Aunt Alice Whiting, great grandfather Will's daughter who never married but spent her time visiting, helping out here and there... Aunt Alice took out her projector again as if the true purpose of life was to show films. (132)

In this case, seeing becomes a positive, healing ability. Yet the power of the spoken word also achieves integral importance in Nellie's healing process, for it is on account of the fact that she "finds her language" that she emerges from her kumbla, in addition to the family stories told by Aunt Alice. However, Nellie's retreat into her kumbla in the first place is partly a result of the destructive use of language which drove her to seek refuge in the closure of a kumbla.

The first Anancy story discussed in relation to Nellie's kumbla in Chapter 2 depicted the destructive aspect of language, and how one may become trapped in the kumbla, as Anancy the spider was destroyed by the echo in the woods. As such, the echoes in the story are connected with Aunt Becca's teachings for Nellie and the whispers and rumours through which she learns about sexuality. The latter Anancy story, in which Anancy survives thanks to language as a kumbla, shows the protective and healing aspects of language through repetition of the phrase "Go eena kumbla." This healing aspect of language connects with the two people who help Nellie to emerge from her kumbla, Alice and Baba. They represent the protection and creativity that Nellie needs in order to break out of the kumbla that she inhabits, and to begin a process of re-creating her identity.

The family history that Nellie learns leads her to the realization that "I saw that if I knew all my kin [...] I could no longer roam as a stranger; that I had to know them to know what I was about" (80). Storytelling and orality are significant in this context: stories by slaves were told as a means of survival, where oral narration also had a healing role. The juxtaposition between echo and repetition in the two Anancy stories can be paralleled with the juxtaposition between rumour and storytelling that take place in Nellie's life. Both echo and rumours (whispers about the unwanted babies discussed in the previous chapter) in this novel have to do with loss: they are sounds that go around and eventually die out; contributing to the destruction of the self – whereas repetition is an important part of the act of storytelling. Stories are transmitted through breath, and they thus have to do with living and survival. In addition, the mnemonic device of repetition adds to the story and helps the audience make better sense of it. Similarly, the stories told by Aunt Alice help Nellie make sense of herself and her life, and they therefore play an integral role in the healing process. The negotiations over the sense-making of Nellie's healing, in turn, are the reader's task in following Nellie's cyclical journey into, and out of, the kumbla.

Who are 'we'?

The lyrics of the novel's eponymous ring game contain a sexual allusion in referring to "this beautiful garden." This highlights the ways in which sexuality is a site of productivity as well as regulation. As Carolyn Cooper points out, one of the most crucial themes of Brodber's *Jane and Louisa* is "female sexuality [...] in both its creative and destructive manifestations."[73] The creativity refers to the positive, productive potential of the sexual woman, but that is turned negative in the image of the womb as a maw and a place to deposit waste. Nellie remarks:

> So the black womb is a maw. [...] The black womb sucks grief and anger and shame but it does not spit. It absorbs them into its body. [...] What an abominable scrap heap thing is this thing womb. (143)

At the end of the narrative, Nellie remarks on the advancement of the process of liberation in the novel: "We are cleaning our garden" (147). For the purposes of participating in Nellie's healing process through reading, it is important to ponder who is being referred to by this phrase as well as the novel's last words, "We are getting ready" (147). The two 'we' sentences provide an interesting example of the interplay of the collective and the individual in linking Nellie's healing process to that of her cousins, Jane and Louisa. Thus, on the one hand, the phrases reveal that Nellie and her cousins have not yet managed to cleanse those gardens of the wrong, distorted image of sexuality they have inherited from their Aunt Becca, along with the rumours of the confined community and their own negative sexual experiences. Instead, they are in the process of doing so.

On the other hand, as Wilentz remarks with regard to another instance in the novel, it is difficult to determine in this multivocal narrative whom the novel's uses of "we" are referring to.[74] Lynne Pearce discusses the use of pronouns in feminist writing, where 'we' has multiple uses besides being "the

---

[73] Cooper, "Afro-Jamaican Folk Elements in Brodber's *Jane and Louisa Will Soon Come Home*," 281.

[74] Wilentz, *Healing Narratives*, 35.

archetypal we of sisterhood."[75] Pronouns have a strategic use in many authors' writing, and they "mean differently in different rhetorical contexts" (21). In the case of Nellie's 'we', it is the reader's task to clarify her personal relationship to the 'we' uttered in the final words of the novel. As Pearce remarks, pronouns work to position readers, and they position their readers variously, based on their particular relationships to the 'we' in question (46).

In this double-voiced discourse, 'we' denotes not only the shared process of unlearning and healing that Nellie, Jane, and Louisa are going through, but the 'we' can also be read to refer to a larger reading audience; attached to the textual other of empathy for a woman's self-realization and liberation from pain. Pearce remarks that Anne McClintock's narrative method in the presentation of her research material is "inductive" and that it "keeps the reader company throughout" (27). Brodber's 'we' draws the reader into the text in a comparable manner, as it is rewarding to feel included in the voicing of a collective identity. The use of the first-person-plural pronoun does invoke a sense of withness, as its articulation entails a certain sense of relationality. Pearce notes that, in some feminist theorizing, 'we' may have dialogic force which then includes the reader in the pronoun's deixis (39). As questions of belonging and participation are an inevitable feature of dialogism, which builds sites for multiple readers, this process of negotiation is particularly relevant in the context of the polysemous 'we' in Brodber's text.

A further instance in Brodber's work which raises a similar question of pronouns and belonging emerges through her definition of the 'I' as black. This time, the question is of the relationship between the writerly 'I' and the readerly 'I'. Brodber discusses the importance of Ethiopianism[76] for black emancipation, and does so in a manner that evokes emotions as a political force and invites us to reflect on how feelings are closely connected to thinking and action. Brodber's essay urges Caribbean intellectuals to turn to Ethiopianism for a "philosophy [...] on which to hang social and spiritual life."[77]

[75] Pearce, *The Rhetorics of Feminism*, 21. Further page references are in the main text.

[76] By 'Ethiopianism', Brodber refers to the afrocentric mind-set of transatlantic black thinkers, writers, and activists such as Marcus Garvey, Una Marson, and C.L.R. James, whose thought mobilizes black solidarity and collectivity. Brodber sees the Rastafarian religion as the epitome of contemporary Ethiopianism, and celebrates the reggae singer Bob Marley's use of Ethiopianist ideology as a political tool.

[77] Erna Brodber, "Re-engineering Blackspace," *Black Renaissance* 2.3 (1999–2000): 157. Further page references are in the main text.

Determining oneself as black or finding one's 'I' makes one feel (pain); assuming this 'I' "brings emotion, brings perspective, brings identification with our forefathers" (159). Despite not naming pain explicitly in calling for a collective identification with the pain and trauma of slavery, Brodber writes: "If you find yourself to be black, you will have great difficulty holding back the tears as you feel the lash on Cudjoe's back" (158). This self-identification leads to action, which will finally change the status of black people.

In other words, it is emotional response to racial injustice and the history of slavery that serves as a political impetus and source of action. It is also the lens through which the world is interpreted for a more just outcome, as Brodber notes: "To feel and to feel attached is not to commit the academic sin of distorting. It is to claim your psychological space" (159). Because Brodber's fiction and non-fiction cannot be viewed separately in terms of their political ideology, it is useful to think about the implications of these statements for a model of affective reading.[78] Those readers who do not see themselves as black surely have difficulty in assuming the 'I' that Brodber writes about when not wanting to appropriate an affective identity that is not reserved for them. The point of negotiation then arises for political agency for those who cannot assume the 'I' that feels Cudjoe's pain. Similarly, there is no reason to believe Brodber's 'we' in *Jane and Louisa* automatically includes a white reader. Quite clearly, a white reader does best to acknowledge her exclusion from the narrative's focus. However, narratorial exclusion does not rule out readerly participation. Thus, the inability to see oneself as black when reading Brodber does not amount to an inability to feel, much less an inability to feel responsively in a generous manner.[79]

Returning to Ahmed's contemplation of relating to the pain of the Other may help in negotiating the reader's relation to Brodber's personal pronouns in a project of the impossible. Ahmed writes about her experience of reading a government document recounting the painful stories of separation by the Stolen Generations of Indigenous children in Australia. Ahmed writes about the pain of one child's mother:

> We can't feel her pain, her ache; and yet, we are moved by the story. It is a hurt that refuses to keep us apart, but also does not bring us together. I know enough of this pain to know the limits of what I can

[78] On Brodber's political ideology in her writing, see Saunders, "The Project of Becoming for Marlene Nourbese Philip and Erna Brodber," 151.

[79] On generosity and response, see Ahmed, *Strange Encounters*, 149.

> know, reading as I am in this time and this place, with this body, arranged as it is, here, now.[80]

The inability to assume the subject-position of the one who feels pain does not lead to the reader's affective immobility. In fact, it teaches us the limits of our knowledge, and at the same time creates an awareness of our own selves in the particular situational context of reading. The process of relating to an Other subject (or subjects) is thus also a process of relating to the self. Thus, Brodber's 'we' in *Jane and Louisa* and her black intellectual's 'I' inevitably invite ontological scrutiny for all kinds of reading subjects.

Nellie's statements "We are cleaning our garden" and "we are getting ready" then mark a place of fundamental ambivalence when in contact with a white reader: she is at the same time excluded from and included in the pronoun's meaning. For Ien Ang, ambivalence in "doing cultural studies at the crossroads" is vital.[81] According to her, it is simply not enough to benevolently 'tolerate' ambivalence, because tolerance is never unconditional and is thus not a valid base for equality.[82] In fact, tolerance only serves to strengthen the (white feminist) epistemic privilege as it attempts to democratize its hegemony.[83] Instead, accepting the paradoxicality of ambivalence presents us, as readers, with a way to engage with texts which seem to both include and exclude us at the same time.

Learning to deal with such an impossible scenario is in line with the utopian drive in feminism that enables us (feminists) to deal with difficult issues without the illusion of a panacea in the form of our answers. Such an impossible scenario is at hand when we see Brodber's 'we' as shorthand for the complex relationships between the potentially multiple agents in the novel's sexual liberation processes and their readers. In reading, we learn the limits of our areas of knowledge, yet we do not cease to look for points of exit from those areas. Ahmed again captures the way in which our readings may shed light on the limits of our knowability:

> It ["The call of pain that cannot be shared"] is a call for action, and a demand for collective politics, as a politics based no on the possibility that we might be reconciled, but on learning to live with the impos-

80 Ahmed, *The Cultural Politics of Emotion*, 38.

81 Ang, *On Not Speaking Chinese*, 187.

82 *On Not Speaking Chinese*, 143.

83 *On Not Speaking Chinese*, 197.

> sibility of reconciliation, or learning that we live with and beside each other, and yet we are not as one.[84]

Gaining the knowledge of existing "beside" and "yet not as one" comes close to Dawn Rae Davis's argument of love as the ability of not knowing:

> love is the impossible experience of knowing across radical difference, and simultaneously, that which requires ethical choice and action even in the face of the impossible.[85]

Davis identifies love as a problem for feminist postcolonial theory and philosophy, because it is based on the benevolence of Christian humanism, which has strong ties with the violent mastery of colonialism. According to her,

> the ability of *not knowing* reconstitutes the *will to know* so that a feminist beholding of the Other woman is a witnessing of the *impossibility* of her appearance in the context of anything demarcated as knowability.[86]

To love the other, in other words, is (not) to know her. Put simply: engaging with the impossible need not be a matter of celebrating ignorance, but rather, a matter of acknowledging our ways of knowing as flawed, imperfect and fundamentally ambivalent.[87]

As Nellie utters the ambivalent words "We are cleaning our garden" towards the end of the narrative, she soon dreams of childbirth, where she is about to deliver a fish; an indigenous symbol of fertility. As the narrative approaches its end, it is getting ready to let Nellie give birth to what has grown inside her throughout the novel; budding womanhood. This idea of giving birth can be parallelled with Brodber's thoughts of the time when she first began writing: "This activity [writing] was to me like vomiting and defecating."[88] As writing comes back to the body and its functions and capabilities, so does Nellie's sexual healing. Yet, the passage ought not to be interpreted as a completion of self traditionally witnessed at the end of a Western, linear, phallocentric *Bildungsroman*. Instead, one can see Nellie beginning to move

---

[84] Ahmed, *The Cultural Politics of Emotion*, 39.

[85] Dawn Rae Davis, "(Love Is) the Ability of Not Knowing: Feminist Experience of the Impossible in Ethical Singularity," *Hypatia* 17.2 (Spring 2002): 146.

[86] Davis, "(Love Is) the Ability of Not Knowing," 155 (italics in original).

[87] "(Love Is) the Ability of Not Knowing," 155.

[88] Brodber, "Fiction in the Scientific Procedure," 165.

into the direction of wholeness.[89] As Saunders notes, Brodber is concerned not so much with the "end result" as with the process of becoming itself.[90]

Thus, when Nellie utters her final words in the novel, "We are getting ready," she uses the present-progressive form highlighting the ongoing process instead of a completed event. Saying "We are ready" would dismantle the processual nature of the narrative and the self, and instead focus on ways of *being* instead of *becoming*. This process of becoming is also crucial to readers: the reading process should not be viewed as an achievement of completion or, to use Sedgwick's terms, as a preoccupation with origin and telos.[91] Rather, reading is a flowing, cyclical activity which contains the promise of a return of joy, belonging, and withness.

⌘

---

[89] See Wilentz, *Healing Narratives*, 35.

[90] Saunders, "The Project of Becoming for Marlene Nourbese Philip and Erna Brodber," 151.

[91] Sedgwick, *Touching Feeling*, 8.

5 Shadow(ing) Men – Visions of Caring Masculinities

Erna Brodber, Opal Palmer Adisa, and Shani Mootoo

WOMEN WHO ARE HEALING from negative sexual affects such as violence and shame need the help of other women as a collective. But Caribbean women writers also often include men in women's liberatory quests as participants: helpers, healers or caregivers. My focus here is on how to read *the men in the shadows* who are also sometimes involved with helping the women heal. Writing against the negative ways in which masculinity is predominantly conceived in the Caribbean, writers who include men (including those whose male sex is ambivalent or shadowed) in the women's healing processes show how women's liberatory quests for (sexual) healing are not self-evidently and solely gynocentric in the Caribbean context.[1] Rather, like the recent interest in men and masculinity in the region, it shows how men are often active participants in these processes, hence also in gender reconfigurations.[2] The oft-noted complementarity of the sexes in the Caribbean[3] becomes expanded when men themselves contest patriarchal limits of agency which in these women writers' creative imaginings also extends to the roles of helper, healer, and nurturer, positions hitherto largely unavailable to men without feminization by default.

---

[1] On masculinity as negative, see Linden Lewis, "Caribbean Masculinity: Unpacking the Narrative," in *The Culture of Gender and Sexuality in the Caribbean*, ed. Linden Lewis (Gainesville: UP of Florida, 2003): 98.

[2] Lewis, "Caribbean Masculinity: Unpacking the Narrative," 121.

[3] "Caribbean Masculinity: Unpacking the Narrative," 120.

Examples of this alternative role of men as helpers, healers or caregivers – or, in general, as human beings with detailed emotions and affective lives – can be seen, for instance, in the character of the Rastafarian Baba in Brodber's *Jane and Louisa*, Reuben in Brodber's *Louisiana*, and Desmond in Opal Palmer Adisa's *It Begins with Tears*. Further examples of men as co-conspirators in the face of female antagonism against women can be seen in Edwidge Danticat's *Breath, Eyes, Memory*, where Sophie escapes her mother's 'testing' into marriage with the African-American musician Joseph, and Martine's boyfriend, Marc, does his best to help her stay sane as her psyche crumbles. In addition, characters such as the transgendered Nurse Tyler in Shani Mootoo's *Cereus Blooms at Night* further manifests the ways in which gender relations are renegotiated in healing processes. As Kaisa Ilmonen notes, in Mootoo's novel as well as in the novels of Lawrence Scott and Michelle Cliff, transgendered characters act as nurses, healers, helpers or caregivers whose task is not only to heal other characters but also "to heal the traumas of history caused by Eurocentric binary thinking while re-signifying the fixed gender structures of colonial modernity."[4] Men, be they traditionally masculine or transgendered, are afforded a similar healing role in the texts mentioned above, when segregation dissolves and traumas become reworked in solidarity between the sexes.

This chapter focuses more closely on the roles of Baba in Brodber's *Jane and Louisa* and Desmond in Adisa's *It Begins with Tears,* as, of the other men characters mentioned above, these two have a similarly peripheral but important role in the narrative quests of healing and liberation. By contrast, Marc in Danticat's novel, for example, does not manage to help Martine, as her traumatized condition is beyond help and she ends up committing suicide.

On the other hand, the formerly male nurse, Tyler, in Mootoo's novel participates in different gender renegotiations from those operating on the complementarity axis, as Baba and Desmond do. Reading Tyler's relationship with Mala, his/her patient, is the topic of the other half of this chapter. In reading the shadow men's participation at a critical moment of crisis in the lives of Nellie, Monica, and Mala, the three healing women in Brodber, Adisa, and Mootoo, I argue that the affective moments between the healing men and the

---

[4] Kaisa Ilmonen, "Healing the Traumas of History: (Trans)sexual Diasporas in Caribbean Literature," in *Seeking the Self – Encountering the Other: Diasporic Narrative and the Ethics of Representation*, ed. Tuomas Huttunen, Janne Korkka, Kaisa Ilmonen & Elina Valovirta (Newcastle upon Tyne: Cambridge Scholars, 2008): 230.

recovering women serve as catalysts for healing and liberation where segregation dissolves and more democratic gender relations can be envisaged. The men's role as minor characters whose function is to help the women recuperate shows how the presence of supportive men does not warrant a takeover but, rather, participation. This reading will shed more light on the "contradictory ways in which sex is viewed in the Caribbean"[5] and show that, at times, moments of gender harmony do exist, even more so when the basis of gender as complementary is called into question, as in Mootoo's novel.

Highlighting non-normative sexualities and shared feelings as a liberating force, Mootoo's novel introduces a special perspective that is central to reading from an affective point of view: the narrative positions the reader in a reparative atmosphere where non-heterosexual feelings serve to create a community, and are thus productive. So far, my treatment of the novels and their reading has been organized by discussing them separately – but here I move towards merging the two in the remaining part of the book.

While the first section of this chapter discusses heterosexual relationships, the other section is an attempt to map Caribbean queer feelings in reading. The ensuing discussion of the relationships of Baba, Desmond, and Tyler with their healing women has a further concern besides interpreting representations of male or transgendered characters as sexual healers of women, and this dual focus of my discussion has to do with how the participation of these men could be read from an outsider reading position. How to negotiate the differently situated reader's access to the text? Men and women come together in cooperation within the novels, but their shared moments of healing also serve to position the reader in a framework that calls for a reconsideration of earlier, essentialist gender relations.

Baba and Desmond, the healing men

The phenomenon of men as healer or helpers can be read as Caribbean women writers' desire and need to reconfigure and re-imagine the lives of men in the Caribbean from women's points of view. The men re-envisaged by women writers are portrayed as caring participants in women's quests to heal from wounds inflicted by internalized misogyny on the part of other women. The oft-neglected role of men as facilitators and nurturers of female sexual healing in the Caribbean challenges the prototypical notion of black

[5] Narain, "Standing in the Place of Love," 336.

Caribbean masculinity as absent or abusive. Lewis maintains that Caribbean men are essentialized in research literature and society as "promiscuous, derelict in his parental duties, often absent from the household and, if present, unwilling to undertake his share of domestic responsibilities."[6] This negative caricature of men is also echoed by media representations, which tend to highlight gangs, street violence, and drug trafficking as men's primary arena of activity. In fact, Erin Skye Mackie makes the point that there is a long history in the Caribbean of celebrating outlaw culture, mostly entailing male figures such as the pirate, the rude boy, or the thug.[7]

When men take part in healing, this further expands our notions of gender relations, and thus also our notions of women as gendered. Casting a look at moments in fiction where gynocentric, woman-headed activities recede in favour of male participation and even guidance will help us see gender relations in the Caribbean as much less restricted and more open to fluctuation than the stereotype of the 'strong Caribbean woman' as solely matrifocal as problematized by Rowley and Momsen.

Baba, the healing Rastafarian

When the protagonist, Nellie, in Brodber's novel experiences a mental and physical breakdown, it is the Rastafarian Baba who cares for her. Burnt-out, Nellie is taken into the home of her childhood friend, Baba Ruddock, who helps her to break the whisper circle and "clean her garden" of the distorted images of sexuality that she has inherited. Maureen Warner–Lewis notes that in Baba's character we can see one of the traditional roles of the Rastafarian as a healer and a caregiver.[8] A healing man like Desmond in Adisa's *It Begins With Tears*, Baba looks after Nellie after her breakdown, but he does not let her take advantage of his caring and his comfortable apartment. Nellie grows frustrated by Baba's word-play, humour, and language.

For example, when Nellie wants to go out for the first time after her breakdown, Baba refuses to go with her. An argument follows in which Nellie hurls

6 Lewis, "Caribbean Masculinity: Unpacking the Narrative," 107.

7 Erin Skye Mackie, "Welcome the Outlaw: Pirates, Maroons and Caribbean Countercultures," *Cultural Critique* 59 (Winter 2005): 24–62.

8 Maureen Warner–Lewis, "Rastafarianism (The Caribbean)," in *Encyclopedia of Post-Colonial Literatures in English* ed. Eugene Benson & L.W. Conolly (London: Routledge, 1994): 1345.

violent insults at Baba, who remarks calmly: "You have found your language."[9] The tenderness and caring he offers to Nellie make her unwilling to leave the safe environment of his house, after all. But he drives her out by destabilizing her sense of comfort and security with the question "aren't you supposed to be going somewhere" (72). Nellie's pride forces her to venture out into the world and experience the flowing, cyclical, and regenerative effects of dance as a social activity that brings enjoyment.

As Nellie's healing advances, she offers Baba a gesture of returning the favour, as with the boy in the cinema earlier on in the novel. She tries to seduce Baba. Showing little respect for her own sexual body, Nellie responds to Baba's care in the only way she knows; sexually:

> I even stripped one night and though he was obviously excited, he said just as matter-of-factly as at any other time:
> –That will come later. After I have met you.–
> Blast him. (69)

In this affective moment, Baba helps Nellie to come to terms with her sexuality, as by turning down Nellie's advances he does not allow her to abuse her self. An illegitimate child himself, Baba is fully aware of the negative image of the womb as a scrap-heap and the whispers and rumours about unwanted babies and their mothers. Refusing to take advantage of Nellie in her time of recuperation, he turns down her sexual approaches:

> I know you want to give yourself but I fear you offer yourself because you don't want you. That's something you throw on a scrap heap. We won't forage for a thing in a scrap heap. (71)

Later, Nellie comes to understand Baba's rejection as an act of caring, whereby he wishes to promote a healthy view of sexuality, where Nellie learns to see herself as desirable in her own right.

Perhaps stemming from his childhood experiences, Baba as therapist wants something better for Nellie than the self-hating and shaming view of sexuality she is possessed by, where she sees her womb as a scrap-heap and a sucker of "grief and anger and shame" (143). By his gentle manipulation of her desire as negative, Nellie realizes that Baba's rejection is in fact meant as a pedagogical gesture. She observes the sexually shamed and abandoned women around her and muses: "He spoke their words for them. So this was what

[9] *Jane and Louisa Will Soon Come Home*, 71. Further page references are in the main text.

Baba knew and was trying to steer me past" (143). Baba's refusal to reproduce the image of female sexuality as a destructive void of no worth helps Nellie to see how his rejection of her advances is an attempt to help her recuperate the long-suffering women's sexual integrity. In this scenario where he "speaks their words for them," Baba does not so much take vocal agency from the women as ventriloquizes what has previously been left unobserved by Nellie, who has been absorbed by her own worries and antagonism towards other shamed women, such as her Aunt Becca. Baba's participation in Nellie's healing shows how, despite highlighting the struggles of female protagonists and women's communities, Brodber does not see healing and emancipation as solely gynocentric but, rather, as complemented by the cooperation of caring men – in Nellie's case, Baba.

Desmond, the adulterous healer

In Adisa's novel, a comparable moment of healing takes place between Desmond and Monica, two adulterous lovers. The morning following the act of violence by the three jealous women, Monica's lover Desmond learns of the violent deed and rushes to Monica's house. In an extended scene of healing, Adisa depicts the curative power of sex and sexuality, as Desmond performs oral sex on Monica in a gesture of healing:

> He blew his love-breath and ran his tongue over every space, every fold, every membrane of Monica's private self, and imagined that he felt her healing under the moist attention.[10]

In this scene with Desmond and Monica, Donna Weir–Soley wishes to privilege the spiritual meaning of Desmond's healing gesture. According to her, in helping Monica by licking her violated body, "Desmond helps to absorb, and thus share, in the pain that is a result of their transgressive lovemaking."[11] At the same time, however, we cannot ignore how this act of oral sex brings a change to the sexual politics that has previously characterized Monica's existence as a provider of pleasure. In this scene, Monica's former role as a prostitute who provides sexual pleasure is set aside as she is depicted as the recipient of sexual pleasure, in contrast to the perpetual giver whose body can be used by men at will.

---

[10] *It Begins With Tears*, 156–57.

[11] Weir–Soley, *Eroticism, Spirituality, and Resistance*, 178.

This scene works as an antithesis to the scene in Brodber's *Jane and Louisa*, where Nellie gives oral sex to a boy in the cinema in seeking to win acceptance. In contrast, Desmond'*s* sexual healing eases Monica's pain and also allows Desmond to take his share of the responsibility for what happened to her, for, as a married man, Desmond was himself the actual adulterer. Adisa's depiction of oral sex stands out in Caribbean women's writing for its explicit presentation of sex as a source of healing. In this scene in particular, she politicizes sex and sexuality as liberatory, as something that sustains and preserves life. In Weir–Soley's view, this scene is the place in the novel where the earlier gender segregation dissolves as Desmond participates in the women's healing ritual by orally removing the pepper from inside Monica.[12] The two contrasting examples of oral sex in Adisa and Brodber's novels are not enough to suggest a paradigm shift regarding oral sex in Caribbean literature. However, from toe-sucking to French kisses and beyond, the recent literary anthology co-edited by Adisa and Weir–Soley, *Caribbean Erotic*, displays a collective deliberation of orality as an aspect of sex that needs to be accounted for in literature which has largely shunned it.[13] In particular, the poems by Adisa and others in the anthology share a striking similarity in enunciating a decidedly oral dimension of sex and love-making, where the act of oral sex is celebrated as liberatory, vital, and stripped of taboos.

Reading healing men in and from the shadows

In reading the intimate healing moments between the men and women in Brodber and Adisa's novels, my ultimate concern is how a feminist reader should, or could, participate in such emancipations. As I argued above, reading the novels' emancipatory processes may cause a feminist reader's emotional investment and attachment to surface. In the case of Desmond and Monica and Baba and Nellie, however, the momentary dissolution of patriarchal gender roles does not signify a likewise dissolution of other difference-based power-structures such as differences in the reader and characters' race, culture or sexuality. It would be all too easy for the affective reader to jump at the chance to melt into the process.

[12] Weir–Soley, *Eroticism, Spirituality, and Resistance*, 183.

[13] *Caribbean Erotic: Poetry, Prose & Essays*, ed. Adisa & Weir–Soley.

Instead of dwelling on feminist attachment in the form of sympathy or compassion in the face of healing relationships, I propose strategies of participating and witnessing without the need to impose oneself on the other. Engaging with the healing men and their women requires a respectful distance for an ethically informed reading, as the caring men's affection to the women they nurture is not a position offered for the Western reader.

When Desmond takes responsibility for Monica's suffering by taking on her pain, he sympathizes with her like the village women who give Monica first aid. Desmond feels Monica's pain in sympathy with her suffering even before he learns of the incident: "The image of Monica pained him."[14] Devastated upon hearing of the incident, Desmond rushes to Monica's side and likewise cries before removing the remaining peppers from inside her, causing him to feel slight consolation, as "the fire was now inside his mouth."[15] Both Desmond's and the women's sympathizing serves as a catalyst for action and reparation. Here, in fact, sympathy (adopting the pain of the other) serves a redeeming function, since it makes others respond to the act of violence to which Monica has been subjected.

In responding to the act of violence, however, the reader should be careful not to cross the limits of the intimate village community. The question in meaning-making through affectivity is thus not only to embrace the affective fallacy but also to know where one's limits of participation are. In this way, the affective fallacy becomes redefined, not as the New Critics meant by reductively rejecting it, but as a feminist tool of reading which serves as a touchstone for knowing one's place in the face of "sticky" affects like a desire to sympathize which can in fact turn into violence.[16] An ethical refusal to take the other's place by adopting Monica's pain becomes especially challenging when Adisa's frequent internal focalization of Monica invites us to sympathize with her, as we are granted full access to her feelings, thoughts, and experience of suffering.

When Nellie in Brodber's novel realizes that she is engaged in a healing process by remarking "We are cleaning our garden," she not only understands what she, Jane, and Louisa are going through but she also learns to come to terms with the larger community of the novel's sexually damaged women, the

---

[14] Adisa, *It Begins With Tears*, 138.

[15] *It Begins With Tears*, 156.

[16] On sticky affects and sympathy as violence, see Ahmed, *The Cultural Politics of Emotion*, 91, 35.

Letitias, Teenas, and Cousin Bs with unwanted babies whom Baba as an abandoned boy knew so well.[17] Desmond and Monica's affective moment of healing in the form of oral sex denotes a similar scenario of ambivalent belonging to that of Brodber's multi-deictic 'we'. There, the sympathy involved in Desmond feeling Monica's pain is not reserved for the reading subject.

While the novel may enjoin the reader to move closer in, it may at the same time reject the Western reader's advances, thereby causing the reader to become a stranger towards and within the text. These differences emerging in and from the reading process have to do with an ongoing dialogue of proximity and distance; the reader is simultaneously close to and far from the 'object' of study. Velma Pollard makes reference to this process of inclusion and exclusion in speaking of "the foreign reader" when discussing the ways in which Caribbean women's writing has transformed painful histories into creative memory.[18] Such an "outsider," according to Pollard, may have difficulties with the creole stylistics in Caribbean women's writing.[19] Pollard's acknowledgment of the differences within a reading audience is important, as it shows how texts themselves and their linguistic strategies (here in the form of creole language use) may invite certain types of readers to feel 'at home' and others to be constructed as 'foreign'.

In the case of reading Baba and Desmond's engagement with their healing women, the question is not only about what kinds of readers are excluded from the narrative's focus through narrative strategies such as creole use. The question is also about the power of fluid stories' agency to glide into their readers through the creative powers of the reader's imagination. In that sense, texts pull their readers in but at the same time can escape the reader's attempts at definition: what follows is a zooming in and out of the reading lens. The reader needs to remain cognizant of her limited role of participating in scenarios which seemingly welcome sympathy and "wish-feelings," but in fact, when applied, may be harmful as a uniform reading strategy.

Visiting literary landscapes as a foreigner conscious of her outsider status thus makes the reader a tourist of sorts. In fact, the reading of postcolonial fiction and the whole postcolonial literary market rely on a "touristic con-

---

[17] Brodber, *Jane and Louisa Will Soon Come*, 143.

[18] Velma Pollard, "History and Caribbean Women's Writing: The Transformation of History by Creative Memory," in *Swinging Her Breasts at History: Language, Body and the Caribbean Woman's Text*, ed. Moira Inghilleri (London: Mango, 2006): 158.

[19] Pollard, "History and Caribbean Women's Writing," 160.

science" developed by its recipients.[20] Comparably, Angeletta Gourdine discusses the Caribbean as a site of identity-transformation for tourists of all kinds. In the formation of the literary tourist, Gourdine includes certain migrant Caribbean authors, such as Edwidge Danticat in one of her non-fiction texts, visiting their homelands as "native tourists."[21] However, the idea of textual touristing and "traveler behavior" can be applied to readers, too.[22] The reader in this model is an outsider or textual tourist; constructed as a stranger in the reading process. But, like tourists engaging in a continuous dialogue between their surroundings and their views of 'home', so do outsider readers connect with texts they read on multiple planes of experience, not just cultural.

If we concentrate on the worst-case scenario in order to tackle the potential risks involved in reading cross-culturally, Gourdine warns that literary tourism may involve

> ritualized behavior that follows the colonial script: modern person travels to premodern historically frozen place, hoping to explore both internal and external unknowns.[23]

This may lead to what Ahmed refers to as "stranger fetishism," referring to an ahistorical, ontological view of the Other as an objectified fetish rather than a contextual figure.[24] Treading the unfamiliar territory of the reading event as a strange encounter then requires the reader to be open to the elements of surprise, conflict, and differentiation. Paying heed to this aspect of differentiation helps the reader to be a conscientious outsider reader; a textual tourist with a consideration for the social markers that assume relevance in that particular context.

In the previous chapter, I adopted Pearce's idea of ghostly reading as a strategy that helps an outsider reader to engage with the novels' gynocentric healing processes without unethically inserting oneself into the culturally situated rituals of healing. A ghostly reader's role enables the reader to take into account how Baba's language and Desmond's love-breath are reserved for Nellie and Monica. While the journeys to healing advance, the reader as a

---

[20] Brouillette, *Postcolonial Writers in the Global Literary Marketplace*, 5.

[21] Angeletta Gourdine, "Caribbean *Tabula Rasa*: Textual Touristing as Carnival in Contemporary Caribbean Women's Writing," *Small Axe* 10.2 (2006): 83.

[22] Gourdine, "Caribbean *Tabula Rasa*," 80.

[23] "Caribbean *Tabula Rasa*," 81.

[24] Ahmed, *Strange Encounters*, 3.

ghost may also be envisaged as a follower on the road to recovery without needing an invitation. Sara Ahmed discusses the condition of following "as a form of commitment as well as a social investment."[25] Seeking a "good" reading requires that we follow directions, our reading strategies, properly, as "bad readings just won't get us there."[26] Building an epistemic line of inquiry from the shadows of Nellie and Monica's paths with Baba and Desmond not only breaks the binary of knowledge-production processes imaged through the metaphors of coming to light from the darkness of ignorance, but also overturns the idea of shadowing as stalking when seen in a performative manner. Here, a shadowing reading can be seen as creating a path to knowledge by observing the signs (the text) closely. As Ahmed explains, a path can be seen as "a trace of past journeys" which then becomes performative by allowing repeated activities such as reading to take place on the same ground but by different steps and treaders.

To illustrate the idea of shadowing as a fruitful reading strategy to engage with the healing women's relationships with their healing men, I adopt Eve Kosofsky Sedgwick's use of cats' behaviour to exemplify a complex philosophical issue.[27] Sedgwick explains how cats, instead of seeking praise, may in fact be offering education to humans with their prey by showing how humans, too, can learn to catch their own food. According to Sedgwick, this is a case of failed pedagogy, as humans narcissistically read the cat's demonstration of predatory behaviour as a gift.[28] Heeding cats may also help us understand how shadowing reading works. As we know, cats often have the tendency to follow a stroller uninvited, but they do so from a distance, occasionally popping into the safety of shadows, bushes, and other pathside shelters. A cat is always on its own, seemingly directionless, journeying even when appearing to follow. In the same way, a shadowing reader takes the scenic route by employing reading as following; always retaining her own identity and experiences even when participating in the formation-processes of others.

---

[25] Sara Ahmed, *Queer Phenomenology: Orientations, Objects, Others* (Durham NC & London: Duke UP, 2006): 17.

[26] Ahmed, *Queer Phenomenology*, 17.

[27] Sedgwick's example deals with Buddhist pedagogy on dying and death, and she illustrates this by turning to two examples of cat behaviour.

[28] Sedgwick, *Touching, Feeling*, 153–54.

This view of reading as shadowing from a respectful distance without stalking may, then, serve to demonstrate how affective engagement with a text may provide us with a "lifeline," as Ahmed sees it: a redemptive reading as "something that saves us."[29]

In this model of reading even moments of disconnection and incommensurability in the text–reader relationship, such as the inability to enter fully into the healing women's relationships, actually serve to *fuel* the dynamic of reading. Sara Ahmed's remark on global feminism is particularly instructive in this respect: "a dialogue must take place, precisely *because* we don't speak the same language."[30] This seemingly paradoxical claim asserts that the project of producing cross-cultural feminist knowledge is a matter of acting in the borderlands of the impossible. It is clear that working with what remains ungraspable in full is always a project of partiality, as Ang suggests.[31] The project of the impossible seems to slip away every time one thinks one has grasped it. Therefore, perhaps it is best to settle for light strokes instead of clenched fists whenever the project of the impossible allows itself to be touched.

In these reparative and participatory men as imagined by Caribbean women writers, we may detect desires to rewrite men as fictional characters beyond monolithic and stereotypical representations, wherein literature serves an affective function, one that opens more ways for 'withness' and empathy between men and women. It is these women writers' perhaps conciliatory way to show how the inclusion of men is indispensable to women's emancipatory endeavours, thus, through their portrayals of these imagined, phantasmatic masculinities, suggesting that in fact men, too, participate in healing feelings. Furthermore, by breaking the complementarity of sexes by which gender is defined in oppositional terms, notions of gender become revised "beyond trite dichotomies."[32] These portraits are also a way to carve out fictional spaces for idealized, caring, intimate relationships between men and women in the Caribbean. In my view, it also suggests that processes of liberation are open for participation and that they can and do take place across differences. These feeling men, in their affective moments with women healing from sexual transgression, violence, and shame, are examples of encoun-

---

[29] Ahmed, *Queer Phenomenology*, 17.

[30] *Strange Encounters*, 180.

[31] Ang, *On Not Speaking Chinese*, 192.

[32] Lewis, "Caribbean Masculinity: Unpacking the Narrative," 107.

ters where participation in the suffering and the healing of the other may serve as a catalyst for more democratic and liberated futures.

In addition to challenging the normative oppositional gender model in the cultural context of the Caribbean, an affective reading of men's participation in women's healing can open up new vistas for reading across cultures. Global readership engaging with literature through differences defining the reading process may gain new and expanded insight into the complex gender relations in Caribbean literature by women, where the contributions of these minor characters, Desmond and Baba, to women's needs at a critical moment in their lives may be seen to serve the function of rehabilitating images of men from the stereotypes that have previously defined their gender in the region. Reading these imagined therapeutic moments of harmony and co-operation, where men and women share common goals and objectives, may allow the shadowing global reader to witness negotiations of gender and thus produce more ethically grounded knowledge and meanings that no longer rely on previous essentialist paradigms.

The ethics of empathy and reading in Shani Mootoo's *Cereus Blooms at Night*

A process of becoming, as in many of the texts discussed in this book, is also at play in Shani Mootoo's novel *Cereus Blooms at Night*. However, the novel differs from the texts discussed so far, in that here the narrator–protagonist, Tyler, narrates his male-to-female gender identity into existence through the telling of Mala Ramchandin's life story. Emerging from the shadows of his male self is a caring (wo)man who engages in a healing relationship with Mala, the aging and ailing woman. Reading *Cereus,* I bring together the idea of the Caribbean queer and affectivity in order to investigate the role of reading in the ethics of empathy at play in Mootoo's novel. The question then becomes that of how to read the "queer feelings" or, as Sara Ahmed claims, "the affective potential of queer."[33] My goals in this section are again twofold and interlinked: to demonstrate that the development of the relationship between the central characters, Tyler and Mala, requires a simultaneous consideration of the dialogic and affective text–reader relationship that arises from the narrative – particularly with respect to Tyler's identification and empathy as a narrator. Mootoo's novel is a prime example of how the reader needs to nego-

[33] Ahmed, *The Cultural Politics of Emotion*, 146.

tiate the ethical implications of Tyler's narrative power in order to continue reading the processes of sexual healing in the way they have been discussed in this chapter.

The extraordinary text–reader relationship arising in the novel from the refusal of the text to explicitly indicate or name certain sexual identities (such as m-to-f transsexual in the case of Tyler, lesbian in the case of Mala Ramchandin's mother Sarah and her Aunt Lavinia, or f-to-m transsexual in the case of Otoh Mohanty) requires consideration, lest the Western reader's readiness to administer labels take over. Arising from Tyler and Mala's relationship, as filtered through Tyler's narration, such a reading sees them in a complex interaction that raises questions of the dialogic power of the narrative to move and position the reading subject. If Tyler's vision of his "shared queerness" with Mala is to be read as nothing but a wish, then it projects its textual positioning onto the reader, too, and potentially produces a reading that is based on a view of empathy as simple identification, as Ahmed's "taking the other's place." An exploration of Tyler and Mala's relationship through consideration of its ethics as implicating the reader's response may shed light on how "a shared queerness" is a form of withness, as theorized by Ahmed, and how the reading process may employ a sense of wonder as a sense-making strategy.

Cereus Blooms at Night highlights the importance of coming to terms with one's queer identity through cooperative sharing – as expressed by its key phrase "shared queerness."[34] Tyler and Mala's relationship in the narrative process is one that practises the act and philosophy of 'withness' discussed above. The affective process of withness then becomes a way of conceptualizing a queer reading of Caribbean feelings.

Tyler's empathy: textual positionings

When Mala Ramchandin is transferred to the nursing home, Tyler assumes the role of caregiver, as the rest of the nursing staff refuse to go near her. In fact, they do not hide their disdain for either of the two; Mala is ostracized because of the rumours about her as the sexually abused (and thus deranged) killer of her father, whereas Tyler is rejected because of his unmanly demeanour. Tyler instantly feels a sense of affinity with Mala; the catatonic,

[34] *Cereus Blooms at Night*, 48.

withering old woman tied to her bed. Tyler narrates his feelings shortly after he has first met Mala:

> She was beginning to perturb me, not because I feared her but rather because I felt an *empathy* for her clenched fists, defiant stare, pursed lips and deep, slow, calculated breathing – an *empathy* that words alone cannot describe.[35]

My attention is drawn here to the word "empathy," which represents for Tyler a force far greater than its verbalization is able to convey. The meaning-potential of Tyler's empathy can work as a method to understand the narrative on (at least) two levels: first, on the level of Mala's story (as told by Tyler) in an effort to reach Mala's sister, Asha, to reconnect with Mala. There, Tyler's affection for Mala in the form of empathy, "shared queerness," helps Tyler make sense of – and come to terms with – himself (as a transgendered individual, although such a term is never mentioned in the novel). At the same time, Mala is very much Tyler's key to entering his chosen profession and, later, his transgendered self. The body of the elderly woman, as an instrument for Tyler's self-actualization, thus also invites ethical scrutiny. Second, and connected with Tyler's empathy for Mala, this empathy can be read as a potential "textual other" through which the story is mediated to the reader.[36] The reader gains access to the text: i.e. Mala's story, only through Tyler's affinity and benevolence towards the old woman. This filtered narration is not without its consequences.

How does the text, Tyler's narrative, position the reader in Tyler's empathy, verbalized as 'shared queerness'? What does it entail? A common identity? Sameness? Or what are the differences that allow the sharing to take place? In narrating his experience of growing up as an individual questioning his gender identity, Tyler recalls his conversation with his grandmother, Nana, who originally told him the story of Mala Ramchandin's incestuous abuse by his father, Chandin Ramchandin. Tyler bases his narrative of Mala's life on his Nana's story, and thus makes it clear how his version is premised on, and filtered through, yet another version of the messy Ramchandin family saga. Tyler narrates:

> I wonder what Nana would think if she knew the positions I was in that enabled me to gain the full story. For there were two: one, *a*

[35] *Cereus Blooms at Night*, 19. (My emphasis.)

[36] Pearce, *Feminism and the Politics of Reading*, 17.

> *shared queerness with Miss Ramchandin*, which gave rise to the other, my proximity to the very Ramchandin Nana herself had known of.[37]

In this passage, Tyler describes his forming gender identity as the facilitator or enabler for his storytelling mission. The narrative, in other words, becomes possible through a shared sense of queerness that he feels connects him with Mala.[38]

Tyler's positionality evoked in the above passage in turn reflects on and affects the reader. When Tyler relates Mala's story, and at the same time begins to make sense of his own gender identity, what fuels Tyler's narrative desire? Is it simply a case of hiss altruistic effort to make Mala's story heard in order for it to reach her sister, Asha? In the novel's prologue, Tyler states that "it is my ardent hope that Asha Ramchandin, [...] will chance upon this book, wherever she may be today, and recognize herself and her family."[39] The purpose of the narrative, then, is to convey a message to a specific person, Asha. In this sense, the novel fails as a missing-persons notice, as by the end of the narrative Asha remains absent. She, too, remains a ghost in the text that she never, so far as we know, came to read.

The narrative of *Cereus* ends with Tyler's direct address to Asha, pleading with her to return for her sister's sake. At the same time, the closing words remind the reader of the absence of the text's intended addressee. This produces the effect of the reader as a substitute interlocutor, and thus a potential carrier of Tyler's message to Asha. Here, the communicative chain inscribed in the text from its beginning becomes ever more evident.

At the same time as he foregrounds Mala's tragic life, Tyler is himself the star in his story. It could in fact be that Tyler's 'disclaimer' in the prologue, "my intention is not to bring notice to myself or my own plight," is the main

---

[37] *Cereus Blooms at Night*, 48. (My emphasis.)

[38] As noted before, the specificity of Tyler's 'queerness' remains obscure in terms of explicit terms or labels used to describe gender and sexual identities. Throughout the novel, this is heavily contrasted by the novel's preoccupation with naming the flora of its setting in detailed Linnaean terms borrowed from colonial natural history, as noted by Grace Kyungwon Hong in "'A Shared Queerness'," 75. See also Alison Donnell's discussion of the covert voicing of sexuality in literature by Caribbean authors who "refuse to trade in (or off) the vocabulary and identity politics" of the West. Donnell, *Twentieth-Century Caribbean Literature: Critical Moments in Anglophone Literary History* (London & New York: Routledge, 2006): 244.

[39] *Cereus Blooms at Night*, 3. Further page references are in the main text.

motivator for his storytelling efforts. However much Tyler emphasizes his being merely "the relater of this story" (3), and however often he reminds the reader of his peripheral role in the story, he inevitably enjoins the reader to adopt him as the protagonist – perhaps even more so than Mala. After telling of the way in which the fellow nursing staff show their disdain for "this pansy" (10), Tyler stops and exclaims:

> The temptation is strong, I will admit, to be the romantic victim. There is in me a performer dying for the part, but I must be strict with myself and stay with my intention to relate Mala Ramchandin's story. (15)

In addressing the way in which he does not want to draw too much attention to himself, Tyler does just that: captures the reader's interest and attention. The reader, in other words, is simultaneously grasped by Tyler when attempting to grasp Mala's story from his narrative.

In this way, Tyler makes the story as much about himself as about Mala. The performer in Tyler does play his part, and the narrative strategy works for his personal motivations as much as it does for relating Mala's story. In aspiring to Asha's recognition of Mala, Tyler also becomes, in fact, a seeker of acknowledgement for his own existence. He sees in Mala someone who recognizes his true self: after Mala has stolen a woman nurse's uniform for Tyler to wear, he rejoices: "She knows what I am, was all I could think. She knows my nature" (77). Thus, Mala and Tyler's 'withness' in the form of "shared queerness" also becomes a form of testimony; as wit(h)ness in their mutual recognition. At the same time, the novel is an amalgam of autobiography and testimony, where the testifying in fact leads to the narrator's, not the 'victim's', self-discovery. Pearce notes that while first-hand testimony is no more authentic than a second-hand one, the latter often leaves the 'victim' largely unknown, in which case there may then be a greater distance between the participants than initially perceived.[40] Because of the lack of reciprocal communication between Tyler and Mala, the mechanism of their wit(h)ness and its implications for an ethics of reading needs further scrutiny.

A "shared queerness" entails an ethical perspective, as it has ramifications for a reading that pays attention to the interaction and special bond between the two characters. After all, this bond becomes related to the reader only by way of Tyler's own relayed interpretation. This may run the risk that the reader will construe Tyler's interpretation of their shared queerness as a form of simple identification; as transference of experience from one person to

[40] Pearce, *The Rhetorics of Feminism*, 201.

another. The question then becomes: does Tyler *make* Mala his double by way of his narration? And if Tyler's way of explaining their bond is an overpowering projection, does Mala's pain then become Tyler's own? As mentioned with regard to Monica's pain in Adisa's *It Begins with Tears*, the pain of the other usurped by a benevolent feeling subject violates the Other's affective experience by taking her place.

Tyler's empathy for Mala, then, may also risk being an unproblematic "seeking to take the other's place."[41] Tyler himself is certainly aware of this, as, when he describes the affective response that he has to Mala during their first encounter, he first articulates his experience of empathy ("I felt *an empathy* for her," 19; my emphasis). After a moment of speculation, however, Tyler comes to think of his empathy as possibly a case of "nothing more than recalcitrant yearning, for I did fancy that she and I shared a common reception from the rest of the world" (20). Tyler is aware of his desire for an ally as the potential motivator for his affective response, but at the same time he is very much seduced by the potential of what working with and caring for Mala can do for him in terms of his professional, as well as sexual, identity. At the same time, then, the reader needs to be constantly aware of the contours and promptings of Tyler's understanding of "a shared queerness," in his desire and empathy for the mentally distraught and severely traumatized, ailing old woman.

Empathy as wonder

If we see Tyler's involvement as participation in the life of the other, we can observe in his actions an openness to the experience of the other. Indeed, an element of surprise and wonder can be seen in Tyler's response to the first time he hears Mala communicate with sound. Mala makes an imitation of the calls of a pair of parrots that happen to fly by as the two take a stroll in the grounds of the nursing home. Tyler immediately lowers himself to Mala's side and marvels at her skill in imitating the birds. When Mala repeats the sound, Tyler narrates: "I looked into her face, my jaw dropped in admiration and disbelief" (24). Tyler's experience of surprise in hearing Mala's bird call draws attention to the unresolved mystery of Mala's traumatized psyche. As Mala cannot speak out her trauma in words (unlike Monica in *It Begins With Tears,* who is able to name her aggressor), the 'parroting' of the parrots'

[41] Ahmed, *The Cultural Politics of Emotion*, 126.

'voice' is her only means of becoming a voiced subject. Therefore, we need to hear her voice as meaningful.

Despite his disbelief, Tyler is thrilled by the sounds made by Mala. Furthermore, the fact that Mala imitates parrots, the bird best known for its own imitative ability, serves to highlight the possibility that Mala herself has detected an affinity between herself and Tyler: the two are similar but not the same, just as a parrot's call is similar to the imitated noise but never the same, always reiterated with a difference. Such openness to surprise by Tyler in the novel recalls Sara Ahmed's thoughts on the affect of wonder when she discusses feminist attachments: "wonder keeps bodies and spaces open to the surprise of others" and forms "an affective relation to the world."[42] Further, this relation involves "the hope of transformation, and the will for politics" and openness to change.[43] An element of wonder then becomes a form of an ethic of empathy in the context of the novel.

Reading Mala and Tyler's "shared queerness" as a form of 'withness', we might see the two existing in interaction 'within' and 'apart from' each other at the same time, as characterized by Ahmed. A new type of collectivity then becomes produced across age, race, and gender difference and suggests that there is space as well as a need for different types of relating and cohabiting than has been available for Caribbean queer subjects. Related to this, the connections between trauma (Mala's sexual abuse and incest) and gender identity (Tyler's transsexualism in Western terms) become central as the negative affect potential at play in the novel. As a larger question that underlines the subject-matter discussed in this section, it is also worth considering the extended collectivity between Tyler, Mala, and, towards the end of the novel, their respective relationships to Ambrose Mohanty (Mala's lover from their youth who reconnects with Mala at the nursing home) and his daughter, Otoh (who was born a girl, but who lives as a man; later becoming the person with whom Tyler falls in love). Several categories of social differentiation (gender, sexuality, age, race, and class) are played out in the novel as a basis for collectivity. The way in which such relationships are formed on the premise of difference may then serve to illuminate how *Cereus Blooms at Night* helps us to envisage alliances and belongingness across non-normative identities. The idea of wonder as a form of ethics might also be a way for the reader to

---

[42] Ahmed, *The Cultural Politics of Emotion*, 183, 179.

[43] *The Cultural Politics of Emotion*, 181.

romance empathy as a textual other without turning the relationship into one of mastery and violence.

It is this question of collective alliances and belonging that becomes central to reading Mootoo's novel, whose narration is made possible by the collectivity of Tyler and Mala's relationship. Tyler's quest to relate Mala's story to a readership involves another crucial relation: the text–reader relationship realized in the act of reading. The in-between character of Tyler is a mediator of "new narrative histories" in the Caribbean context.[44] He provides the reader with access to a story that would otherwise remain unheard. In the process, Tyler's own story absorbs the reader and serves to educate her about his own particular way of embodying the Caribbean queer. Rosamond S. King notes that "the reader cannot escape Tyler," nor can Tyler escape the reader – as without her, too, the story would fail to exist. This crucial relation of the text and its reader is a key to understanding the queer Caribbean as expressed in literature. King laments the failure of Caribbean authors to portray trans lives in full in their writing,[45] but it is hardly fair to make such demands on literary fiction as an artform. Instead, it is our opportunity as well as responsibility as readers to go to the heart of the effects that these lives have on our readings, and thus on our views of queer lives in the Caribbean.

Applying the idea of feminist attachment with its related affects of empathy, withness, wonder, and love as the premise for a cross-cultural text–reader relationship, the process of affective meaning-production is based on a mode of knowing that does not impose itself on the experience of the Other and works as a reparative, wondering, and participatory relation to the world. However, further questions arise from this attempt at reading different sexualities reparatively: how does such a reading open up to non-normative forms of sexuality? Addressing the potential ways in which we might read sexual identities as existing on the continuum of ambivalent, contested sexual markers provides the focus of the next and final chapter of our journey into Caribbean sexual feelings and their readings.

⌘

[44] Ilmonen, "Healing the Traumas of History," 245.

[45] King, "Re/presenting Self & Other," 598.

6

'Caribbean Passion' – The Hypersexual and the Asexual Woman as Reparative Tropes

Opal Palmer Adisa and Erna Brodber

As established throughout this book and argued by many critics, Caribbean sexuality in literature by women is frequently presented as problematic and paradoxical. In this final chapter, I take up two examples of such polarization in another attempt to look for ways in which sexuality could be read reparatively. The respective female protagonists, Monica and Ella, in Opal Palmer Adisa's *It Begins With Tears* and Erna Brodber's *Louisiana* represent, roughly speaking, two different types of sexual being and doing: one hypersexualized, the other ostensibly asexual. The alternative visions these two prototypes have to offer beyond their dichotomy become readable through an intimate reparative reading that prompts the reader to remain open and impressionable (even vulnerable) to the element of the unexpected in the reading event. Texts, in other words, in this reading practice are seen to have the capacity to influence us in ways that fall outside the restraints of the categorical or, indeed, prototypical.

My point is not to test whether or not these female characters can be considered liberating or liberated. Rather, I again begin with the assumption that a reparative reading may be situated in between juxtaposed, disputed fields of debate; perhaps therefore challenging, demystifying, and questioning fixed notions and values. My purpose here is to explore the ways in which Monica and Ella are seen to behave in a reparative reading. What alternatives do they offer to their pre-constructed typologies, the hypersexual and the asexual, respectively?

The title of this chapter is drawn from the title of a poetry collection by Opal Palmer Adisa. Employing the word 'passion' in her poetry in its dual senses of erotic lust and of pain and suffering, Adisa foregrounds a politics of sensuality, both physical and spiritual. The notion or metaphor of Caribbean passion can be applied to the protagonists in my two sample texts. In Adisa's novel, the figure of the prostitute Monica may be read in reparative terms where she does not open to the reader with a paranoid practice alone. To do so would be to foreground her role – as prostitute and adulterer – as a problematically loose, unchaste woman, to be moralized and rejected. Instead, in a reparative reading practice, her multiple sensations position the reader in the narrative with seduction as its affective force. This energy can be understood as a textual philosophy aiming at a larger reparative mission: the communal women's healing process which takes place at the end of the novel (as discussed in Chapter 4).

An alternative take on passion emerges in the kind of disembodied spirituality provided by Brodber's *Louisiana*, in which Ella leads a life of seemingly asexual passion as she is transformed into Louisiana; a psychic and seer of people's past. The asexuality of Ella's character should not be interpreted simply as such; rather, it should be recognized as yet another, non-normative form of sexuality, hence worthy of consideration from the point of view of theorizations on sexuality. Whether dubbed asexual or not, Ella's multiple passions as she experiences "the hegemony of the spirit" in the course of her transformation display a slanting of orientation and thus skew the normativity of (hetero)sexuality.[1] In acting "out of line,"[2] the asexual presents an alternative to the sensitive and sensual Afro-Caribbean body as differently oriented.

Underlying this chapter as a larger reader-theoretical framework is the idea of Caribbean passion as a metaphor for motivations and desires that might fuel a cross-cultural feminist reading of Caribbean fiction by women. Caribbean passion can thus provide a way to conceptualize the ethical dimension of the text–reader relationship and prompt the reader to adopt reparative reading practices in places where they might not seem pertinent.

Reading Monica, the hypersexual woman

In one of the main plot-lines in *It Begins With Tears*, Monica, a retired prostitute in her forties, returns to her rural home village to live comfortably in a house paid for by a lover. What is striking about Monica's characterization is

[1] Brodber, *Louisiana* (London: New Beacon, 1994): 98. On sexuality as an orientation, see Ahmed, *Queer Phenomenology*.

[2] *Queer Phenomenology*, 66.

that she is represented throughout as a sensual woman: "Everything about Monica was sensual, like heat rising from the sun," and "Monica was like a bitch in heat, and no matter what activity a male was engaged in, he would smell her a mile away and stop work to attend to the itch in his groin."[3] In the absence of a controlling, moralizing narratorial voice, she is depicted as someone for whom erotic passion is not merely a livelihood but a philosophy – and a pleasurable way of life. In fact, erotic passion is presented as foundational to Monica's subjectivity, not just as something that she happens to practise.

In fact, we are told it was precisely Monica's sexual desirability that made her leave the constraints of the Kristoff village community at the age of fourteen, when her budding sexuality did not conform to the community's moral views on ideal womanhood. Monica's mother's accusations, coupled with the village women's disapproval and the constant attention from village men, made her want to leave home. I wish to ignore for the moment Weir–Soley's characterization of Monica before her sexual punishment and the subsequent healing as someone with "an overdeveloped sexual nature" as something inherently problematic and a sign of "spiritual and psychological imbalance."[4] Instead, I examine Monica's sexuality and sensuality as a seductive force engaging the reader in a relationship with her. In this relationship, Monica comes to be understood as an embodiment of sensual passion who embraces her sexuality and eroticism – in Audre Lorde's famous characterization, "the lifeforce of women."[5]

Dangerous liaisons: seduction and soliciting in reading

When we first meet Monica in the novel with her return to the village after more than twenty years, her views on passion are made explicit in interior monologue:

> The act [of sex] had been relegated to night, to privacy and secrecy, but Monica would have none of that. She liked doing it during the day, preferably just before lunch. She threw back her head and laughed a deep belly-laugh. *Passion should never be private or secret. It wasn't*

[3] Adisa; *It Begins With Tears*, 57, 25.

[4] Weir–Soley, *Eroticism, Spirituality, and Resistance*, 169.

[5] Audre Lorde, *Sister Outsider: Essays and Speeches* (Freedom CA: Crossing Press, 1984): 55.

> *meant to be*. Sexual acts engaged in undercover invariably came to light, usually in the form of a protruding stomach. Laughter racked her body. She used the back of her hand to wipe the tears that trailed down her face. It was too funny. This passion.[6]

Monica reflects upon herself as a woman of open sexuality, for whom passion is neither private nor secret. Lack of concealment emerges from this passage as the main philosophy of Monica's sexual tour de force. In addition, her laughter privileges the comic or joyous over the serious – quite the opposite of what we are used to seeing in Caribbean literature, as noted by O'Callaghan in commenting that sexuality is typically represented as a traumatic or negative issue.[7] Rather, laughter, as an act of carnivalism in the face of something potentially negative (bearing in mind the polysemy of the word 'passion'), resembles that of the female grotesque in its transgression of norms.[8]

Monica's carnivalesque and carnal, body-racking, and tear-inducing laughter exposes her unruliness: sex and sexuality are a laughing matter. Reminiscent of the laugh of the Medusa, Monica's laugh depicts the polymorphous-perverse woman evoked by Cixous: "you can't talk about *a* female sexuality, uniform, homogeneous, classifiable into codes."[9] Monica's sexuality, accordingly, cannot be reduced to the singular. Instead, the sexuality embodied in Monica seems to emanate from female drives as overflowing and multiple. The way Cixous characterizes the political implications of a writing woman's sexuality fits Monica very well: "Her libido will produce far more radical effects of political and social change than some might like to think."[10] This is particularly the case towards the end of the novel, where Monica's healing ritual of helping the participating women to recover from their own traumas heals the community. However, Monica's open sexuality does not sit well with certain village women, who openly judge her when she first returns

---

[6] *It Begins With Tears*, 25. (My emphasis.)

[7] O'Callaghan, "'Compulsory Heterosexuality' and Textual/Sexual Alternatives in Selected Texts by West Indian Women Writers," 297.

[8] See, for example, Mary Russo, *The Female Grotesque: Risk, Excess and Modernity* (New York & London: Routledge, 1995).

[9] Hélène Cixous, "The Laugh of the Medusa" (1975), tr. (1976) Keith & Paula Cohen, in *Feminisms: An Anthology of Literary Theory and Criticism*, ed. Robyn Warhol & Diane Price Herndl (New Brunswick NJ: Rutgers UP, 1997): 347.

[10] "The Laugh of the Medusa," 352.

home. In other words, the carnivalesque evokes resentment which deems it abject; that is to say, feminine, carnal – even immoral.

Monica's character cannot easily be seen as either harmful or liberatory. Few feminists outside the radical-sexuality movement would venture to claim that the figure of the prostitute is ever emancipatory or free of connections to relations of domination.[11] A pro-Monica reading therefore raises the question: if the narrative leads us to make no moral judgment on Monica, does it, then, follow that the sexually active female subject can automatically be read as a herald of sexual liberation? How does Monica, the ex-prostitute, become readable in problematic yet reparative terms in a particular cultural context? A Caribbean woman prostitute read through an emphasis on her passion, lust, and enjoyment of sexuality runs the serious risk of reproducing the stereotype of black women as sexually promiscuous. The common view of sexually generous Caribbean women is that of hypersexual, exotic beauties, who "are not, in the minds of [Western sex tourist] men, prostitutes who are having sex for money, but are perceived to be poor women who genuinely enjoy sex."[12] This obviously leads to a hypersexualized image of Caribbean women, and, like the emphasis on women's libidinal enjoyment during the sexual-liberation movement of the 1960s, has its downside in strengthening the patriarchal status quo. This is a risk, however, that a reparative reading position has to take.

According to Sedgwick, "reparative motives and positionalities" by their susceptible nature form a practice which "undertakes a different range of affects, ambitions and risks."[13] This mention of the risks involved suggests Sedgwick's awareness of the naive ways in which previous reparative vocabulary in reading has been too "sappy, aestheticizing, defensive, anti-intellectual or reactionary," for which, in turn, no allowance is made in the depen-

---

[11] Sex-radical feminism questions all sexual norms that may close off women's options to express themselves in whatever sexual way they desire, particularly in terms of maximizing pleasure and promoting active sexual agency. Sex-radical (sometimes, controversially, 'sex-positive') feminism may also involve sex work and prostitution as means of furthering women's sexual autonomy. "From a sex radical perspective, feminists should demand that fully consenting partners whose sex is neither exploitative nor abusive have the opportunity to practise whatever gives them sexual satisfaction"; Linda LeMoncheck, *Loose Women, Lecherous Men: A Feminist Philosophy of Sex* (Oxford: Oxford UP, 1997): 70.

[12] Kempadoo, "Theorizing Sexual Relations in the Caribbean," 178.

[13] Sedgwick, *Touching Feeling*, 150.

dence on the depressive position of the paranoid.[14] This means that a reparative reading does not exist without its paranoid counterpart.[15] In short, the reliance of the reparative on the paranoid eludes the kind of vocabulary shunned by Sedgwick, and so makes a reparative reading of the hypersexualized Monica a risk worth taking.

Resistance and the erotic as power

Lynne Pearce's idea of textual positioning[16] is again useful here in considering the desires that might move a reparative reader of Monica. Questioning the various positions that the narrative offers the reader may help expand the view of Monica as a sexual being beyond dominant patriarchal definitions. As discussed earlier, texts have the capacity to position their readers in many ways. This would prompt a paranoid reader to consider whether the text of the novel positions, or attempts to position, the reader in a sex-work-positive context. The paranoid reader then sets out anxiously to expose the ways in which s/he, like Monica's male admirers, is seduced by Monica into reading her sexuality in a positive light. After all, Monica is characterized as a "woman who, even when she least intended it, created a sensation."[17] What, then, are the sensations (not just the drama meant here) created by Monica in the reader? Could Monica be read favourably as expressing an exoticized, sexual cultural experience similar to that of the sex-tourist men who, according to Kempadoo, recount their sexual extravaganzas on internet message boards; acclaiming their unforgettable encounters with sexually generous and open Caribbean women? In other words, being seduced by Monica, or even actively soliciting her as a reader would mean reading her in precisely the same way that sex tourists view their Caribbean paid sexual partners on the internet message board: as exotic, hypersexual beauties who just happen to like a bit of cash in exchange for an innocent moment of pleasure.

If it were the case that a favourable reading-position parallels that of the male sex-tourist on the internet, can it then be inferred that such a reading is male-lensed? Alternatively, could this seduction be dubbed a lesbian reading, where the line between desire and identification is blurred? As we know,

[14] Sedgwick, *Touching Feeling*, 150.

[15] *Touching Feeling*, 136.

[16] Pearce, *Feminism and the Politics of Reading*, 12.

[17] Adisa, *It Begins With Tears*, 25.

readings are not simply the product of the reader's or the text's dominance in meaning-production. This leads to a questioning of the contours of such impressionability: to what degree can texts do something to us? Can they do anything that they want – even seduce us? What would be the consequences of such seduction?

Just as Pearce deals with reading in the affective framework of romance, I have looked at other types of reading relationships that feature sexuality. In my reading of Monica within this framework of sexual feelings, I am prompted to consider her and her philosophy as a textual other; an object of textual desire that conditions the reader's judgment. Perhaps Monica's allure, as in the case of the adulterous Desmond with whom she has a relationship, has worked its magic through the absence of any guiding narratorial judgment to create the sensation that – despite her adultery, her unorthodox profession, and her promiscuity – she is, in fact, quite okay?

Would it then follow that we should now become resistant readers of fiction by women, too, if the fiction in question does not conform to politically correct feminist emancipations? It was the belief of resisting feminist readers that by challenging the representations in canonical male literature we can achieve emancipatory readings.[18] Rita Felski argues, however, that at the moment there is perhaps not such a strong need for the feminist reader to stand on her guard as a resisting reader, and textual pleasure need not lead to a loss of "capacity for critical thought."[19] According to Felski, the pitfall in resorting to resisting reading is to evade affectivity and thus reject the potential for being inspired or changed by a literary encounter – *any* literary encounter.[20] Cutting oneself off from being affected by Monica is hardly a viable objective here; heeding the sensations created by literature is certainly a fruitful reading strategy in itself. At the same time, the questioning of the reader's textual positioning resembles the resisting reader's suspicion of a literary text. Just as paranoid and reparative reading practices coexist side by side, in constant interaction, at the same time it is only sensible to maintain a sceptical attitude toward prostitution as an institution, and a reparative openness toward the figure of the prostitute as an individual.

---

[18] See Judith Fetterley, *The Resisting Reader: A Feminist Approach to American Fiction* (Bloomington: Indiana UP, 1978).

[19] Rita Felski, *Literature After Feminism* (Chicago & London: U of Chicago P, 2003): 35.

[20] Felski, *Literature After Feminism*, 36.

The reader tracing Monica's sensations will not be left unsatisfied, since her experiences of pleasure in the novel are multiple. The literary sensations experienced and created by Monica have to do with attuning oneself to the bodily senses. For example, taste in the novel is conveyed as inseparable from sexual arousal: when Monica first meets Desmond, the narrator remarks that temptation is "sweet like sour-sop."[21] Similarly, sweet taste is again referred to as Monica thinks of Desmond "making her feel so sweet, honey didn't know what nectar was."[22] The role of the senses, sensuality, and sensation is inextricably linked to processes of meaning-production. Scholars like Eve Kosofsky Sedgwick and Vivian Sobchack remind us that the sense-making experience – whether reading a novel or watching a film – always evokes the interaction of senses, as it is always also an embodied, carnal, and material experience.[23]

Attuning oneself to the embodied experience of reading Monica may allow us to see her in the same way as Myriam Chancy reads the erotic principle in Afro-Caribbean women's writing, based on Audre Lorde's arguments.[24] Chancy sees the erotic principle as a powerful force inscribed in the tradition of African-derived women's history and remembering. Lorde emphasizes the connection between the erotic and the spiritual, whereby the erotic can be seen in relation to African New World cosmologies, where the sensual and the spiritual are inextricably linked. Most importantly, however, the power of the erotic is about the "black female body as the site of our ultimate empowerment," as Chancy eloquently puts it.[25]

Weir–Soley also sees a link between the erotic in Adisa's novel and Lorde's influential idea of the power of the erotic. She refers to sexuality in Adisa as "the erotics of change," which clearly brings out the relationship between politics and sexuality. Weir–Soley argues thus:

> the erotic, then, becomes an enabling source of female resistance against the spiritual and physical death that inevitably accompanies absolute notions of ownership and possessiveness that lead to the kind

[21] *It Begins With Tears*, 31.

[22] *It Begins With Tears*, 79.

[23] See, for example, Sedgwick, *Touching Feeling*, 15, and Sobchack, *Carnal Thoughts*, 60.

[24] Chancy, *Searching for Safe Spaces*, 123. Chancy cites Audre Lorde's seminal essay "Uses of the Erotic: The Erotic as Power," in her collection *Sister Outsider*.

[25] Chancy, *Searching for Safe Spaces*, 123.

> of excessive jealousy and murderous rage that precipitate heinous acts of violence such as the one visited upon Monica.[26]

The character of Monica, then, can be read as an antithesis to the idea of an individual's sexuality as something that can be owned, or contained by institutions or regulations. Monica's untamed erotic energy before her peppering can be read as empowering and exemplary. This unique portrayal of female sexuality in Caribbean women's writing shows us that the erotic female body can in fact be a site of empowerment for reading women, at the same time as it receives contradictory meanings among their textual sisters. These contradictions inherent in Caribbean female sexuality – and, as Weir–Soley indicates, to Caribbean subjectivities in general[27]– are seen in the next section from a seemingly opposite angle when Monica's hypersexuality is mirrored by another type of sexual identity – that of *a*sexuality.

Re-orienting desire in reading *Louisiana*

If, for the sake of argument, we were to conceptualize the two characters under scrutiny in this chapter (Monica and Ella) in dichotomous terms, then the sensual Monica finds her seemingly polar opposite in the cerebral Ella in Erna Brodber's *Louisiana*. Patricia Saunders views Ella as the "literary descendant" of the protagonist in Brodber's *Myal*, Ella O'Grady.[28] At the end of that novel, Ella plays her part in changing the colonial education system as a schoolteacher; teaching her pupils to unlearn the legacy of colonialist epistemologies. *Louisiana* has a similar lesson about the faultiness of white Western knowledge-systems. However, the novel's protagonist and partial namesake, Ella Townsend, also bears a striking resemblance to another young female scholar in the 1930s, gathering folklore knowledge from the rural black inhabitants in her native Florida. Zora Neale Hurston's project, documented in her *Mules and Men*, is the historical counterpart to Ella Townsend's documentation project in *Louisiana*.[29] However, Ella's scholarly en-

---

[26] Weir–Soley, *Eroticism, Spirituality, and Resistance*, 179.

[27] *Eroticism, Spirituality, and Resistance*, 181.

[28] Saunders, "The Project of Becoming for Marlene Nourbese Philip and Erna Brodber," 152.

[29] Angeletta Gourdine, "Carnival-Conjure, *Louisiana*, History and the Power of Women's Ethnographic Narrative," *ARIEL: A Review of International English Literature* 35.3–4 (2004), 139 n2.

deavour as a young anthropologist takes a drastically different turn as she is taken on a "journey into knowing" when the voices on the interview tape engage her in a transformation of self into Louisiana, the psychic who can see other people's pasts.[30]

The function of magical realism in the novel is to signify the partiality and limitedness of scientific knowledge, which simply fails to provide a successful set of tools with which to unravel issues that elude traditional Western notions of rationality and reason. In fact, as Mary Chamberlain suggests, spiritual metaphors, surreal elements, and folk rhetoric "all signify values and priorities, ways of looking at the world and interpreting it. They are often symbolic shorthand for a particular [cultural] worldview."[31] In *Louisiana*, the connections to the ancestral lineage teach us that community is not simply tied to the here and now but, rather, to the past and beyond, which can be reached by undertaking the journey into knowing that transforms the individual's sense of self into one that is plural and mediative.[32]

Asexuality as an alternative passion

Denise DeCaires Narain suggests that a shift can be detected in Brodber's fiction from material corporeality towards a more spiritual, disembodied state. This shift culminates in *Louisiana*: Ella Townsend withdraws from embodiment by becoming the transhistorical psychic Louisiana. Narain notes: "Ella's sexual presence is de-emphasized and her body represented as the *asexual vessel* through which the community can find expression and healing."[33] This is certainly true: Ella lends her body for the good of a larger cause, uncovering the connection between black people in the Caribbean and the USA in the first decades of the twentieth century, as told to and through her by Sue Ann King (also known as Mammy) and her friend Louise (also known as Lowly). Brodber's fusion of genres, voices, registers, and references is a carefully constructed mosaic, identifying with Africa-derived spiritual and political ideo-

---

[30] *Louisiana*, 38.

[31] Mary Chamberlain, "The Global Self: Narratives of Caribbean Migrant Women," in *Feminism and Autobiography: Texts, Theories, Methods*, ed. Tess Cosslett, Celia Lury & Penny Summerfield (London: Routledge, 2000): 159.

[32] See Chamberlain, "The Global Self," 161.

[33] Narain, "The Body of the Woman in the Body of the Text," 113. (My emphasis.)

logies at its centre. The community tales told by Brodber are not homogeneous, despite their collective character.

As such, *Louisiana* highlights a shift away from a protagonist's individual identity and subjectivity in favour of moving towards and submerging herself in the collective and the individual. Having 'got over' as Louisiana, the woman formerly known as Ella Townsend constantly transcends the boundaries of coherent human personhood and denounces autonomous subjectivity, in the service of a project whose philosophical foundation is African cosmology and world-view. But if Ella is an "asexual vessel," as DeCaires Narain suggests, and if sexuality is tied to sensuality and embodied experience, what are the contours of Ella's passion when she becomes Louisiana, the "talking drum" that transmits people's histories to them?[34] What is the direction of her desires?[35]

Certainly, it would be quite easy to place Louisiana in Rowley's "homogenous typeface of Caribbean womanhood," where the figure of the obedient Mammy, in circulation since chattel slavery, appears as the antithesis of the hypersexual Monicas, Jezebels, and black Venuses.[36] The mammy, according to Patricia Hill Collins, is decidedly asexual, hence unthreatening.[37] In terms of the binary contradiction created by this polarization, is Louisiana, supposedly de-sexed and chaste, the antithesis of Monica, hence readable only in disembodied, spiritual terms, with no room for corporeal desires?

It can be argued that neither Monica nor Louisiana can be reduced to the polar opposites assigned to her by stereotypical representation systems stemming from colonial history. On the one hand, sexuality here comes to be understood as existing beyond these narrow options, in order to provide a resistant reading of the dualism associated with black female sexuality. On the other, a reparative reading highlights the alternatives that Louisiana has to

[34] *Louisiana*, 36.

[35] On the "direction of our desire," see Ahmed, *Queer Phenomenology*, 1.

[36] Rowley, "Reconceptualizing Voice," 22. On black women's sexual polarization, see, for example, Patricia Hill Collins, *Black Sexual Politics: African Americans, Gender and the New Racism* (New York & London: Routledge, 2004): 140, and Evelyn Hammonds, "Toward a Genealogy of Black Female Sexuality: The Problematic of Silence," in *Feminist Genealogies, Colonial Legacies, Democratic Futures*, ed. M. Jacqui Alexander & Chandra Talpade Mohanty (New York & London: Routledge, 1997): 172.

[37] Patricia Hill Collins, *Black Feminist Thought: Knowledge, Consciousness, and the Politics of Empowerment* (New York & London: Routledge, 1991): 74.

offer for black female sexuality as not target-oriented and therefore more fluid and fluctuating.

For an account of disembodied spirituality in conjunction with sexuality and passion, we need to consider the nature of asexuality in this context. We need to discuss what is meant exactly by Ella's asexuality or her body as an "asexual vessel."[38] According to Anthony F. Bogaert, asexuality refers to "the state of having no sexual attraction for either sex."[39] When sexual orientation becomes located in a specific target (either sex), as it does according to this logic, then asexuality becomes constructed as a non-entity. However, if, like Ahmed, we perceive the constitution of sexual identity as the ways in which we are oriented (i.e. the ways in which we reach for objects, become directed, or inhabit space), then asexuality might be conceptualized as having no target, but as having an orientation: hence, having (or, rather, doing) *a* sexuality – asexuality.

A point of view that does not wish to construct a hierarchy of sexual identifications may be helpful in seeing the possibilities of sexual variability as something other than a disorder – rather, as another means of expressing individual human sexuality. Ahmed's phenomenological account of sexual orientation has its counterpart in Bogaert's analysis of a national probability sample, where it similarly emerges that we tend to understand sexuality only in terms of directionality and motility, always in connection with an end or an objective:

> Traditional sexual orientation questions have an inherent "target-oriented" view of sexual response and arousal; that is, they imply that sexual response and arousal must be directed toward or targeted to someone or to a particular sex. These questions may not adequately capture the nature of some women's sexuality.[40]

In *Louisiana*, there is a similar uncertainty and openness about precisely what it is that Louisiana actually desires. In the part of the novel entitled "Louisiana," to mark Ella's transition, Louisiana ponders on her mission as one who

---

[38] Narain, "The Body of the Woman in the Body of the Text: The Novels of Erna Brodber," 113.

[39] Anthony F. Bogaert, "Asexuality: Prevalence and Associated Factors in a National Probability Sample," *Journal of Sex Research* 41.3 (August 2004): 279.

[40] Bogaert, "Asexuality: Prevalence and Associated Factors in a National Probability Sample," 285.

delivers: "I don't know when or even what, but I know that I will deliver."[41] Such ambivalence might suggest that our objects of desire are not always clear-cut, or even in knowable existence, nor do they have to be. The point about Louisiana is therefore perhaps not that she is asexual per se, but that she is automatically assumed to be and interpreted as such, because our ways of thinking about sexuality are too narrow to accommodate those who experience non-conformist passions.

"Experiencing the hegemony of the spirit," as Ella describes her metamorphosis, is referred to by Madame Marie, Ella's mentor in New Orleans, as "getting over." The section of the novel where Ella undergoes transformation, entitled "I got over," most likely alludes to the gospel song "How I got over" made famous by Mahalia Jackson, where "my soul looks back and wonders how I got over." Indeed, as Ella looks back into people's pasts while at the same time seeing her own childhood in Jamaica, she is in fact 'getting over' in multiple senses of the word: to overcome or recover,[42] to reconcile oneself, to become accustomed, or to move or travel across.

The novel's use of the phrase "get over" in the sense of moving or travelling across, refers to the physical migration of people; not only of slaves forced to cross over on the Middle Passage, but also of their descendants, such as Ella Townsend and her parents, who crossed over from the Caribbean to the USA and established new lives there. Therefore, bearing in mind the ubiquitous interconnectedness of elements in Brodber, the community tale that is being conveyed by Mammy and Louise through Louisiana is, with the help of her husband Reuben, also the communal tale for all New World blacks, even if the story is only a fragment of their experience.

Another link in the word-play of getting over is provided in *Louisiana* by the scene depicting Louise's funeral in Jamaica, where the idea of 'being translated' has the more literal sense of 'carrying over' or 'moving to the other side'. There, death does not signify the end of things, ultimate closure, but, rather, 'being translated' as a movement into a different sphere, where one can experience and perceive things differently. Brodber writes that in African religious world-views brought to the New World, physical death did not mark the end of life, but was a new beginning and an opportunity for an

---

[41] Brodber, *Louisiana*, 97.

[42] In Ebonics, getting over, or 'gittin ovuh', refers to survival – both spiritual and material. Geneva Smitherman, *Talkin That Talk: Language, Culture and Education in African America* (London & New York: Routledge, 2000): 199.

ancestor to exercise power over mortals.[43] This is what is meant in the novel by the idea of "passing the lifeline."[44] As Ella is taken over by the hegemony of the spirit, she also comes to terms with the fact that the spirit world outweighs the scientific world, and the story begins to unfold when she simply succumbs to following her "journey into knowing."

Listening to Louisiana's vocal subjectivity

In considering how to "reorient our reading practices,"[45] which Puri calls for, we can see *Louisiana* as a novel opening itself to a cross-cultural reading by a listening strategy, as it teaches a lesson about the importance of voice and listening through its central motif, the tape recorder. The recorder is supposed to be a tool for Ella's academic work, but instead it becomes an important device in its own right when Mammy and Louise communicate with Ella through it. The novel's opening chapter, entitled "I heard a voice from heaven say," contains Ella's transcription of the bizarre voices that she hears on the tape recorder. The tape begins with the voice of Louise, the long-deceased friend of Mammy King, telling the latter about her "translation" (death). Louise explains how there was a "voice calling me home," God's voice, which, in the form of the traditional funeral song, invites the dying older woman to abandon her living body and join the ranks of heaven.[46] Evoking a strong sense of spirituality with the Biblical reference underlining God's authority over human agency, voice and orality throughout the novel carry a higher message than that which any individual mind is able to convey. The tape recorder thus presents a medium for communicating those voices through the act of listening to the tape.

Lynne Pearce opens her discussion of dialogic thought by employing the telephone as a metaphor for dialogism. This is analogous to Brodber's use of the tape recorder in *Louisiana*, as the telephone is "an instrument of communication that can *only* function through the interaction of two people: the caller can speak only when the person being dialled picks up the receiver."[47] In this way, a telephone conversation is premised on the notion of dialogic-

---

[43] Brodber, "Re-engineering Blackspace," 160.

[44] Brodber, *Louisiana*, 28.

[45] Puri, *The Caribbean Postcolonial*, 140.

[46] Brodber, *Louisiana*, 10.

[47] Pearce, *Reading Dialogics*, 2.

ality, where "a discursive recipient of some kind is always present."[48] Dialogically, the phone conversation is communication per se, always constructed by the (un)awareness of an addressee.[49] As a medium restoring communicative events, the tape recorder captures Ella's conversations with Mammy and Lowly. Through these conversations, Ella's subjectivity is transformed into Louisiana. Seen in this way, Ella's rebirth as Louisiana is dialogic at its very core. Thus, it is not only Louisiana but also the reader who becomes produced in these conversations, as the tape recorder functions as a means of communication similarly dependent on the interactive process of listening.

However, at first when Ella begins to analyse the unexpected data of the voices on her tape recorder, she uses systematic methods of anthropological data-processing, such as creating schemes of each of the voices and names heard on the tape. The process of trying to connect the names, song stanzas, and other material on the tapes turns frustrating and futile, and she realizes that she will not find the answers by following traditional Western methods of knowledge-production. Instead, it dawns on her that there are knowledges opening to her that cannot be grasped with the scholarly rationale and education that she was taught at Columbia University. The way Ella's vision of knowledge is therefore expanded is by learning to heed the teaching of the Anancy story, as told by the New Orleans healer, Madam. In the story, Anancy has a magic pot that cooks food well enough. But alas, when Mrs Anancy discovers its magic, she uses it to make food for her family, and, following her everyday custom, washes the pot – on account of which it loses its magic. Through the story, Ella learns that the "magic pot cannot be cleaned" and comes to "accept this recording machine as the magic pot."[50] In other words, Ella, too, is forced to learn that her world-view, as based on earlier lessons of objective scientific methodology, is not enough. After this realization, she is able to finish the transcribing task in two weeks.

The reader, too, has to abandon her eurocentric meaning-production and turn instead to a more flexible process of signification – and, like Ella "open to the story *as it tells itself*."[51] In fact, to apply a term borrowed from Brod-

---

[48] Pearce, *Reading Dialogics*, 3.

[49] *Reading Dialogics*, 3.

[50] Brodber, *Louisiana*, 80.

[51] Evelyn O'Callaghan, "Cultural Penetration, Arts and Sciences: A Review of Erna Brodber's *Louisiana*," *Journal of West Indian Literature* 7.2 (1998): 73 (emphasis in original).

ber's story "One Bubby Susan"[52] to *Louisiana*, 'communication knowledge' may refer here to oral wisdom transmitted through different media – be it the tape recorder or Ella (the talking drum) – towards an end transcending the realm of human subjectivity. Indeed, while the message, "the community tale," is communicated by voices that "pass the lifeline," the reading, too, needs to be heard "on other frequencies."[53]

The prominence of listening and voice in the novel once again brings out Cavarero's philosophy of vocal expression, where she states that in concentrating on the written word, logocentric Western philosophy has neglected the role of voice in subject-formation. A brief sub-chapter in Cavarero's book is dedicated to the contemplation of non-Western meanings attributed to voice. Cavarero brings in the Caribbean context by borrowing famous assertion by the poet and historian Kamau Brathwaite that "the hurricane does not roar in pentameter."[54] As Denise DeCaires Narain remarks in her article on Caribbean woman poets, Brathwaite's famous articulation denotes how "the steady rhythms of the pentameter cannot give voice to the volatile geography of the Caribbean."[55] Cavarero, for her part, tries to explain the ways in which the voice does not merely correspond to sound in this context. Rather, "it is always the voice of someone as it vibrates in symphony with the natural and artificial sounds of the world in which she or he lives."[56] Cavarero points out that poets like Brathwaite are best received by listening to their works read aloud.[57]

Having read Cavarero's book, I heard Brathwaite speak at a conference some years ago and decided to pay special attention to the quality and rhythm

---

[52] Orality is central in Brodber's short story, "One Bubby Susan," which calls for "communication knowledge" in its counternarrative about the origin of an Arawak cave carving in rural Jamaica. The narrator pleads with her narratee to turn to knowledge not found in books, communication, knowledge, but, rather, in "people who really know the land" (49).

[53] Brodber, *Louisiana*, 28.

[54] Kamau Brathwaite, *History of the Voice: The Development of Nation Language in Anglophone Caribbean Poetry* (London & Port-of-Spain: New Beacon, 1984): 10. Quoted by Cavarero, *For More than One Voice*, ch. 2.6.

[55] Denise DeCaires Narain, "Landscape and Poetic Identity in Contemporary Caribbean Women's Poetry," *ARIEL: A Review of International English Literature* 38.2–3 (2007): 42.

[56] Cavarero, *For More than One Voice*, 148.

[57] *For More than One Voice*, 150.

of his voice. Revisiting my notes from this keynote lecture, I discovered that I had not managed to reproduce in my own writing what I had heard – save for a few initial remarks, in which I am clearly echoing Cavarero when commenting on a "deep, sonorous voice, which in itself does things: it convinces, takes you along, wraps you around it and comes from deeper than the lungs or the throat." At the end of this description, as if for emphasis, I had written: "from somewhere deeper." What, or where, this 'somewhere' is, I assume refers to Cavarero's understanding of Brathwaite's vocality as imitating the environment in and from which the voice arises. Cavarero refers to this phenomenon – of the voice and sound as fundamentally bound to the space and time of their occurrence – as the "sonorous universe."[58] The idea of reading as listening is highlighted by the important silences and other forms of non-verbal communication on the tapes, which can be regarded as the sonorous universe of Mammy and Lowly's conversations. As Saunders remarks, "there are lessons to be learned from the unspoken, silenced spaces in Mammy's experiences."[59] In fact, these 'silences' contain

> laughs and gestures which express ideas and emotions; voids, which at first appearance seem to be empty spaces; and articulations which render themselves in registers beyond Ella's interpretive strategies.[60]

Ella has the habit of letting the tape run during silences in Mammy's interview. The "sonorous universe" previously construed as silence by Ella becomes filled with voices and sounds when she begins to listen to the tapes. The listening activity becomes an act of translating, when Ella acts as the translator of those silences, as well as the one who becomes translated.

Ella cannot make sense of the voices on the tape by transcribing the dialogue and analysing it with scientific procedures. Instead, the only way to understand the voices is to be absorbed in the communication process; first as a listener and later as a healer educated to her task with the help of Mammy's and Louise's words and experiences. It is Ella's husband, Reuben, who convinces Ella in the beginning that she is not mentally ill in hearing the voices on the tape, as he hears them, too. Ella comments:

> Thank God for Reuben. But for him I might have handed myself over to a psychiatrist. It was he who pointed out to me that I hadn't heard

[58] Cavarero, *For More than One Voice*, 147.

[59] Saunders, "The Project of Becoming," 156.

[60] "The Project of Becoming," 156.

> any more voices than he had; that the voices on the reel were there for all to hear and verify.[61]

Reuben confirms that Ella is not crazy through the evidence provided by the recorder: hearing and the act of listening serve to verify the actuality of the events. Therefore, Ella and the reader need not doubt the authenticity of the tapes, and when Ella follows the journey into knowing in her own life, the reader also embarks on a journey into knowing by following and listening to the narrative.

Instead of becoming a mother in the biological, reproductive sense through her marriage to Reuben, Ella becomes involved in a marriage and a birth, but in a way that falls outside the confines of the heterosexual institution of marriage and reproduction. The novel offers an interesting portrayal of Ella's transformation as a form of (re)birth, with Lowly and Mammy as her mothers. This indicates that it is indeed possible to think of sexuality as more than something that is directed towards specific, known objects. As Ella begins her process of transformation into Louisiana, she frequently communicates across the lifeline in fits of passion. The lines that she follows and crosses are not straightforward, as evidenced by the difficulty of the process. Sara Ahmed discusses the importance of lines for sexual orientation, as, by following the straight ancestral lineage, the reproduction of offspring is ensured.[62] Sexual orientation has to do with investment in following certain lines: Ella becomes the linking tool for the broken lines provided by Mammy and Lowly's conversations, and cannot therefore be seen as following a straight line herself.[63] Indeed, her translation in the form of crossing the lifeline back and forth may be seen as an example of a queer (a)sexual desire acting "out of line" [64] and which blurs straight lines between various forms of existence. Ella-as-Louisiana may thus be said to take place through a re-orientation of desires in the form of an all-woman conception and rebirth.

Upon her first experience of the vocal forces of Lowly and Mammy (also known in the novel as Louise and Sue Ann) communicating to and through her, Ella observes: "The venerable sisters had married themselves to me – given birth to me, – they would say."[65] Two women marrying a third in this

---

[61] Brodber, *Louisiana*, 31.

[62] Ahmed, *Queer Phenomenology*, 17.

[63] On lines, see Ahmed, *Queer Phenomenology*, 17.

[64] *Queer Phenomenology*, 66.

[65] Brodber, *Louisiana*, 32.

equation leads to an all-female conception; the result of which is Ella-turned-Louisiana. Lowly remarks on this unusual form of reproduction: "Two places can make children! Two women sire another?"[66] Louise expresses the idea of two women conceiving a child as a question, while not questioning the truth-value of the idea of two places making children. This highlights connections between different locations as Mammy and Lowly, the spiritual mothers, give birth to Louisiana through their guiding voices and stories.

The two places that can make babies refer not only to the American state of Louisiana, but also to the plantation named Louisiana in the parish of St. Mary in Jamaica.[67] Mammy's friend Louise had been there before coming to the USA and connecting with Mammy (Sue Ann), who hails, conversely, from the parish of St. Mary in the state of Louisiana. When Ella finally gives up her personal agency and surrenders herself to the "hegemony of the spirit" (98), she gives a powerful manifesto untangling the web of names, places, and ideas:

> I am the link between the shores washed by the Caribbean sea, a hole, yet I am what joins your left hand to your right. I join the world of the living and the world of the spirits. I join the past with the present. In me Louise and Sue Ann are joined. Say Suzie Anna as Louise calls Mammy. Do you hear Louisiana there? Now say Lowly as Mammy calls Louise and follow that with Anna as Louise sometimes calls Mammy. Lowly-Anna. There's Louisiana again, particularly if you are lisp-tongued as you could well be. Or you could be Spanish and speak of those two venerable sisters as Louise y Anna. I was called in Louisiana, a state in the USA. Sue Ann lived in St. Mary, Louisiana, and Louise in St Mary, Louisiana, Jamaica. […] I am Louisiana. I give people their history. I serve God and the venerable sisters. (124–25)

The quotation highlights Ella's transformation, the process completed once she becomes Louisiana, the medium which, like the recording machine, can record a polyphony of voices and then transmit them. Having fully come to terms with her role as a mediator between the living and the dead, Louisiana

---

[66] Brodber, *Louisiana*, 17. Further page references are in the main text.

[67] The Jamaican plantation named Louisiana did exist in real life, as emerges from Brodber's history of her home village, *The People of My Jamaican Village, 1817–1948* (Kingston, Jamaica: U of the West Indies P, 1996). See also Alison Donnell, "What it Means to Stay: Reterritorialising the Black Atlantic in Erna Brodber's Writing of the Local," *Third World Quarterly* 26.3 (April 2005): 479–86, repr. in *Connecting Cultures*, ed. Emma Bainbridge (Abingdon & New York: Routledge, 2008): 93–100.

(as the character of Ella/Louisiana, the voices of Louise and Anna, the American state, the plantation in Jamaica – and, indeed, as the novel) unites transatlantic black people. As the narrative unfolds, the voices ultimately add up to a "community tale" of Mammy's and Lowly's involvement with the Jamaican-born Marcus Garvey's UNIA, the Universal Negro Improvement Association, in the early twentieth century. Merging time-lines, senses, and continents, and in telling people their history, Louisiana denotes how there is "a paradigm for centuries of unnoticed collaboration, communication, and family connections,"[68] and this paradigm involves a simultaneous vision of the past and the present as polyphonic.

Location as the breeder in Louise's declarative thus suggests that we can conceptualize desire in ways that look more to the spaces inhabited in desire than to the specific inhabitants of those spaces. It is space itself, here particularized as the location "two places" – meaning the two Louisianas where Sue Ann and Louise originate: one as the state in the USA, the other a plantation in Jamaica – that becomes the site and the object of desire. At the same time, Ella's body as the locus of Lowly's and Mammy's narrative desire results in her delivering not only their common history but many others' as well. Ella, however, is not solely the spawn of Lowly and Mammy's passionate vocal engagement: she is also a subject whose desires reside in multiple locations, not just in a sexed body. Apart from her human, target-oriented desire for her husband Reuben, Ella's desire is flowing and disoriented, to the extent that it even approaches the possible connotations of passion as suffering when, towards the end of the narrative, her health begins to fail. Ella continues to hear the voice from heaven in the popular refrain, calling her home, which circulates throughout the narrative. As the heavenly voice strengthens, her own voice weakens, as Reuben notes when (with Ella's corporeal weakening and spiritual strengthening) he takes on scribal duty.[69]

Despite the ostensibly asexual nature of Ella's character, she leads a life of passion, taken over by the spiritual forces that enable her to fulfil her mission of transmitting the stories she has been given. The childless Ella/Louisiana should not be read merely as sacrificing her womanhood and, as such, being a victim of her mission. Here, Judith Butler's idea of ecstasy is relevant. Butler writes of sexuality and gender as a "mode of being dispossessed," and, in writing about the limits of sexual autonomy, she contends that neither sexual-

[68] James, *The Maroon Narrative*, 113.

[69] Brodber, *Louisiana*, 147.

ity nor gender is a wholly autonomous entity.[70] Rather, they always exist in relation to one another, wherein one becomes dispossessed when "transported beyond oneself by passion" or when one becomes "*beside oneself* with rage or grief."[71] Using the affect of grief as her example, Butler shows that when we are beside or not at one with ourselves, we are beyond the limits of self-control. Moving beside oneself is Ella's frequent experience, particularly when the spiritual passions take over. Yet, these ruling passions are not wholly subjectivity-dismantling, for when Ella's transformation is complete, she does not simply give up personal agency in surrendering herself to the "hegemony of the spirit."[72] The manifesto "I am Louisiana" (125) in Ella's journal entry, namely, could not be uttered as a declarative sentence without a first-person subject-position from which it can be articulated.

The narrative comes full circle when Louisiana herself begins to hear the voice from heaven calling her home. Her tape recorder long since replaced by a pendant through which she sees the stories that she transmits to those who wish to re-live their pasts, she not only hears heaven but *sees* it: "I look through my pendant often these days. I see heaven" (136). As when Louise migrated across the material to the spiritual, Louisiana hears and sings the same song, "*I hear a voice from heaven say*," as she hands over the narrating duties to her husband, Reuben. Reuben narrates Louisiana's passing when he, too, finally comes to understand the main teaching of the events:

> I know now what she knows: Mammy would not tell the president nor his men her tale [of her involvement in Garveyism] for it was not hers; she was no hero. It was a tale of cooperative action; it was a community tale. We made it happen. (161)

Reuben's realization may serve as guidance for the reader, too: *Louisiana* ought not to be read as the story of Louisiana, also known as Ella Kohl – for, as Mammy is no hero, nor is Louisiana the heroine of the story in the traditional, literary sense. A jointly told community tale disarticulates narrative subjectivity as Western literary theory understands it, and brings polyphonic oral tradition to the foreground; to be heard and received by the reader.

Towards the end of *Louisiana*, 'moving' in both senses (physical and emotional) is highlighted in a passage where Lowly and Sue Ann connect with Louisiana for one last time. Mammy remarks: "She moves too back to her old

---

[70] Judith Butler, *Undoing Gender* (New York & London: Routledge, 2004): 19.

[71] Butler, *Undoing Gender*, 20 (italics in original).

[72] Brodber, *Louisiana*, 98. Further page references are in the main text.

Louisiana. We had some touching times then" (160). This obscure remark can be interpreted as both referring to moving back to the US state of Louisiana, where Ella Townsend first encounters Louise and Mammy, and to the Louisiana in St Mary, Jamaica, to which Ella's ancestry goes back. In any case, Mammy refers to moving into a place and time where one is moved ("We had some touching times then"). Certainly, from what Reuben writes as he becomes Ella's ammanuensis when she begins to weaken, this place and time involve a commitment to interaction and cooperation. With Ella's passing, we gather from Reuben's account that Ella's voice can be heard in the chorus of song that accompanies her final journey:

> My wife's voice was there too. Different chords, different tunes, different octaves. Sheer jazz. One sound. From one body. A community song. (161)

In terms of the construction of vocal subjectivity, we can see how, after Cavarero, the voice that is transmitted through breath and sound is a vital element in telling the community tale of *Louisiana.*[73]

Caribbean passion as a reading strategy turns our focus towards these two seemingly polarized representations of women's sexuality (Monica and Louisiana), as I have tried to find ways in which they can, like Sedgwick's reparative reading, "provide the self with pleasure and nourishment in an environment that is perceived not particularly to offer them."[74] The perceived non-hospitality created by the political implications of these two figures, the hypersexual and the asexual, can be challenged by reparative reading strategies. In a reparative reading, Monica and Louisiana do not, in fact, seem all that different; despite being situated at opposite ends of the continuum of sexuality. Passion is an affect which can unite seemingly disparate sexual identities when a traditional, patriarchal view of sexuality as target-oriented and in need of regulation fails. Monica and Ella's sexual orientations, read beside each other, challenge the reader in ways that have not yet been read.

In addition to being a reading strategy, there are plenty of reparative moments in the novels themselves, such as the women's healing ritual in the river in *It Begins With Tears* or Louisiana's ability to help people by giving them their histories. Although Sedgwick writes about reparative reading as a practice – and as a method – rather than as a textual quality, it may be that some texts are reparative in their own right. Lasse Kekki remarks that Sedg-

---

[73] Cavarero, *For More than One Voice*, 150.

[74] Sedgwick, *Touching Feeling*, 137.

wick does not seem so interested in texts with a reparative quality (despite naming certain authors whose works may feature it), and suggests in his reading of Tony Kushner's *Angels in America* that the play is an example of reparative writing "open to surprises and other new developments."[75] Echoing Kekki, I recognize a reparative impulse in Adisa's and Brodber's fiction; both of them offer us a world-view that is open to elements of wonder and surprise – in terms of both negative and positive affect. Reading with passion can be seen as a form of wonder which entails an openness to be surprised by the Other.[76] The element of surprise in reading Monica and Louisiana, I suggest, achieves the important outcome that the reader may become open to sexual orientations that in fact lie beyond immediate, easy reach.

If we wish to turn to an affective reading where the reader opens herself to the narrative, the mechanics of such affective desires need to be considered. I suggest that one way to do this is to turn once more to the preposition 'beside', which is the one preferred by Eve Kosofsky Sedgwick to, for example, 'beyond' or 'beneath'.[77] According to Sedgwick, 'beside' is a preposition that rejects dualism and linear logic and enables the simultaneous existence of several different forms of experience. A paranoid reading operates by anticipating a self-explanatory, oppressive outcome to any given phenomenon; a reparative reading is less poised to jump to conclusions. Seemingly polarized categories, such as the hypersexual and the asexual, do not in themselves denote identities that are self-evident or essential, nor do they contain a pre-conceived 'whatness'. Rather, the two ways of *doing* sexuality in the form of Caribbean passion do not exist *beyond* or *beneath* the terms used to describe them – nor do they exist beyond or beneath each other. Rather, the multiple forms of passion at play in these representations of sexuality exist *beside* one's vocabulary and *beside* one another. Perhaps, then, 'beside' is a location for a writerly and readerly orientation as well: a text is a space for the unleashing of desire, a reaching for an object that is realized only in the act of its reading. An attempt to orient oneself by inhabiting textual spaces, then, becomes an attempt to exist – like Ella and Monica in this reading – beside one another.

⌘

[75] Kekki, *From Gay to Queer*, 309.

[76] Ahmed, *The Cultural Politics of Emotion*, 183.

[77] Sedgwick, *Touching Feeling*, 8.

7
Sisters Together and Apart

Towards an Affective Phenomenology of Reading

WHEN COMING TO THE END of a process such as this study, it is customary to look both forward and back; to where one began and to what lies ahead. Ahmed observes that such an orientation toward something "is determined by our location; it is a question of the phenomenality of space."[1] The preposition 'towards' then points to directionality, to what we are facing.[2] I began this foray into sexual feelings with Shalini Puri's call for a re-orientation of our reading practices when reading postcolonial Caribbean literature.[3] Such a re-orientation has to do with the ways in which we gravitate towards objects, the texts we read, as Ahmed's phenomenological argument goes. Reader theory in its inception was a phenomenological endeavour, as theorists facing texts they read were concerned about how meaning became constructed in the dimensionality of time and space.[4] Having discussed literary orientation in the final chapter of this study, I feel I am moving toward something that is both old and new at the same time: the phenomenality of reading. An affective phenomenology of reading takes into account the role of emotions in meaning-production in a way that is about orientations toward those emotions. This work, I feel, has only just begun.

Perhaps, then, I am not so much going toward as much as I am 'around': this cyclical preposition, according to Ahmed, suggests a kind of immersion, wherein we are "taken up by something," and making "that thing central, or

---

[1] Ahmed, *Queer Phenomenology*, 115.

[2] *Queer Phenomenology*, 115.

[3] Puri, *The Caribbean Postcolonial*, 140.

[4] Raman Selden, Peter Widdowson & Peter Brooker, *A Reader's Guide to Contemporary Literary Theory* (1985; London: Prentice Hall, 1997): 51.

as being at the center of one's being or action."[5] For isn't reading in this manner an activity where the reader is at the centre of her action? Such 'being around' also orientates the self "*toward* certain kinds of objects," when "we not only face those things, but those things face us" (115) and this dialogic, interactive nature of reading affectively takes us not only toward and around, but also beside – as I have suggested throughout this study. In accordance with Sedgwick, Ahmed discusses what it means to be 'beside' something or someone. Observing the interracial male couple in a poem by Countee Cullen walking side by side, she remarks: "perhaps this is a different kind of politics of sides: one is not asked to 'take sides' when one is 'beside' – one walks beside and alongside" (115). But at the same time, being beside someone is a constant negotiation over sides, in the sense that politics comes into play whenever we are beside someone or something. The walks beside and alongside also construct the very 'besideness' that is seen as existing in that process of walking.

Existing or attempting to exist beside something in this book has been an excursion into the orientations of sexual feelings for the reader and the text. But this study has been as much about disorientation, the condition of being lost (6–7), as the location of beside is not always accessible. I agree with Ahmed when she writes that "moments of disorientation are vital" (157). Such moments can in fact re-orientate the (reading) subject so that she comes to inhabit a new place as a result of disorientation. Finding one's way may in fact take place through disorientation, because in such moments we articulate wonder, which opens up the possibilities of new homes (24). Elsewhere, Ahmed writes, of wonder, that it is

> an encounter with an object one does not recognize; or wonder works to transform the ordinary, which is already recognized into the extraordinary. As such, wonder expands our field of vision and touch.[6]

Wonder comes close to the epistemology of love, where the acknowledgement of the limits of one's knowledge ushers in a more ethical, loving way of (not) knowing.[7]

Wonder, then, as an emotional response to the affective stranger encounter of reading, is an extremely 'useful' emotion in critical work. Certainly, this

---

[5] Ahmed, *Queer Phenomenology*, 115. Further page references are in the main text.

[6] Ahmed, *The Cultural Politics of Emotion*, 179.

[7] See Davis, "(Love Is) the Ability of Not Knowing."

realization is nothing new to black feminism, as is noted by Ahmed.[8] For example, we find this in Patricia Hill Collins' afrocentric feminist epistemology, with its ethic of caring calls for "talking with the heart"[9] – which, as an ethical premise for knowledge-production, can thus be taken to demonstrate the true roots of the feminist affective turn.

In this study, I have argued for an affective, dialogic, feminist reader theory, with an investment in sexual feelings. This version of Pearce's implied and contextual reader theory has viewed the act of reading as a strange encounter as formulated by Ahmed. The birth of the reader has, since Barthes, chiefly raised issues of ontology, the coming into being or becoming of reading subjects. These reading subjects in turn negotiate meaning and knowledge-production and thus raise questions of epistemology. Questions of reading are ultimately always questions of epistemology and ontology beside one another: not separate, but not necessarily submerged, either. The process of reading in this study is the place of coming-together of the Caribbean cultural context and the white Western reader. In this encounter, sexuality becomes a site of affect in multiple ways, constructing both the reader and her 'object' of study. Ambivalence of sexuality in formation, the negative view of sexuality as destructive, and ways of negotiating sexual healing as well as the passionate continuum of hypersexuality and asexuality – all present ways of reading sexuality as, and through, affect. Thus, complex sexual feelings such as the kumbla, sexual shame, and the ethic of empathy and wonder serve as reading tools or strategies in the affective text–reader relationship.

Such a reading scenario presents the reader with ethical considerations, as the simple act of sympathizing with the texts' affects is not sufficient, since it takes on the other's subject-position. Instead, we need to turn to empathy, which accepts the Other on his or her own terms.[10] This leads to a communicative ethic, an awareness of the way in which we approach non-Western literary constructs via Western paradigms – particularly the way in which we approach Caribbean women's writing from the perspective of Western feminism, since this relationship has been problematic on account of the different historical contingencies of the two areas. In an attempt to reconcile while also venturing some risk, I have followed the lead of certain white feminists' bold critical stances, where they have urged white feminist scholars to "be 'bad'

[8] Ahmed, *The Cultural Politics of Emotion*, 182.

[9] Collins, *Black Feminist Thought*, 215.

[10] Bennett, "Overcoming the Golden Rule."

feminists whose global manners are always revealed for contestation."[11] In this way, the "troubling business" of white feminism (to which my work belongs) may become less troubling and, as I have argued throughout, more reparative.[12]

Particularly in the case of Brodber's Nellie, identity is about becoming rather than being. Accordingly, this book, too, must end on a note that promises new beginnings and further consideration instead of achievement or completeness. I would therefore like to propose a few additional titles as examples of Caribbean women's writing that lends itself to affective scrutiny. For example, in Oonya Kempadoo's second novel, *The Tide Running*, we can see sexuality and affectivity at play in the relationship between an older woman and a younger man.[13] Set in Tobago, the novel highlights a budding friendship between a British-Tobagonian couple settling down to live on the island and a young local man. A sexual relationship develops between the mother and wife, Bella, and the (supposedly) sexually mature twenty-year-old, Cliff, continuing Kempadoo's theme of ambivalent sexual affects. This time it is youthful masculinity, not female adolescence, that is rendered mysterious and contradictory; the reader never really gets full access to Cliff's mind and thus remains uncertain who, if anyone, in the novel is the abuser or the abused. Kempadoo's novel serves to again further ambivalence and expand Caribbean masculinities beyond the usual options reserved for men.

Continuing with the theme of alternative masculinities, we can see further examples of men as healers, helpers or collaborators in Caribbean fictional contexts hitherto unmentioned. The character of Gilbert in Andrea Levy's *Small Island* is an obvious example; he is caring, conscientious, and well-rounded, while his wife, Hortense, nurtures grand delusions about the kind of life she wants for herself in England.[14] Less obviously, Julie Moody–Freeman argues how, in Paule Marshall's fiction, men are not to be read as unequivocally the enemies of women, but how, rather, Marshall "encourages a more complex understanding of human relations in the African Diaspora/Caribbean."[15] Another example of caring men, this time combined with questions

---

[11] Haggis & Schech, "Meaning Well and Global Good Manners," 397.

[12] See Moreton–Robinson, "Troubling Business."

[13] Oonya Kempadoo, *Tide Running* (London: Picador, 2001).

[14] See Andrea Levy, *Small Island* (New York: Picador, 2004).

[15] Julie E. Moody–Freeman, "Un/Silencing African Diasporic Women's Voices: Contesting Power and Silence in Paule Marshall's *Daughters*," in *Seeking the Self –*

of sexual otherness, can also be seen in Patricia Powell's *A Small Gathering of Bones*,[16] which subtly highlights non-heterosexuality by portraying its protagonists' tragic struggle with AIDS in its early days in Jamaica. As gay men, Ian and Dale (connected by a former lover) are faced with the disease as victim, carer, and, as the novel alludes, as a potential unfortunate future victim. Not only is gay sexuality treated in a Caribbean setting, thus providing access to identities denied and tabooed, but the novel also continues the theme of men as carers, when Dale assumes this role for the ailing Ian. I propose that more consideration ought to be devoted to how men have historically and culturally participated in (women's as well as men's) healing processes in the Caribbean, and how these participations unsettle dichotomies, polarizations, and axioms of gender and sexuality in the region, creating spaces for more balanced gender relations, cooperation, and recuperation.

Further, we can see how reading and affectivity come into play when Caribbean identities are removed from the islands and become migrant and metropolitan. In the Dominican-American Angie Cruz's *Let It Rain Coffee*, we can see the struggle of the protagonist, Esperanza Colón, for the American Dream as seen on her favourite television show, *Dallas*, compromised by her low-wage care job and family worries in the metropolis, *Nueva York*.[17] Although Esperanza fails to live up to the impossible standards she has set herself, the novel's presentation of failure as a creative activity (as envisaged by Judith Halberstam) challenges the hegemony of capitalism and globalization.[18] Instead of reading the novel in terms of the two extremes of success or failure which typically characterize migrant narratives, a focus on Esperanza's "middle ranges of agency" shows how the stock terms in which migration is often presented fail to capture the nuances of immigrant experience at odds with the promise of the metropolis.[19]

Encountering the Other: Diasporic Narrative and the Ethics of Representation, ed. Tuomas Huttunen, Janne Korkka, Kaisa Ilmonen & Elina Valovirta (Newcastle upon Tyne: Cambridge Scholars, 2008): 69.

[16] Patricia Powell, *A Small Gathering of Bones* (Oxford & Portsmouth NH: Heinemann, 1994).

[17] Angie Cruz, *Let It Rain Coffee* (New York: Simon & Schuster, 2005).

[18] Judith Halberstam, *The Queer Art of Failure* (Durham NC & London: Duke UP, 2011).

[19] On the extremism of migrant narratives, see Pearce, "Beyond Redemption?," and, on middle ranges of agency, see Sedgwick, *Touching Feeling*, 13. For a full reading of Cruz's novel, see Elina Valovirta, Lydia Kokkola & Janne Korkka, "The Smell of an

Mootoo's second novel, *He Drown She in the Sea*, is another migrant fiction that lends itself to an affective, dialogic reading. The reader finally encounters Asha Ramchandin, Mala's elusive sister from *Cereus Blooms at Night*, in Canada through quite different circumstances.[20] In the novel, the protagonist (a landscape designer of Caribbean origin) steps into a gardening store and narrates:

> One day we went to a place name Asha's Garden Center. Is a woman who had emigrated from Lantanacamara who owns it. She was the reserved type, secretive for so. [...] She had a good few varieties of the cereus plant, ent you know the night-blooming cactus?[21]

The description fits Mala's sister, but as the novel makes no further reference to Asha, Mala or, indeed, Tyler, who searches for Asha with his story in *Cereus*, it is only the reader who connects the characters in the two novels. In other words, the reader – as discoverer of and witness to Mala and Asha's lives – becomes an integral, dialogic, "reciprocating 'other'"[22] for the stories' constitution. In lieu of Asha, the reader is, then, the facilitator and enabler of Tyler's narrative in *Cereus*. S/he is also the connecting point between the missing sisters, who never meet again in the narrative, but who come together and are placed beside one another in the reader's imaginative consciousness.

Finally, in order to end on a circular note, as has been the arch of this research narrative, Erna Brodber's fourth novel, *The Rainmaker's Mistake*, brings together many of the themes of gender, body, and sexuality discussed in this book – childhood and adolescence coupled with puberty, bodily taboos (such as menstruation, ejaculation, and flatulence), and non-normative sexual orientation.[23] The novel is an emancipatory narrative about the freed slaves in

---

Impossible Dream – *Dallas*, Migration and Failure in Angie Cruz's *Let It Rain Coffee*," *Journal of Commonwealth Literature* (September 2014, forthcoming).

[20] Shani Mootoo, *He Drown She in the Sea* (New York: Grove, 2005).

[21] Mootoo, *He Drown She in the Sea*, 54.

[22] *Reading Dialogics*, 20.

[23] For example, Woodville sexually abuses young Queenie, who does not understand what it means when "milk came out of this independent organ!"; Brodber, *The Rainmaker's Mistake*, 35. Later on, she wonders why "blood start to come out between my legs" without injury that would cause it (53). Another character, unaware of Western names for sexual identity categories, remarks that "they called me a homosexual – there is a gross word they use I will not mention here; they called me eunuch; they called me a-sexual" (116).

Jamaica struggling to come to terms with their new-found independence. Amnesia, lack of history, and access solely to white social norms and future[24] characterize the lives of the eight protagonists, who alternate in narrating the fantastical story of their people's quest for freedom. All of the confusing experiences make the characters understand the prohibitions of society that limit their and others' bodies: "there are taboos. Taboos exist" (104). Confusion as the novel's outlining affect illustrates the cataclysmic effect that slavery had on Africans in the New World. Queenie narrates, anticipating changes, but is unsure of what will happen: "We are on the brink of something" (6). Later on, confusion gives way to determination, when she remarks, in a way that brilliantly captures the phenomenality (i.e. the orientations and directions) of knowledge-seeking endeavours that has also sustained this book: "I needed to head in the direction where answers were to be found" (97). That, I hope, is the direction in which we are all headed.

⌘

[24] The characters travel to what in the novel is referred to as "the Future and the Norm," the former referring to time-travel across decades to see what life will be like later on, and the latter referring to the white Western world of education, where Queenie, for example, studies to become a doctor (133).

Works Cited

Abel, Elizabeth. "Black Writing, White Reading: Race and the Politics of Feminist Interpretation," in *Female Subjects in Black and White: Race, Psychoanalysis, Feminism*, ed. Elizabeth Abel, Barbara Christian & Helene Moglen (Berkeley: U of California P, 1997): 102–31. Originally in *Critical Inquiry* 19.3 (Spring 1993): 470–98.

Adisa, Opal Palmer. *Caribbean Passion* (Leeds: Peepal Tree, 2004).

——. *Eros Muse: Poems & Essays* (Trenton NJ: Africa World Press, 2006).

——. *It Begins With Tears* (Oxford: Heinemann, 1997).

——, & Donna Weir–Soley, ed. *Caribbean Erotic: Poetry, Prose & Essays* (Leeds: Peepal Tree, 2010).

Ahmed, Sara. "Communities that feel: Intensity, difference and attachment," in *Conference Proceedings for Affective Encounters: Rethinking Embodiment in Feminist Media Studies*, ed. Anu Koivunen & Susanna Paasonen (Media Studies, Series A; Turku: University of Turku, School of Art, Literature and Music, 2001): 10–24.

——. *The Cultural Politics of Emotion* (Edinburgh: Edinburgh UP, 2004).

——. *Differences That Matter: Feminist Theory and Postmodernism* (Cambridge: Cambridge UP, 1998).

——. "Phantasies of Becoming (the Other)," *European Journal of Cultural Studies* 2.1 (January 1999): 47–63.

——. *Queer Phenomenology: Orientations, Objects, Others* (Durham NC & London: Duke UP, 2006).

——. *Strange Encounters: Embodied Others in Post-Coloniality* (London & New York: Routledge, 2000).

Ahokas, Pirjo, & Eila Rantonen. "Feminismin muukalaiset: Rodun ja etnisyyden haasteet" [The strangers of feminism: The challenges of race and ethnicity], in *Naissubjekti ja Postmoderni* [The female subject and the postmodern], ed. Päivi Kosonen (Tampere: Gaudeamus, 1996): 65–88.

Alexander, Simone A. James. *Mother Imagery in the Novels of Afro-Caribbean Women* (Columbia: U of Missouri P, 2001).

Ang, Ien. *On Not Speaking Chinese: Living Between Asia and the West* (London & New York: Routledge, 2001).

——. *Watching Dallas: Soap Opera and the Melodramatic Imagination*, tr. (1985) Della Couling (London: Routledge, 1991).

Ashcroft, Bill. *Post-Colonial Transformation* (London & New York: Routledge, 2001).

——, Gareth Griffiths & Helen Tiffin. *The Empire Writes Back: Theory and Practice in Post-Colonial Literatures* (London & New York: Routledge, 1989).

——. *Key Concepts in Post-Colonial Studies* (London & New York: Routledge, 1998).

Bennett, Milton J. "Overcoming the Golden Rule: sympathy and empathy," in *Basic Concepts of Intercultural Communication*, ed. Milton J. Bennett (Yarmouth & London: Intercultural, 1998): 191–214.

Bhabha, Homi K. "DissemiNation: time, narrative, and the margins of the modern nation," in *Nation and Narration*, ed. Homi K. Bhabha (London: Routledge, 1990): 291–32.

——. *The Location of Culture* (London & New York: Routledge, 1994).

Bogaert, Anthony F. "Asexuality: Prevalence and Associated Factors in a National Probability Sample," *Journal of Sex Research* 41.3 (August 2004): 279–87.

Brah, Avtar. *Cartographies of Diaspora: Contesting Identities* (London: Routledge, 1996).

——, & Ann Phoenix. "Ain't I a woman? Revisiting intersectionality," *Journal of International Women's Studies* 5.3 (2004): 75–86.

Brathwaite, Kamau. *History of the Voice: The Development of Nation Language in Anglophone Caribbean Poetry* (London & Port-of-Spain: New Beacon, 1984).

Brodber, Erna. *The Continent of Black Consciousness: On the History of the African Diaspora From Slavery to the Present Day* (London: New Beacon, 2003).

——. "Fiction in the Scientific Procedure," in *Caribbean Women Writers: Essays from the First International Conference*, ed. Selvyn R. Cudjoe (Wellesley MA: Calaloux, 1990): 164–68.

——. *Jane and Louisa Will Soon Come Home* (London & Port of Spain: New Beacon, 1980).

—— *Louisiana* (London & Port of Spain: New Beacon, 1994).

——. *Myal* (London & Port of Spain: New Beacon, 1988).

——. "One Bubby Susan," in *The Penguin Book of Caribbean Short Stories*, ed. E.A. Markham (Harmondsworth: Penguin, 1998): 48–53. Originally in *Jamaica Journal* 22.4 (1989–90): 52–53.

——. "Oral sources and the creation of a social history of the Caribbean," *Jamaica Journal* 16.4 (July 1983): 2–11.

——. *The People of My Jamaican Village, 1817–1948* (Kingston, Jamaica: U of the West Indies P, 1996).

——. *The Rainmaker's Mistake* (London: New Beacon, 2007).
——. "Re-engineering blackspace," *Black Renaissance/Renaissance Noire* 2.3 (1999–2000): 154–65.
——. "Sleeping's Beauty and the Prince Charming," *Kunapipi* 9.3 (1989): 1–4.
——. *The World is a High Hill: Stories about Jamaican Women* (Kingston, Jamaica: Ian Randle, 2012).
Brouillette, Sarah. *Postcolonial Writers in the Global Literary Marketplace* (Basingstoke & New York: Palgrave Macmillan, 2007).
Burrow, Sylvia. "The Political Structure of Emotion: From Dismissal to Dialogue," *Hypatia* 20.4 (Autumn 2005): 27–43.
Butler, Judith. *Gender Trouble: Feminism and the Subversion of Identity* (New York & London: Routledge, 1990).
——. *Undoing Gender* (New York & London: Routledge, 2004).
Campbell, Sue. *Interpreting the Personal: Expression and the Formation of Feelings* (Ithaca NY & London: Cornell UP, 1997).
Cavarero, Adriana. *For More than One Voice: Toward a Philosophy of Vocal Expression*, tr. Paul A. Kottman (*A Più voci: Per una filosofia dell'espressione vocale*, 2003; Stanford CA: Stanford UP, 2005).
Chamberlain, Mary. "The Global Self: Narratives of Caribbean Migrant Women," in *Feminism and Autobiography: Texts, Theories, Methods*, ed. Tess Cosslett, Celia Lury & Penny Summerfield (London: Routledge, 2000): 154–66.
Chancy, Myriam J.A. "'No Giraffes in Haiti': Haitian Women and State Terror," in *Écrire en pays assiégé: Haïti / Writing Under Siege*, ed. Marie–Agnès Sourieau & Kathleen M. Balutansky (Francopolyphonies 1; Amsterdam & New York: Rodopi, 2004): 303–21.
——. *Searching for Safe Spaces. Afro-Caribbean Women Writers in Exile* (Philadelphia PA: Temple UP, 1997).
Chevannes, Barry. *Rastafari. Roots and Ideology* (Syracuse NY: Syracuse UP, 1994.
Cixous, Hélène. "The Laugh of the Medusa," tr. (1976) Keith & Paula Cohen, in *Feminisms: An Anthology of Literary Theory and Criticism*, ed. Robyn Warhol & Diane Price Herndl (New Brunswick NJ: Rutgers UP, 1997): 347–62. Originally as "Le Rire de la Méduse," *L'Arc* 61 (1975): 39–54.
——. *Stigmata: Escaping Texts*, foreword by Jacques Derrida, preface "On Stigmatexts" by Hélène Cixous (London & New York: Routledge, 1998).
Collins, Patricia Hill. *Black Feminist Thought: Knowledge, Consciousness, and the Politics of Empowerment* (New York & London: Routledge, 1991).
——. *Black Sexual Politics: African Americans, Gender and the New Racism* (New York & London: Routledge, 2004).
Conner, Marc C. "Introduction: Aesthetics and the African American Novel," in *The Aesthetics of Toni Morrison: Speaking the Unspeakable*, ed. Conner (Jackson: UP of Mississippi, 2000): ix–xxviii.

Cooper, Carolyn. "Afro-Jamaican Folk Elements in Brodber's *Jane And Louisa Will Soon Come Home*," in *Out of the Kumbla: Caribbean Women and Literature*, ed. Carole Boyce Davies & Elaine Savory Fido (Trenton NJ: Africa World Press, 1990): 277–88.

——. *Noises in the Blood: Orality, Gender and the 'Vulgar' Body of Jamaican Popular Culture* (Warwick University Caribbean Studies; London: Macmillan, 1993).

——. "'Something Ancestral Recaptured': Spirit Possession as Trope in Selected Feminist Fictions of the African Diaspora," in *Motherlands: Black Women's Writing from Africa, the Caribbean and South Africa*, ed. Susheila Nasta (London: Women's Press, 1991): 64–87.

Crenshaw, Kimberlé. "Mapping the Margins: Intersectionality, Identity Politics, and Violence against Women of Color," *Stanford Law Review* 43.6 (July 1991): 1241–99.

Cruz, Angie. *Let It Rain Coffee* (New York: Simon & Schuster, 2005).

Dance, Daryl Cumber. "Go Eena Kumbla: A Comparison of Erna Brodber's *Jane and Louisa Will Soon Come Home* and Toni Cade Bambara's *The Salt Eaters*," in *Caribbean Women Writers: Essays from the First International Conference*, ed. Selvyn R. Cudjoe (Wellesley MA: Calaloux, 1990): 169–84.

Danticat, Edwidge. *Breath, Eyes, Memory* (London: Abacus, 1994).

Davies, Carole Boyce. *Black Women, Writing and Identity. Migrations of the Subject* (London & New York: Routledge, 1994).

——, & Elaine Savory Fido. "Introduction: Women and Literature in the Caribbean: An Overview," in *Out of the Kumbla: Caribbean Women and Literature*, ed. Carole Boyce Davies & Elaine Savory Fido (Trenton NJ: Africa World Press, 1990): 1–22.

——, ed. *Out of the Kumbla: Caribbean Women and Literature* (Trenton NJ: Africa World Press, 1990).

Davis, Dawn Rae. "(Love Is) the Ability of Not Knowing: Feminist Experience of the Impossible in Ethical Singularity," *Hypatia* 17.2 (Spring 2002): 145–61.

Delaney, Janice, Mary Jane Lupton & Emily Toth. *The Curse: A Cultural History of Menstruation* (1976; Urbana & Chicago: U of Illinois P, 1988).

Derrida, Jacques. "The Double Session," in Derrida, *Dissemination*, tr. Barbara Johnson (*La Dissémination*, 1972; tr. 1981; London & New York: Continuum, 2004): 187–316.

Donnell, Alison. *Twentieth-Century Caribbean Literature: Critical Moments in Anglophone Literary History* (London & New York: Routledge, 2006).

——. "What it Means to Stay: Reterritorialising the Black Atlantic in Erna Brodber's Writing of the Local," *Third World Quarterly* 26.3 (April 2005): 479–86, repr. in *Connecting Cultures*, ed. Emma Bainbridge (Abingdon & New York: Routledge, 2008): 93–100.

DuBois, Andrew. "Close reading: An introduction," in *Close Reading: The Reader*, ed. Frank Lentricchia & Andrew DuBois (Durham NC: Duke UP, 2003): 1–40.

Dyer, Richard. *White* (London: Routledge, 1997).

Eeva, Sara. "Kreolinaisen heteroseksuaalisuuden 'pakollinen' ja melankolinen rakentuminen Jean Rhysin romaaneissa *Voyage in the Dark* ja *Siintää Sargassomeri*" [The "compulsory" and melancholy construction of Creole female heterosexuality in Jean Rhys' *Voyage in the Dark* and *Wide Sargasso Sea*], in *Pervot pidot: Homo-,lesbo- ja queer-näkökulmia kirjallisuudentutkimukseen* [Queer feast: Perspectives into gay, lesbian and queer literary studies] ed. Lasse Kekki & Kaisa Ilmonen (Helsinki: Like, 2004): 312–338.

Feagin, Susan. *Reading With Feeling: The Aesthetics of Appreciation* (Ithaca NY: Cornell UP, 1996).

Felski, Rita. "The Doxa of Difference," *Signs* 23.1 (Autumn 1997): 1–21.

——. *Literature After Feminism* (Chicago & London: U of Chicago P, 2003).

Feng, Pin-chia. "Rituals of Rememory: Afro-Caribbean Religions in *Myal* and *It Begins with Tears*," *MELUS* 27.1 (Spring 2002): 149–75.

Fetterley, Judith. *The Resisting Reader: A Feminist Approach to American Fiction* (Bloomington: Indiana UP, 1978).

Fuller, Danielle. "Reading as Social Practice: The Beyond the Book Research Project," *Journal of Popular Narrative Media* 1.2 (October 2008): 211–17.

——, & James Procter. "Reading as 'social glue'? Book Groups, Multiculture and the *Small Island Read 2007*," *Moving Worlds* 9.2 (2009): 26–40.

Forbes, Curdella. "Fracturing Subjectivities: International Space and the Discourse of Individualism in Colin Channer's *Waiting in Vain* and Jamaica Kincaid's *Mr. Potter*," *Small Axe* 12.1 (2008): 16–37.

Foucault, Michel. *The History of Sexuality*, vol. 1: *An Introduction*, tr. Robert Hurley (*Histoire de la sexualité*, I: *La Volonté de savoir*, 1976; New York: Vintage, 1980).

Francis, Donette A. *Fictions of Feminine Citizenship: Sexuality and the Nation in Contemporary Caribbean Literature* (Basingstoke & New York: Palgrave Macmillan, 2010).

——. "'Silences too horrific to disturb': Writing Sexual Histories in Edwidge Danticat's *Breath, Eyes, Memory*," *Research in African Literatures* 35.2 (Summer 2004): 75–90.

Gates, Henry Louis, Jr. *The Signifying Monkey: A Theory of African-American Literary Criticism* (New York & Oxford: Oxford UP, 1988).

Glave, Thomas. "Toward a Nobility of the Imagination: Jamaica's Shame (An Open Letter to the People of Jamaica)," *Black Renaissance/Renaissance Noire* 2.3 (1999–2000): 77–81.

Goldberg, Jonathan. *Tempest in the Caribbean* (Minneapolis: U of Minnesota P, 2003).

Gourdine, Angeletta K.M. "Carnival-Conjure, *Louisiana*, History and the Power of Women's Ethnographic Narrative," *ARIEL: A Review of International English Literature* 35.3–4 (July–October 2004): 139–58.

——. "Caribbean *tabula rasa*: Textual touristing as carnival in contemporary Caribbean women's writing," *Small Axe* 10.2 (June 2006): 80–96.

——. *The Difference Place Makes: Gender, Sexuality and Diaspora Identity* (Columbus: Ohio State UP, 2002).

Grosz, Elizabeth. *The Nick of Time: Politics, Evolution and the Untimely* (Durham NC & London: Duke UP, 2004).

——. *Time Travels: Feminism, Nature, Power* (Durham NC & London: Duke UP, 2005).

Gwin, Minrose. *The Woman in the Red Dress: Gender, Space and Reading* (Urbana & Chicago: U of Illinois P, 2002).

Haggis, Jane, & Suzanne Schech. "Meaning Well and Global Good Manners: Reflections on White Western Feminist Cross-Cultural Praxis," *Australian Feminist Studies* 15/33 (2000): 387–99.

Halberstam, Judith. *The Queer Art of Failure* (Durham NC & London: Duke UP, 2011).

Hall, Stuart. "Negotiating Caribbean identities," in *New Caribbean Thought: A Reader*, ed. Brian Meeks & Folke Lindahl (Kingston, Jamaica: U of the West Indies P, 2001): 24–39. Originally in *New Left Review* 209 (January–February 1995): 3–14.

Hammonds, Evelyn. "Toward a genealogy of black female sexuality: The problematic of silence," in *Feminist Genealogies, Colonial Legacies, Democratic Futures*, ed. M. Jacqui Alexander & Chandra Talpade Mohanty (New York & London: Routledge, 1997): 170–82.

Hemmings, Clare. "Invoking Affect: Cultural Theory and the Ontological Turn," *Cultural Studies* 19.5 (September 2005): 548–67.

Henderson, Mae Gwendolyn. "Speaking in Tongues: Dialogics, Dialectics, and the Black Woman Writer's Literary Tradition," in *Changing Our Own Words: Essays on Criticism, Theory, and Writing by Black Women*, ed. Cheryl A. Wall (New Brunswick NJ: Rutgers UP, 1989): 16–37.

Henry, Paget. *Caliban's Reason: Introducing Afro-Caribbean Philosophy* (London & New York: Routledge, 2002).

Hogan, Linda, & Sasha Roseneil. "Gendering ethics/the ethics of gender," *Feminist Theory* 2.2 (August 2001): 147–49.

Hong, Grace Kyungwon. "'A shared queerness': Colonialism, transnationalism, and sexuality in Shani Mootoo's *Cereus Blooms at Night*," *Meridians: Feminism, Race, Transnationalism* 7.1 (2006): 73–103.

hooks, bell. *Feminist Theory: From Margin to Center* (Cambridge MA: South End, 1984).

Hunter, Lynette. "Listening to situated textuality: Working on differentiated public voices," *Feminist Theory* 2.2 (August 2001): 205–17.

Huttunen, Tuomas, Janne Korkka, Kaisa Ilmonen & Elina Valovirta, ed. *Seeking the Self – Encountering the Other: Diasporic Narrative and the Ethics of Representation* (Newcastle upon Tyne: Cambridge Scholars, 2008).

Ilmonen, Kaisa. "Healing the traumas of history: (Trans)sexual diasporas in Caribbean literature," in *Seeking the Self – Encountering the Other: Diasporic Narrative and the Ethics of Representation*, ed. Tuomas Huttunen, Janne Korkka, Kaisa Ilmonen & Elina Valovirta (Newcastle upon Tyne: Cambridge Scholars, 2008): 229–46.

Iser, Wolfgang. *The Act of Reading: A Theory of Aesthetic Response* (Baltimore MD & London: Johns Hopkins UP, 1978).

James, Cynthia. *The Maroon Narrative: Caribbean Literature in English Across Boundaries, Ethnicities, and Centuries* (Portsmouth NH: Heinemann, 2002).

Jennings, La Vinia Delois. *Toni Morrison and the Idea of Africa* (Cambridge & New York: Cambridge UP, 2008).

Kekki, Lasse. *From Gay to Queer: Gay Male Identity in Selected Fiction by David Leavitt and in Tony Kushner's Play "Angels in America I–II"* (Bern: Peter Lang, 2003).

Kempadoo, Kamala. "Theorizing sexual relations in the Caribbean: Prostitution and the problem of the 'exotic'," in *Confronting Power, Theorizing Gender: Interdisciplinary Perspectives in the Caribbean*, ed. Eudine Barriteau (Kingston, Jamaica: U of the West Indies P, 2003): 159–85.

Kempadoo, Oonya. *Buxton Spice* (London: Orion, 1998).

——. *Tide Running* (London: Picador, 2001).

King, Rosamond S. "Re/presenting Self & Other: Trans Deliverance in Caribbean Texts," *Callaloo* 31.2 (Spring 2008): 581–99.

Koivunen, Anu. "An affective turn? Reimagining the subject of feminist theory," in *Working with Affect in Feminist Readings: Disturbing Differences*, ed. Marianne Liljeström & Susanna Paasonen (London & New York: Routledge, 2010): 8–28.

——. "Preface: The affective turn?," in *Conference Proceedings for Affective Encounters: Rethinking Embodiment in Feminist Media Studies*, ed. Anu Koivunen & Susanna Paasonen (Media Studies, Series A; Turku: University of Turku, School of Art, Literature and Music, 2001): 7–8.

——, & Susanna Paasonen, ed. *Conference Proceedings for Affective Encounters: Rethinking Embodiment in Feminist Media Studies* (Media Studies, Series A; Turku: University of Turku, School of Art, Literature and Music, 2001). E-book at http://www.utu.fi/hum/mediatutkimus/affective/proceedings.pdf.

Lang, Anouk. "'Enthralling but at the same time disturbing': Challenging the Readers of *Small Island*," *Journal of Commonwealth Literature* 44.2 (June 2009): 123–40.

——. "Reading race in *Small Island*: Discourse deviation, schemata and the textual encounter," *Language and Literature* 18.3 (August 2009): 316–30.

Leusmann, Harald. "An interview with Oonya Kempadoo," *World Literature Written in English* 39.1 (2001): 107–15.

LeMoncheck, Linda. *Loose Women, Lecherous Men: A Feminist Philosophy of Sex* (Oxford: Oxford UP, 1997).

Lentricchia, Frank, & Andrew DuBois, ed. *Close Reading: The Reader* (Durham NC: Duke UP, 2003).

Levy, Andrea. *Small Island* (New York: Picador, 2004).

Lewis, Linden. "Caribbean Masculinity: Unpacking the Narrative," in *The Culture of Gender and Sexuality in the Caribbean*, ed. Linden Lewis (Gainesville: UP of Florida, 2003): 94–125.

——. "Envisioning a politics of change within Caribbean gender relations," in *Gendered Realities: Essays in Caribbean Feminist Thought*, ed. Patricia Mohammed (Kingston, Jamaica: U of the West Indies P & Centre for Gender and Development Studies, 2002): 512–30.

——. "Exploring the intersections of gender, sexuality, and culture in the Caribbean: An introduction," in *The Culture of Gender and Sexuality in the Caribbean*, ed. Linden Lewis (Gainesville: UP of Florida, 2003): 1–21.

——, ed. *The Culture of Gender and Sexuality in the Caribbean* (Gainesville: UP of Florida, 2003).

Liljeström, Marianne, ed. *Feministinen tietäminen: Keskustelua metodologiasta* [Feminist knowing: Conversations on methodology] (Tampere: Vastapaino, 2004).

——, & Susanna Paasonen, ed. *Working with Affect in Feminist Readings: Disturbing Differences* (London & New York: Routledge, 2010).

Locke, Jill. "Shame and the Future of Feminism," *Hypatia* 22.4 (Fall 2007): 146–62.

Lorde, Audre. *Sister Outsider: Essays and Speeches* (Freedom CA: Crossing Press, 1984).

McDonald, Antonia. "Coming Home to Mama's Garden: Creative Fellowship in *Jane and Louisa Will Soon Come Home*," *MaComère* 6 (2004): 13–18.

McKay, Nellie. "Introduction" to *Critical Essays on Toni Morrison*, ed. McKay (Boston MA: G.K. Hall/Twayne, 1988): 1–15.

Mackie, Erin Skye. "Welcome the Outlaw: Pirates, Maroons and Caribbean Countercultures," *Cultural Critique* 59 (Winter 2005): 24–62.

Mardorossian, Carine. *Reclaiming Difference: Caribbean Women Rewrite Postcolonialism* (Charlottesville: UP of Virginia, 2005).

Markee, Patrick. "The tree that knew too much," *New York Times* (11 July 1999): 12, http://query.nytimes.com/gst/fullpage.html?res=9A0CE7DD143DF932A25754C0A96F958260 (accessed 26 August 2013).

Mohanty, Chandra Talpade. "'Under Western eyes' Revisited: Feminist Solidarity Through Anticapitalist Struggles," *Signs* 28.2 (Winter 2003): 499–535.

Momsen, Janet. "The double paradox," in *Gendered Realities: Essays in Caribbean Feminist Thought*, ed. Patricia Mohammed (Kingston, Jamaica: U of the West Indies P & Centre for Gender and Development Studies, 2002): 44–55.

Moody–Freeman, Julie E. "Un/Silencing African Diasporic Women's Voices: Contesting Power and Silence in Paule Marshall's *Daughters*," in *Seeking the Self – Encountering the Other: Diasporic Narrative and the Ethics of Representation*, ed. Tuomas Huttunen, Janne Korkka, Kaisa Ilmonen & Elina Valovirta (Newcastle upon Tyne: Cambridge Scholars, 2008): 52–71.

Mootoo, Shani. *Cereus Blooms at Night* (London: Granta, 1996).

——. *He Drown She in the Sea* (New York: Grove, 2005).

Moreton–Robinson, Aileen. "Troubling business: Difference and whiteness within feminism," *Australian Feminist Studies* 15/33 (2000): 343–52.

Morrissey, Marietta. "Explaining the Caribbean family: Gender ideologies and gender relations," in *Caribbean Portraits: Essays on Gender Ideologies and Identities*, ed. Christine Barrow (Kingston, Jamaica: Ian Randle, 1998): 78–90.

Narain, Denise DeCaires. "The Body of the Woman in the Body of the Text: The Novels of Erna Brodber," in *Caribbean Women Writers: Fiction in English*, ed. Mary Condé & Thorunn Lonsdale (London: Macmillan, 1999): 97–115.

——. "Body talk: Writing and speaking the body in the texts of Caribbean women writers," in *Caribbean Portraits: Essays on Gender Ideologies and Identities*, ed. Christine Barrow (Kingston, Jamaica: Ian Randle, 1998): 255–75.

——. "Landscape and Poetic Identity in Contemporary Caribbean Women's Poetry," *ARIEL: A Review of International English Literature* 38.2–3 (April–July 2007): 41–64.

——. "Standing in the place of love: Sex, love and loss in Jamaica Kincaid's writing," in *Gendered Realities: Essays in Caribbean Feminist Thought*, ed. Patricia Mohammed (Kingston, Jamaica: U of the West Indies P & Centre for Gender and Development Studies, 2002): 334–57.

Newson, Adele S., & Linda Strong–Leek. "Introduction" to *Winds of Change: The Transforming Voices of Caribbean Women Writers and Scholars*, ed. Adele S. Newson & Linda Strong–Leek (New York: Peter Lang, 1998): 1–9.

——, ed. *Winds of Change: The Transforming Voices of Caribbean Women Writers and Scholars* (New York: Peter Lang, 1998).

Nordlund, Taru, Tiina Onikki-Rantajääskö & Toni Suutari, ed. *Kohtauspaikkana kieli: Näkökulmia persoonaan, muutokseen ja valintoihin* [Language as a meeting place: Aspects of persona, change and choices] (Helsinki: SKS, 2006).

O'Callaghan, Evelyn. "'Compulsory heterosexuality' and textual/sexual alternatives in selected texts by West Indian women writers," in *Caribbean Portraits: Essays on Gender Ideologies and Identities*, ed. Christine Barrow (Kingston, Jamaica: Ian Randle, 1998): 294–319.

——. "Cultural penetration, arts and sciences: A review of Erna Brodber's *Louisiana*," *Journal of West Indian Literature* 7.2 (April 1998): 70-80.

——. "Interior schisms dramatised: the treatment of the 'mad' woman in the work of some female Caribbean novelists," in *Out of the Kumbla: Caribbean Women and Literature*, ed. Carole Boyce Davies & Elaine Savory Fido (Trenton NJ: Africa World Press, 1990): 89–109.

Paravisini–Gebert, Lizabeth. "Women Against the Grain: The Pitfalls of Theorizing Caribbean Women's Writing," in *Winds of Change: The Transforming Voices of Caribbean Women Writers and Scholars*, ed. Adele S. Newson & Linda Strong–Leek (New York: Peter Lang, 1998): 161–68.

Patterson, Anita Haya. "Contingencies of pleasure and shame: Jamaican women's poetry," in *Feminist Consequences: Theory for the New Century*, ed. Elisabeth Bronfen & Misha Kavka (New York: Columbia UP, 2000): 254–82.

Pearce, Lynne. "Beyond redemption? Mobilizing affect in feminist reading," in *Working with Affect in Feminist Readings: Disturbing Differences*, ed. Marianne Liljeström & Susanna Paasonen (London & New York: Routledge, 2010): 151–64.

——. *Feminism and the Politics of Reading* (London: Arnold, 1997).

——. *Reading Dialogics* (London: Edward Arnold, 1994).

——. *The Rhetorics of Feminism: Readings in Contemporary Cultural Theory and the Popular Press* (London: Routledge, 2004).

——. *Romance Writing* (Cambridge: Polity, 2007).

Pollard, Velma. "History and Caribbean women's writing: The transformation of history by creative memory," in *Swinging Her Breasts at History: Language, Body and the Caribbean Woman's Text*, ed. Moira Inghilleri (London: Mango, 2006): 150–61.

Powell, Patricia. *A Small Gathering of Bones* (Oxford & Portsmouth NH: Heinemann, 1994).

Probyn, Elspeth. *Blush: Faces of Shame* (Sydney: U of New South Wales P, 2005).

Puren, Nina. "Hymeneal Acts: Interrogating the Hegemony of Rape and Romance," *Australian Feminist Law Journal* 5 (1995): 15–26.

Puri, Shalini. *The Caribbean Postcolonial: Social Equality, Post-Nationalism, and Cultural Hybridity* (New York: Palgrave Macmillan, 2003).

Reddock, Rhoda. "Conceptualizing 'difference' in Caribbean feminist theory," in *New Caribbean Thought: A Reader*, ed. Brian Meeks & Folke Lindahl (Kingston, Jamaica: U of the West Indies P, 2002): 196–209.

Roberts, June E. *Reading Erna Brodber: Uniting the Black Diaspora Through Folk Culture and Religion* (Westport CT: Greenwood, 2006).

Robertson, Claire C. "Cultural Materialism: Reflections on a Theoretical Odyssey from Africa to the West Indies," *Journal of Women's History* 11.1 (Spring 1999): 167–80.

Rojola, Lea. "Puhetta *siitä*: Lukijuuden rakentuminen Maria Jotunin novellissa Rakkautta" [Speaking about *it*: The construction of readership in Maria Jotuni's short story Rakkautta], in *Kohtauspaikkana kieli. Näkökulmia persoonaan, muutokseen ja valintoihin* [Language as a meeting place: Aspects of persona, change and choices], ed. Taru Nordlund, Tiina Onikki-Rantajääskö & Toni Suutari (Helsinki: SKS, 2006): 475–99.

——. "Sukupuolieron lukeminen: Feministinen kirjallisuudentutkimus" [Reading gender difference: Feminist literary criticism], in *Feministinen tietäminen. Keskustelua metodologiasta* [Feminist knowing: Conversations on methodology], ed. Marianne Liljeström (Tampere: Vastapaino, 2004): 25–43.

Rowley, Michelle. "Reconceptualizing voice: The role of matrifocality in shaping theories and Caribbean voices," in *Gendered Realities: Essays in Caribbean Feminist Thought*, ed. Patricia Mohammed (Kingston, Jamaica: U of the West Indies P & Centre for Gender and Development Studies, 2002): 22–43.

Russo, Mary. *The Female Grotesque: Risk, Excess and Modernity* (New York & London: Routledge, 1995).

Saunders, Patricia. "The Project of Becoming for Marlene Nourbese Philip and Erna Brodber," in *Caribbean Cultural Identities*, ed. Glyne Griffith (Lewisburg PA: Bucknell UP, 2001): 133–159.

Scott, Helen. *Caribbean Women Writers and Globalization: Fictions of Independence* (Aldershot & Burlington VT: Ashgate, 2006).

——. "Ou libéré? History, transformation and the struggle for freedom in Edwidge Danticat's *Breath, Eyes, Memory*," in *Écrire en pays assiégé: Haïti / Writing Under Siege*, ed. Marie–Agnès Sourieau & Kathleen M. Balutansky (Francopolyphonies 1; Amsterdam & New York: Rodopi, 2004): 459–478.

Sedgwick, Eve Kosofsky. *Touching Feeling: Affect, Pedagogy, Performativity* (Durham NC & London: Duke UP, 2003).

——, & Adam Frank. "Shame in the cybernetic fold: Reading Silvan Tomkins," in *Touching Feeling: Affect, Pedagogy, Performativity*, Eve Kosofsky Sedgwick (Durham NC & London: Duke UP, 2003): 93–121.

Selden, Raman, Peter Widdowson & Peter Brooker. *A Reader's Guide to Contemporary Literary Theory* (1985; London: Prentice Hall, 1997).

Sheller, Mimi. *Consuming the Caribbean: From Arawaks to Zombies* (New York & London: Routledge, 2003).

Smith, Faith, ed. *Sex and the Citizen: Interrogating the Caribbean* (Charlottesville & London: UP of Virginia, 2011).

Smitherman, Geneva. *Talkin That Talk: Language, Culture and Education in African America* (London & New York: Routledge, 2000).

Sobchack, Vivian. *Carnal Thoughts: Embodiment and Moving Image Culture* (Berkeley: U of California P, 2004).

Spivak, Gayatri Chakravorty. "Can the Subaltern Speak?" in *Marxism and the Interpretation of Culture*, ed. Cary Nelson & Lawrence Greenberg (Basingstoke: Macmillan Education, 1988): 271–313.

Stein, Mark. *Black British Literature: Novels of Transformation* (Columbus: Ohio State UP, 2004).

Stump, Jordan. *Naming and Unnaming: On Raymond Queneau* (Lincoln: Nebraska UP, 1998).

Taylor, Orville."Cultural Considerations for Social Workers in the Jamaican Inner City: A Sociological Perspective," *Caribbean Journal of Social Work* 1 (March 2002): 65–76.

Terada, Rei. *Feeling in Theory: Emotion after the "Death of the Subject"* (Cambridge MA & London: Harvard UP, 2001).

Tiffin, Helen. "Cold Hearts and (Foreign) Tongues: Recitation and the Reclamation of the Female Body in the Works of Erna Brodber and Jamaica Kincaid," *Callaloo* 16.4 (Autumn 1993): 909–21.

Tomkins, Silvan S. *Affect Imagery Consciousness*, vol. 2: *The Negative Affects* (New York: Springer, 1963).

Valovirta, Elina. "The Kumbla Revisited: Reading Erna Brodber's *Jane and Louisa Will Soon Come Home* as Post-Colonial *écriture féminine*," *Atlantic Literary Review* 3.2 (April–June 2002): 130–42.

——, Lydia Kokkola & Janne Korkka, "The Smell of an Impossible Dream – *Dallas*, Migration and Failure in Angie Cruz's *Let It Rain Coffee*," *Journal of Commonwealth Literature* (September 2014, forthcoming).

Warner–Lewis, Maureen. "Rastafarianism (The Caribbean)," in *Encyclopedia of Post-Colonial Literatures in English*, ed. Eugene Benson & L.W. Conolly (London: Routledge, 1994): 1344–45.

Weedon, Chris. *Feminism, Theory and the Politics of Difference* (London & Malden MA: Blackwell, 1999).

Weir–Soley, Donna Aza. *Eroticism, Spirituality, and Resistance in Black Women's Writings* (Gainesville: UP of Florida, 2009).

Wilentz, Gay Alden. *Healing Narratives: Women Writers Curing Cultural Dis-ease* (New Brunswick NJ: Rutgers UP, 2000).

Wimsatt, W.K. *The Verbal Icon: Studies in the Meaning of Poetry* (Lexington: U of Kentucky P, 1954).

Woodward, Kathleen. "Traumatic Shame: Toni Morrison, Televisual Culture, and the Cultural Politics of the Emotions," *Cultural Critique* 46 (Autumn 2000): 210–40.

Wynter, Sylvia. *The Hills of Hebron* (London: Jonathan Cape, 1962).

⌘

Index

⌘